REPENTANCE

REPENTANCE

A Comparative Perspective

Edited by
AMITAI ETZIONI
and
DAVID E. CARNEY

Sponsored by the Communitarian Network

ROWMAN & LITTLEFIELD PUBLISHERS, INC.
Lanham • New York • Boulder • Oxford

ROWMAN & LITTLEFIELD PUBLISHERS, INC.

Published in the United States of America
by Rowman & Littlefield Publishers, Inc.
4720 Boston Way, Lanham, Maryland 20706

12 Hid's Copse Road
Cummor Hill, Oxford OX2 9JJ, England

British Library Cataloguing in Publication Information Available

Library of Congress Cataloging-in-Publication Data
Repentance: A comparative perspective / edited by Amitai Etzioni and David
Carney.
    p.   cm.
    Includes bibliographical references and index.
    ISBN 0-8476-8470-9 (cloth : alk. paper). — ISBN 0-8476-8471-7
(pbk. : alk. paper)
    1. Repentance—Comparative studies.   I. Etzioni, Amitai.
II. Carney, David.
    BL476.7.R46   1997
    291.2′2—dc21   96-51904
                                                            CIP

ISBN 0-8476-8470-9 (cloth : alk. paper)
ISBN 0-8476-8471-7 (pbk. : alk. paper)

Printed in the United States of America

Contents

Acknowledgments

First and foremost, I would like to thank the Lilly Endowment, Inc., for its support for this project, "Civic Repentance." Sr. Jeanne Knoerle, my project director at Lilly, and before her, Edward Queen III, provided me with much encouragement and stimulation.

I am grateful to the following scholars for commenting on drafts of papers included in this volume: Bryce Christensen, Paul Courtwright, Amy-Jill Levine, Seyyed Hossein Nasr, Donald Shriver, and Don Swearer. Several essays that were prepared under the auspices of this project, but which could not find their way into this volume, will appear in our future publications as this project continues.

David E. Carney worked with me throughout the compilation of this book with much patience, insight, and fine research. Jessica Mayer conducted research for the introduction and helped to edit it, and also brought the manuscript to press.

Introduction

Civic Repentance: Just and Effective

When my children were young, I tried to encourage them to be virtuous, to appreciate when they lived up to their commitments, and to celebrate their achievements. Focusing on the positive came readily to me, as I remembered all too vividly the experience of growing up in a very strict home. While positive inducements for my children were effective, they did not suffice; occasionally a punishment seemed unavoidable. However, punishments were structured in such a way that after the children received their penalty and made amends, there was a ritual of reconciliation. It was made clear to the children that they had fully regained good standing in the family and that bygones were, well, bygone.[1]

I am struck by the absence of concepts and processes of repentance (and of reconciliation) in Western civic culture. Civic culture refers to the set of shared values, mores, and rules that guide our life, especially but not only in our public life.[2] Currently, in Western civic culture, we condemn people who violate our values; we drive politicians out of public office; we send those who offend our sensibilities into the social isolation of Coventry; we incarcerate criminals. Yet even after these offenders have paid their dues to society in full, there are still no established social processes through which they can be restored to full and legitimate membership in the community. For example, convicts who have served their term become "ex-cons"; their status is permanently diminished both in terms of citizens' rights and socioeconomic rights (e.g., membership in several professions is denied to them). Further, their social standing remains inferior, as is evidenced by the suspicion and rejection with which they are treated. In other words, their crime

1

stays with them. This is true also for public figures, who often remain under scrutiny, semi-ostracized, decades after they were driven from public office, even if they have engaged in no additional behavior that offends the community.

Case in point: Senator Gary Hart had to withdraw from the presidential race in 1988 when he was caught having an extramarital affair. (He was also criticized for lying to the press, and thus to the public, for maintaining that he had had no affairs, before he was caught red-handed.) His penalty was considerable, having to give up a chance at the highest office in the land; and while his remorse might not have been in strong evidence, he seems to have led a "normal" life ever since. Still, seven years later, when Senator Hart tried to become politically active again, he met with almost universal derision. Responding to a 1995 report that Hart might campaign for a Senate seat, Colorado GOP chair Don Bain declared, "We want him to run. . . . The polls we've seen show that anybody beats him." National Republican Senatorial Committee executive director John Heubusch added, "We know our counterparts . . . are desperate . . . , but we never suspected they'd try to dredge up a liberal and discredited political retread like Gary Hart."[3]

The difficulties inherent in attaining civic repentance, and the lack of structured processes by which to seek such repentance, are illustrated by a description of *Nightline*, a television program—hardly a place where one would typically seek or expect to find repentance, nor a place accessible to most members of the community who violate mores. Howard Kurtz of the *Washington Post* observes, "It has become an almost religious experience: the sinner appears, confesses to Father Ted [Koppel] and seeks absolution from the television audience."[4] The report continues that one "supplicant" was Janet Cooke, a *Washington Post* reporter who "vanished in disgrace" after a prize-winning story she wrote was exposed as a hoax. "Koppel, sitting in judgment on behalf of the media establishment, was not letting her off easy."[5] The fact that we allow a television personality to play such a role indicates to sociologists that we are craving opportunities for structured repentance within the civic culture.

The actual story of Janet Cooke further illustrates my main point. Despite considerable remorse and attempts at a reconstructed life, Cooke has had great difficulties in finding employment over all these years; she claims to have resorted to working for six dollars an hour at a department store in Kalamazoo, Michigan, since no one would hire her as a journalist.[6] She admits that what she did was "horrible," but expresses bitterness toward her seemingly permanent status as an outcast. She laments, "I've . . . lost half my life. I'm in a position where cereal has become a viable dinner choice."[7]

Much more complicated case studies in the lack of structured repentance are those of Richard Nixon and Robert McNamara. While Nixon's Watergate offense was quite a bit more serious than having an extramarital affair or concocting a press report, and his remorse was somewhat scant, he worked rather hard at manipulating a self-rehabilitation. For example, he pursued only "selected" biographers who would paint him in a favorable light, such as British Parliament member and longtime friend, Jonathan Aitken. In the book *Nixon, A Life*, Aitken touts the ex-president as having "a strong claim to being America's finest foreign policy president of the 20th century."[8] In the years following his resignation, Nixon also worked hard to serve as an "unofficial" presidential adviser.[9] Nixon had to improvise, however, because there were no obvious steps in the civic culture that he could undertake to pay his dues, make amends, and be forgiven. He died without being reintegrated into the community, at least under some cloud if not in a state of disgrace. Tourists at the Vietnam Memorial, when asked what they would remember Nixon for, gave the following replies. First man: "Watergate." First woman: "Watergate." Second woman: "Unfortunately, Watergate." Second man: "I think it's ludicrous that the entire country will be shut down on Wednesday to honor a man who was forced to resign from the presidency."[10] I am not suggesting that Nixon was remorseful, or that his repentance was adequate, or that the society was at fault in its attitude toward Nixon even at his death. I am only pointing to the fact that there was no well-defined avenue to guide him, steps to follow, or reintegration to hope for.

Robert McNamara tried to make his way for the role he played in Vietnam by writing the book *In Retrospect: The Tragedy and Lessons of Vietnam*, but his efforts, too, were not well received, to put it carefully.[11] Many felt that his apology came too late (after nearly thirty years) and was far from expansive. In a review of the book, David Halberstam comments, "Twenty-eight years ago, [McNamara] was deceiving millions . . . of . . . Americans. Now with this book, he is merely deceiving himself."[12] Charles Colson is one example of a public figure who did find his way back into the good graces of the community, yet this was largely the result of following a religious, rather than a civic, course.

From a sociological and human viewpoint, this deficiency in civic repentance is damaging to the moral foundations of society and unjust to those involved. We must expect that individuals who violate society's mores and who pay their dues in full, but continue to be denied full membership in the community, will be resentful. We must expect that they will feel unfairly punished, as if their sentence is interminable, and that they will react by limiting their contact with law-abiding members of the community (who treat ex-cons as second-class citizens and persons) and narrowing their focus to others who violated the law or are somehow considered deviant or inferior. Subsequently, they are likely to be less motivated to complete their social rehabilitation, and to have less incentive to avoid new acts that might further undermine their standing in the community than they would if full restoration to good citizenship were available. I say all this hypothetically because there seems to be no direct evidence for these points. Indeed, it might be said that there could not be, because, given that there currently exist no structured opportunities for civic repentance in our culture, one cannot compare those who availed themselves of such opportunities with those who did not. It seems reasonable, however, to expect that such assertions are true.

A Sociological Perspective

There is a considerable amount of sociological thinking behind the preceding analysis of civic repentance and social order that should be briefly explained. Social science in general, and sociology in particular, has long been preoccupied with the question of how to account for social order, since the traditional, religion-based social order has weakened with the onset of modernity and rise in secular thinking.[13] Theories that have been proposed include a reliance on the state and its policing powers, and economic inducement (contracts and negotiated agreements). Alternatively, I join those who emphasize values, arguing that unless the members of a society share a set of core values, internalizing them in their personalities and having them further reinforced by social rites and institutions, social order will be unreliable.[14]

According to this line of reasoning, it has been assumed that if the members of a community internalize a given set of shared values and embody them in social institutions, then the members will seek to abide by the behavioral implications of these values, that the values will act as a powerful motivational force. It has been understood, however, that even under very favorable social circumstances, some members of most communities will not live up to the mores of their culture, the normative expectations of their peers, and in many cases, even those they hold themselves. Thus, there arises a need to deal with behavior that conflicts with the moral culture.

To begin, we must recognize that if mores-violating behavior is ignored, it will expand. If one tolerates loud playing of boom boxes in public squares, for example, more and more people will bring their radios along. The same holds for drug abuse, driving at dangerous speeds, and much more serious offenses—hence the continuous need to curb offending behavior.

True, not all behavior that a community frowns upon is damning or should be exorcised in one way or the other; some of it is morally innovative, such as desegregation. In other words, sometimes it is to the benefit of society to allow a change in mores to legitimize behavior that was, until then, considered illegitimate. But this opens a whole different subject; here I focus on the violation of those mores that are deemed just both by the community itself and by considered ethical judgment.[15]

Responses to unacceptable behavior take the form of penalties, incarceration, and even execution. But these are all problematic in that they lead to further alienation, and are costly and often ineffectual, as the war against drugs demonstrates.[16] (The inability of authorities to curb drug transactions in prisons is particularly illuminating, since it suggests that even in a police state, there would still be a considerable amount of drug dealing.)

To take another approach, we learn from studies in social science that people deeply seek the approval of others. One can assume that offenders (I use this word to refer to violators of laws and violators of mores) at some time receive approval from other offenders, such as members of a gang, fellow inmates, and companion drug abusers. But what of the offender who wants to reform his deviant behavior? Once he departs from a life of crime, he loses the affirmation of other miscreants. If he then finds that the doors to acceptance by law-abiding members of the community, those who uphold mores, are, in effect, locked, his rehabilitation is paralyzed. This "locked door" is one reason that offenders are pushed back, as indeed they often seem to be in our society, into their previous, deviant, social circles. By contrast, if offenders could complete the steps of repentance, and then be fully accepted by the upright community, this would serve as significant incentive for offenders to embark on the road to repentance, see it through, and become and remain productive members of the community.

Of special interest to this discussion is the impact that the new "information age" has had on the possibility of civic repentance. In past, more communitarian ages, people lived in small communities and knew each other personally. If a fellow member of the community transgressed, but then restructured his or her life, people had a fairly detailed understanding of these events, and could treat this person accordingly. In the complex modern society, however, people change residences frequently and often know each other rather little. This makes the reliance on documentation and former statuses much greater, and contributes to the staying power of the notation "ex-con," as opposed to more communitarian ages.

Further along these lines, the development of new instruments of communication technology introduces another major change: it gives the general public relatively easy access to personal records. Thus, previously an ex-con could relocate to another part of the country and gain de facto rehabilitation, since poor communication and information retrieval systems allowed a virtual escape from the past. (A fear of being recognized by someone from his or her previous life was usually quelled by some change in appearance.) These individuals, while "on the run," were often found to be leading exemplary lives—arguably as much as the result of a desire not to be detected, as of the unique opportunity to be reintegrated into a community, which an altered identity affords. Contemporary criminals, by contrast, face the technological advances of fingerprint tracking, DNA analysis, and rapidly growing databases. Without formal rehabilitation, it is much more difficult to achieve civic repentance in today's world, and, I fear, one is even less inclined to try.

While this discussion emphasizes the need to adapt social processes to technological advances, we should not trivialize the significance of criminals who successfully alter their public identities and restructure their lives. Those in hiding can be considered experiments in what might happen if offenders were given a chance at full repentance.

Note that it is not assumed that all or even most offenders will seek to regain the good graces of the community and to be reintegrated into it; it is only suggested that if offenders do seek to embark on such a repenting course—for whatever utilitarian or principled reasons—the lack of civic repentance will make their course harder, furthering the detriment to the community and persons involved.

Support for this analysis of civic repentance comes from the fact that unending social punishment offends our sense of justice. People who have truly repented, our moral sense informs us, have redeemed themselves with respect to a particular violation, and should cease to be judged in light of it. On a personal level, the ethical view that instructs us to "do unto others as we would have done unto us" allows us to conceive of a life in which we are *ourselves* subject to unjust treatment and excessive—above all, interminable—penalties; this empathy increases our awareness of the moral merit of finding or evolving a vehicle of civic repentance.

In short, then, civic repentance, if it were available when the proper prerequisites were met, promises to be a strong element of a good social order. We expect that it would motivate people to abide by shared mores, and do so at low economic and psychological cost.

Transposing Religious Rituals into a Civic Culture

Repentance in a religious context is a rather clearly understood concept, at least in the Judeo-Christian tradition and several others, as the essays collected in this volume show. Yet, as we saw, civic culture contains no explicit definition of repentance nor of the social processes that it requires. We occasionally make loose reference to the idea in a civic sense: for instance, after a reluctant Donald Wubs, thirteen-million-dollar embezzler of a Christian savings club, faced the courtroom and declared, "I admit to the fact that I lied and misled people," a district judge considered him "repentant" and lightened his sentence.[17] However, to the extent that the term is being applied at all, civic repentance has no generally agreed upon meaning, legitimacy, or above all the needed social specification of the processes that an "ordinary" individual or public leader must undergo to be fully restored to membership in the community. The notion of "rehabilitation" comes close—we say that an offender who has mended his ways is "rehabilitated"—but this term is loaded with other meanings such as physical rehabilitation (the regimen required to get a person up and walking after a crippling illness) and the former Soviet rehabilitation (the ritual of confessing to political transgressions in public, often under the threat of being otherwise shipped off to a labor camp in Siberia or worse). For the sociological reasons already stated, then, it seems evident that the civic society and its members would be better off if the concept of repentance could be more effectively transposed from the religious to the moral culture.

Other religious concepts have made a similar journey of transposition, and have become such an integral part of the civic culture that we often overlook their religious origins and meanings. An example is the notion of "stewardship." In the Christian tradition it embodies the concept that "the Lord God took man and put him in the garden of Eden to till it and keep it" (Genesis 2:15); it is the idea that since all of creation belongs to God, and humans only possess things on a conditional basis, we should be "stewards" of the earth—tend to it—while devoted to the higher purposes of the Lord.[18] Recently, "stewardship" has been used by environmentalists, with little reference to its religious connotations, to refer to our moral obligation to pass the earth on to our children at least not in a worse condition than it was given to us. Organizations that have adopted the idea include the World Stewardship Institute, whose mission is to alter the environmental behavior of the world's international corporations in "benign and restorative" ways, and the Environmental Stewardship Program, which aims at teaching young people ecological terminology and environmental awareness.[19] Likewise, the concept of "reconciliation," found in various religious traditions, is frequently employed by conflict resolution and mediation mavens in the absence of any religious attribution. Gestures of reconciliation, for instance, were attributed to both the Americans and the Japanese in the aftermath of World War II: Japan formally apologized for wartime activities before the United Nations General Assembly, and the United States sought to compensate Japanese Americans who were interned during the war with small, but symbolic, cash payments.[20]

When I write that I favor the transport of repentance from the religious to the civic realm, I do not mean to imply that we should here, too, ignore or deny religious sources. One may well be able to adapt the concept and acknowledge its roots. The concept and the processes it entails, though, will need to be modified to some extent in the process. This is best understood if the elements of religious repentance are examined one at a time.

The Elements of Religious Repentance

What defines repentance? Much of this volume shows that different religions approach repentance in rather different ways. For the purpose at hand, to enhance transposition, I focus on three elements that seem crucial; two are commonly recognized even by those who do not study religious concepts or are otherwise unfamiliar with them, while the third one is surprisingly often overlooked.

True Remorse

Those who seek repentance must first of all show *true remorse* as a way of paying homage to (i.e., recognizing the legitimacy of) both the mores that they have violated and the fellow members of the community whom they have offended. Without this evidence, the community will not validate the offenders' claims of being ready to abandon their deviant conduct, mend their ways, and seek a return to full membership in the community. Furthermore, those who are not remorseful are viewed as if they offended the community twice: once in whatever offense they have committed and, second, in their refusal to acknowledge that mores were violated.

Here a dilemma immediately arises: How can one determine that remorse is true? Many people, when faced with the apologies of politicians, criminals, and even friends and spouses, have doubts as to the motivation behind such expressions. One might think that a possible reason why civic repentance is so rare is that remorse is doomed to be suspect in a world of public relations experts, spin doctors, and a jaded and cynical population. Actually, before passing judgment about the sincerity of remorse, one should recognize a whole range of repentant behavior.

At one extreme are violators of mores who make little effort to disguise their lack of remorse. An example of this is the Menendez brothers during their trial for the murder of their parents. Lyle and Eric claimed that, in effect, the murders were their parents' own fault, that the brothers resorted to the use of machine guns in response to repeated sexual abuse. (No reliable evidence to this effect was presented.) Referring to others who show no remorse, James Q. Wilson describes "youngsters who [commit crimes and] afterwards show us the blank, unremorseful stare of a feral, presocial being."[21] Many public figures, when caught red-handed, present a Menendez-like defense: to prevent the blame from falling on their shoulders, they attack the laws by which they are charged and the public mores that they violate. President Reagan's former political director Lyn Nofziger, when convicted for using White House contacts for influence-peddling, trivialized his crime (it's "like violating a stop sign") and attacked the law as "lousy" and "stupid."[22] Such behavior leaves little doubt about the lack of remorse.

Other offenders utter apologies, but with defeating qualifications. In response to accusations of sexual harassment, former senator Bob Packwood said, "Am I sorry? . . . Of course, if I did the things that they say I did."[23] Following his trial, the infamous Oliver North declared that he was repentant—up to a point: lying to Congress was a mistake, but only because maintaining the deception "created a whole bunch of new responsibilities."[24] Former national security adviser Robert C. McFarlane remorsefully admitted to deceiving Congress and being involved in the Iran-Contra cover-up, but claimed that he was pleading guilty to four misdemeanors only because a long and costly trial would have made any ultimate victory a hollow one.[25] Linguist Deborah Tannen reports that her husband said to her one day, "I am sorry I hurt your feelings." But because he was grinning as he spoke these words, this "left open the possibility—indeed strongly suggested—that he regretted not so much what he did but my emotional reaction."[26]

Before continuing, though, one should note that even faked remorse might—at least under some conditions—be better than no remorse at all. Fake remorse shows that the party is at least aware of the community's censure and seeks to make amends, even without truly accepting responsibility for the aggrieving act. The advantage of false remorse stands out when one compares it to brazen displays of unremorseful self-righteousness.

Fortunately, true remorse does have its indicators; on many levels one can find signs that help to validate or invalidate remorse. Prolonged remorse, for example, is more compelling than short-lived remorse. Also, one can draw upon personal knowledge of an individual, as Tannen does when she refers to her husband's grin. While others may not be quite sure what a grin means in this context, Tannen knows him, she writes, as someone who "thinks that the earth will open up and swallow him if he admits fault."[27]

In other cases, the affect of those who express remorse provides a clue: those who fake it sound empty, rehearsed, and unconvincing, while those who are truly sorry seem humbled. A relevant case is that of a sixteen-year-old Maryland boy who was serving time in a juvenile-detention center for the sexual molestation of his nine-year-old sister. When told that his release was contingent upon feeling genuine shame for what he had done, the boy's first response was flippant, nominal, affect-less: "Sorry, Sarah" [name changed]. Yet this was judged to be insincere, and the boy's retention continued. In a following therapy session, the boy dropped to his knees and uttered with much pain, "Sarah, I'm sorry for taking advantage of you. I'm sorry for sexually molesting you. I'm sorry for getting on top of you. I'm sorry for blaming it on you. And I'm sorry for not apologizing last time."[28] Granted, there is not definitive proof that the second expression was authentic and not conjured up or rehearsed in order to win release. However, it is clear that such expressions are more likely to reflect remorse than the first dismissive reaction, and there is some reason to suggest that even if such remorse is initially produced for self-serving purposes, it may have some rehabilitative effect.

In another example, Lee Atwater, on his deathbed, sought forgiveness from Michael Dukakis for making Willie Horton his running mate, and for other dirty tricks that Atwater employed. Deathbed confessions are often granted special weight, and the same might be said about deathbed remorse. One can of course argue that Atwater became remorseful merely to build up points for his next "campaign," but those who believe that there is an afterlife probably understand that fake remorse is not going to add to their standing in that world. Indeed, Atwater, facing death from brain cancer at age forty, seemed to be seriously consumed by misgiving. All this is not to deny, however, that remorse that is offered when there is little to be directly gained from its expression is often the most convincing of them all.

A final note on the topic of remorse as an element of repentance: With remorse, as in all matters of repentance, there are clear cultural differences. Tannen reminds us that remorse is highly ritualized in Japan, while it is much less a part of Western culture.[29] It is more formal and external in cultures that emphasize shame, but more internal in those that focus on guilt as a mechanism of social control. We can conclude, then, that there is no single process for the expression of remorse by repentant persons, but that most cultures recognize, to some degree, that it is essential to the process of forgiveness.

Doing Penance and/or Making Amends

The second component of repentance involves "paying one's dues." Those who transgress must pay their dues to society by making restitution to the victims and/or to the community; they must be punished and get their "desert." Punishment serves several functions, including deterrence (discouraging nonoffenders from offending and the offender from repeating the offense) and making the victims and the community whole (e.g., by exacting financial penalties from the offenders). Punishment also provides structured opportunities to recommit to the values that have been offended.

Careful attention to repentance reveals that the process of punishing offenders often entails making them feel guilty, subjecting them to public criticisms for their offense, and so on. While at the *end* of successfully completed repentance, there is forgiveness, reconciliation, and reintegration into the community, during the process itself those who repent are made to suffer, which is an element of the penalty. Religious repentance often concurs, with punishments that range from social isolation to self-flagellation.

While not formally committed to remorse, the civic culture is quite clear about the need for punishment, focusing more on the punitive model than on the restorative one. If an offender is properly punished according to the prevailing mores, some members of the community often seem quite satisfied, as if punishment were an end in itself. This optimism is defeated, though, when confronted by the fact that reha-bilitation in prison occurs infrequently.[30] Indeed, one might argue that prisons serve as the finishing schools and colleges of crime for young offenders; convicts "graduate" hardened, more committed to a life of crime, and equipped with more criminal skills, knowledge, and con-tacts than when they entered prison. There are now only the first signs of interest in a rather different model of criminal justice, one that pays attention to ensuring that offenders will be not only punished but also "changed" and reintegrated into the community.[31] Those interested in restorative justice will find the study of repentance of special value.

Restructuring One's Life

Many discussions of repentance include only these two elements, re-morse and punishment. Take, for instance, the often told narrative of Canossa, part of religious education for centuries.

Canossa is a castle in northern Italy, made famous by an encounter of longtime enemies, Pope Gregory VII and Emperor Henry IV. The background is this: In 1072, the emperor usurped the church's au-thority by appointing a relative as archbishop. The pope's swift re-sponse was to excommunicate the emperor and install another man in the archbishop position. Five years passed. At last, having lost his following, Henry crossed the Alps in midwinter and presented himself to the pope barefoot and in penitent's garb. The emperor spent three days suffering in the inclement weather, at which point he was granted pardon by the pope and restored to his throne. In other words, the emperor was judged to be sincerely repentant by having displayed re-morse and being humiliated and exposed to the cold; accordingly, he was forgiven.[32]

A third component, often overlooked, is actually of critical impor-tance: To fully repent, "sinners" must *restructure their lives* in line with the prevailing mores.[33] It is not enough for an adulterous person to show remorse on Sunday and recite twelve Ave Maria's as punishment; the person must stop committing adultery. Otherwise, the first two elements of repentance will not suffice to reinforce the moral culture; we risk that showing remorse and absorbing penalty will simply become part of the cost of doing whatever crooked business an offender is involved in. In order to avoid this type of truncated repentance, *true reintegration must not be granted until a period has passed in which guilty parties have had a chance to demonstrate that they have restructured their lives and themselves.*

This element is the one that is most lacking in the civic culture. Take, again, the example of ex-cons. Even if all three conditions of repentance are met—perhaps in the case of a young offender who dealt drugs in college but deeply regretted his misdeeds, served a long jail term, and then, ten years later, has had no new scrapes with the law, holds a legitimate job, pays taxes due, takes care of his children, and does volunteer work—in short, leads an exemplary life in civic terms— that person will still not be fully integrated into society.

This is evident in several ways. In many states a criminal offense is sufficient cause to be denied a license in the occupations of accountant, barber, real estate broker, pharmacist, physician, and embalmer, to name a few.[34] A majority of jurisdictions refuse felons the right to vote or run for public office. Barring the rare examples where offenders are granted legal pardon by the governor or president, or the conviction is overturned, ex-convicts are permanently marked by records that seriously affect their life chances. If ex-cons show on their resumes that they were incarcerated, this is held against them. If they leave a lacuna in their resumes, this raises suspicions. If they lie to try to hide their ex-con status, they are committing a new moral and legal violation of mores.

A point I leave for future deliberations is whether this unending "branding" of violators takes place because the culture lacks *rituals of closure* that certify one's completed repentance. Many religions may not have such a ritual because they never consider a person free of sin, never completely repentant. One religion that provides some ritual of closure is Judaism: the end of fasting at sundown on Yom Kippur, in a sense, marks the end of that round of atonement; there is no assumption, however, that from then on, the person who atoned is on a different plateau until he or she explicitly sins again.

In summary, while civic culture is rife with punishments and has a few opportunities for showing remorse (especially at sentencing and in some rare opportunities for reconstructive justice), the third, missing, element is the one that is most needed if civic repentance is to be fostered.

Free Will in Religious versus Civic Repentance

There is much to be gained from transposing the concept of repentance from the religious realm to the civic one, yet it cannot, and need not, be simply a transfer. At issue is an important distinction between religious and civic culture that stems from the built-in assumptions about free will. Several religions have a very complex and nuanced view of the relationship between the person who seeks to repent, and a redeemer—such as in Christianity, Jesus Christ—who elevates the person to be more virtuous than he or she would be otherwise. The specifics of this relationship are critical, for the more a theology relies on the redeemer to attain repentance, the less room there is for free will, individual action, and personal responsibility. Some religions, as essays collected in this volume show, lean fairly far in the direction of presuming some superior force that shapes the direction of our lives. (It is this kind of thinking that inspires the questions "Why does God allow bad things to happen to good people?" and "If God is all-knowing and all-powerful, then how could He allow a Holocaust or genocide to take place?") The implicit assumption here is that human beings are relatively powerless to control their fate. No religion, however, intends to provide a blanket exemption to its members that releases them from efforts to abide by mores and contribute to the common good. Hence, complicated formulas have been evolved by various religions according to which people must choose what is "right" in order to be redeemed, yet which allows for the fact that there are limits to the extent to which they can affect their destiny, at least in this world.

Civic culture, especially in the West, tends to be much more voluntaristic. It assumes that people have the ability to control their behavior and that they must take responsibility for their intentions and the consequences of their acts (although it makes various exceptions for categories of people: children, mentally handicapped patients, and people acting in great passion are presumed to be less in control of themselves). True, in recent decades there has been a tendency to draw on the sociological and psychotherapeutic notions of blaming "the system," the parents, the culture, the media, or the government for people's misconduct. But a functional civic culture cannot countenance such deterministic approaches. Therefore, a strong communitarian reaction to "victimology" has been to acknowledge that while there are external factors that mitigate guilt, no one is wholly exempt from taking responsibility for his or her wrongful acts, or from achieving repentance with regard to them. In short, while religious and civic culture's versions of free will are not entirely distinct—religions allow for some free (human) will, and civic culture for some determining factors—the shift of emphasis to the importance of personal responsibility is essential for the transposition of repentance from one realm to the other.

Developing Civic Repentance: Megalogues and Policies

To proceed with the transposition of repentance, two developments must take place. First, we need a moral megalogue on civic repentance. A "moral megalogue" is a moral dialogue projected onto a larger scale; a "moral dialogue" is the process by which we identify shared fundamental values that guide our lives.[35]

One may wonder how societies could possibly come together to affirm a set of values by means of a moral megalogue. The process occurs by linking millions of local conversations (between couples, in neighborhood bars or pubs, in coffee or tea houses, next to water coolers at work) into societywide networks and shared public focal points. The networking takes place during regional and international meetings of many thousands of voluntary associations in which local representatives participate in dialogues; in political party caucuses; and increasingly via electronic links (such as groups that meet on the Internet). Several associations, including the National Issues Forum, the Public Agenda Foundation, and the League of Women Voters, are explicitly dedicated to nourishing megalogue.

Megalogues are often fueled, accelerated, and affected by events such as public hearings (the Thomas-Hill hearing focusing discussion on what constitutes sexual harassment and the morally proper response to it), trials (the 1925 Scopes trial challenging the teaching of evolution), demonstrations (the efforts to undermine the normative case for the war in Vietnam), and marches (marches in the 1960s to change views on racial discrimination). While fireside chats and other speeches from the "bully pulpit" of the presidency play much less of a role than is often attributed to them, especially when one expects that a president could change the direction of a country with a few well-honed speeches, they do serve to inspire nationwide dialogues. The discussions are often extensive, disorderly (in the sense that there is no clear pattern to them), and have an unclear beginning and no clear or decisive conclusion. Nevertheless, in societies that are relatively communitarian, megalogues lead to significant changes in core values.

A brief illustration will serve. Until 1970, the environment was not considered a shared core value in Western societies (nor in many others). This is not to say that there were not studies, articles, and individuals who saw great value in it; but the society as a whole paid it little systematic heed, and it was not listed among America's core values.[36] As is often the case, a book—Rachel Carson's *Silent Spring*—triggered a nationwide dialogue.[37] A massive oil spill and the ensuing protests in Santa Barbara, California, and the Three-Mile Island nuclear power plant incident further impressed the subject on the national normative agenda. Thousands of people gathered in New York City to listen to pro-environment speeches and to pick up garbage along Fifth Avenue. Two hundred thousand people gathered on the Washington Mall in 1970 to demonstrate concern for the environment on "Earth Day."[38] The same process of moral megalogue could strengthen any one country's commitment to civic forgiveness.

Also necessary for the transposition of repentance are changes in policy; these changes have been little studied and even less often experimented with. We must establish whether it will set back the justice system significantly (there are always a few instances) if criminal records could be "sequestered" after a period of, say, twenty years if the person has no record of having committed additional crimes. I suggest sequestered rather than expunged, because the records should be available under certain circumstances (for instance, if a previous offender has been convicted of a new crime after the given period, before sentencing, it might be proper to reopen the file).

Other policy changes would include full readmission to the rights to vote, run for office, and practice all professions after a given period that may be shorter than the one at the end of which files will be sequestered. The reason rehabilitation should be staggered is to provide a continuous stream of approbations, recognitions, and rewards for those who repent.

The next step would be to deem colleges and places of employment as engaging in discriminatory behavior if they reject ex-cons who have repented by the given standards. No such antidiscriminatory laws seem to currently exist in the United States; not only is it an employer's right to refuse to hire a convicted felon, but in some cases, the employer would be considered legally negligent if employment were offered.[39]

Most difficult would be to change the social connotations of being an ex-con. The sociological record of the way we speak of and view people of different races, gender, or sexual orientation, as well as people with disabilities (among others once considered inferior or deviant), shows that one can largely edit culture through moral megalogue. Only after we develop the concept of civic repentance, highlight the new orientation with said changes in public policy, and accompany these processes with a recognition of the social and personal losses that are inflicted when full repentance is not available—might the elevation of status from "ex-con" to "normal" member of the community be possible. The same holds true for other offenders of the law and mores.

Oversteering

The art of redirecting societies is still a rather primitive one. Societies that seek to correct their course often end up grossly overcompensating in the opposite direction. This is illustrated by public policy debates, which are too often couched in simplistic dichotomous terms. When we debate if we should rely on the private sector or the government, for instance, we ignore huge and important third sectors that include hundreds of thousands of not-for-profit corporations and a similar number of community-based action groups, as well as numerous hybrids. In fact, most successful social entities are some mixture of the three elements—for instance, our best hospitals, universities, museums, and charities. In deliberating repentance, there is a similar danger that we are thinking about it as being lacking or present, rather than being in need of extension (to include the third element of recalibrating one's life and reaching a point of closure). As a result we tend to force the corrections to the corrections system to go overboard.

A demonstration of this is the District of Columbia, which seems to assume repentance is synonymous with time spent in prison, and restores most of the offender's rights as soon as he or she exits the prison door. In the specific field of practicing law, for example, the District of Columbia has no published character and fitness standards, no ban on felony convicts, and no special conditions for applicants with chemical dependencies.[40] Additionally, the District of Columbia restores full franchisement rights upon completion of one's sentence. Thirteen other jurisdictions are similarly quick to do so, including Florida, Nevada, and New Jersey.[41] These local authorities do not fully whitewash the offense, but this is largely because some elements of the process are not under their control; the federal government mandates certain levels of punishments and limits some conditions for parole. The moral message such lax local standards send is that, given half a chance, some authorities would make civic repentance rather easy to acquire, long before ex-offenders have the chance to reconstruct their lives and show that they have been rehabilitated.

The danger of moving from the unavailability of full civic repentance to easily acquired reintegration is the same that arises when repentance is turned into amnesty by which violators' transgressions are wiped out without requiring offenders to go through the three steps of repentance (or when they are allowed to zip through them). France, for one, has an established tradition of granting amnesty to thousands of minor offenders and millions of violators of traffic laws at the time of presidential elections. The result? Significantly increased speeding and parking offenses, plus a sharp increase in the number of deaths on French roads, in election years.[42]

In short, the three elements of repentance serve a dual purpose. They identify the opportunities that ex-offenders should have access to, in terms of opportunities to gain full membership in the community, and they outline the steps that must be undertaken (with no small effort) before repentance can take place. True repentance cannot be attained without genuine remorse, some punishment, and above all, opportunities to show that one's life has been reconstructed. While religious repentance guides the evolution to civic repentance, it will have to evolve in its own way, stressing personal responsibility without ignoring—indeed respecting—forces that exist beyond any one individual.

Notes

1. For additional discussion see John Braithwaite, *Crime, Shame, and Reintegration* (New York: Cambridge University Press, 1989).

2. For the origins of this term, please see *The Civic Culture* by Gabriel A. Almond and Sidney Verba (Boston: Little, Brown, and Co., 1963). Also of interest may be *Beyond Belief: Essays on Religion in a Post-Traditional World* by Robert N. Bellah (New York: Harper & Row, 1970), 168–189; in this book Bellah defines the now-famous concept of "civic religion."

3. "Hart Unlikely to See Issues-Oriented Campaign," *Hotline*, 24 August 1995, Senate Watch section.

4. Howard Kurtz, "Ted Koppel Firmly Anchored," *Washington Post*, 28 May 1996, 2(B).

5. Ibid.

6. Bernard Weintraub, "Of Politics and News: Two Films from Life," *New York Times*, 15 August 1996, 11(C).

7. Leigh Behrens, "Shortcuts," *Chicago Tribune*, 9 June 1996, 10.

8. Robert Shogan, "The Jury Is Still Out on Nixon's Place in History," *Los Angeles Times*, 26 April 1994, 1(A).

9. Ibid.

10. Howard Berkes, "Varying Views and Memories about Richard Nixon," *All Things Considered* (National Public Radio), 24 April 1994, transcript number 1462–5.

11. Robert McNamara, *In Retrospect: The Tragedy and Lessons of Vietnam* (New York: Times Books, 1995).

12. David Halberstam, "Dead Wrong," *Los Angeles Times Book Review*, 16 April 1995, 11.

13. See Dennis Wrong, *The Problem of Order* (New York: The Free Press, 1994).

14. Talcott Parsons, *The Structure of Social Action* (New York: McGraw-Hill, 1937); Robert Bellah, *The Good Society* (New York: Alfred A. Knopf, 1991); Amitai Etzioni, *The New Golden Rule* (New York: Basic Books, 1997).

15. For a discussion of the way such judgments can be made see Etzioni, *The New Golden Rule*, chapter 8.

16. For documentation see Amitai Etzioni, *A Comparative Analysis of Complex Organizations*, rev. ed. (New York: Free Press, 1975), 28–30.

17. Matt O'Conner, "Head of a Religious Savings Scam Gets Four Years," *Chicago Tribune*, 26 July 1994, 1(D).

18. Loren Wilkinson et al., *Earth Keeping: Christian Stewardship of Natural Resources*, ed. Loren Wilkinson (Grand Rapids, Mich.: William B. Eerdmans Publishing Co., 1980), 75, 224.

19. Internet addresses: http://www.sonic.net/wsi/ and http://www.fourh-council.edu/wenvtop.html.

20. Nicholas Tavuchis, *Mea Culpa: A Sociology of Apology and Reconciliation* (Stanford, Cal.: Stanford University Press, 1991) 106–8.

21. James Q. Wilson as quoted by John J. DiIulio, Jr., "Stop Crime Where It Starts," *New York Times*, 31 July 1996, 15(A).

22. Amitai Etzioni, "Say 'I'm Sorry' Like a Man," *New York Times*, 23 March 1988, 178(B).

23. Wire Reports, "Packwood, in Interview, Still Refuses to Repent," *Baltimore Sun*, 11 September 1995, 3(A).

24. Doyle McManus, "Ollie North: Semper Fi; Iran Contra: The Former Marine Still Believes in the Reagan Legacy, but His Cloak-and-Dagger World Is No More," *Los Angeles Times*, 24 October 1991, 1(E).

25. Etzioni, "Say 'I'm Sorry,' " 178.

26. Deborah Tannen, "I'm Sorry, I Won't Apologize," *New York Times Magazine*, 21 July 1996, 6.

27. Ibid.

28. Jonathan Alter and Pat Wingert, "The Return of Shame," *Newsweek*, 6 February 1995, 21.

29. Tannen, "I'm Sorry," 6.

30. See D. A. Andrews et al., "Does Correctional Treatment Work?" *Criminology* 28, no. 3 (1990): 369–87.

31. See Burt Galaway and Joe Hudson, eds., *Restorative Justice: International Perspectives* (New York: Criminal Justice Press, 1996).

32. Diana Butler, "Dole and Robertson Repeat Mistake Made by King, Pope in 1072," *Star Tribune*, 28 September 1996, 7(B).

33. The conditions under which mores may be legitimately challenged has already been addressed.

34. David Rudenstine, *The Rights of Ex-offenders* (New York: Avon Books, 1979), 171–94.

35. For further discussion see Etzioni, *The New Golden Rule*, chapter 5.

36. Robin M. Williams, Jr., *American Society: A Sociological Interpretation* (New York: Alfred A. Knopf, 1952).

37. Rachel Carson, *Silent Spring* (Boston: Houghton Mifflin, 1962).

38. Marc Mowery and Tim Redmond, *Not in Our Backyard: The People and Events That Shaped America's Modern Environmental Movement* (New York: William Morrow and Co., 1993), 39.

39. Personal correspondence with Stephen Saltzburg, George Washington Law School professor, 28 September 1996.

40. American Bar Association Section of Legal Education and Admissions to the Bar and the National Conference of Bar Examinations, *A Comprehensive Guide to Bar Admissions Requirements, 1995–96* (Chicago: American Bar Association, 1995), 6–9.

41. Brian Hancock, ed., *Federal Election Commission Journal of Election Administration*, vol. 17 (District of Columbia: Federal Election Commission, 1996).

42. "A Quaint Custom," *The Economist*, 22 April 1995, 50.

1

Repentance and Forgiveness: A Christian Perspective

Harvey Cox

Ye who do truly and earnestly repent you of your sins, and are in love and charity with your neighbors, and intend to lead a new life, following the commandments of God, and walking from henceforth in his holy ways: Draw near with faith, and take this holy Sacrament to your comfort; and make your humble confession to Almighty God, devoutly kneeling.

—Invitation to Communion, Book of Common Prayer

Roots of Repentance

The need for repentance is hardly peripheral to Christianity. The first sentence attributed to Jesus in Mark, the oldest of the canonical Gospels, is "The time has arrived; the kingdom of God is upon you." The second and immediately following sentence is "Repent, and believe the Gospel." There is every indication that those who heard these words of Jesus recognized what he was asking for, although not all were willing to comply. Any Jew of the time, even those with a minimal exposure to their religious heritage, would have known that repentance involves genuine regret for one's transgressions, sorrow and remorse for the injury they have caused, an essential element of contrition, and a deeply felt desire to avoid repeating the offense.

All this would have been familiar to most of Jesus' hearers. What

21

was different, at least in some measure, was his urgent tone and the immediacy of the demand for repentance. The coming reign of God—which the pious prayed for—was beginning now, he was saying, and therefore the change of heart it required could not be postponed. Jesus' parables and sayings carry this same tone of immediacy and urgency. Today, now, this moment, is the time for repentance. The kingdom of God is in the midst of you.

During the nearly two thousand years since the earthly ministry of Jesus the various Christian churches have developed highly complex theologies of repentance and intricate penitential systems. But the core of the Christian understanding of the matter is well summarized in the ancient invitation to the commemoration of the Lord's Supper—later the Mass or the Eucharist—which eventually found its way into the English Book of Common Prayer and is used with some variants by a wide variety of denominations and churches. It is quoted at the head of this essay. Scrutinizing its elements reveals the underlying theology that can be summarized in five parts as follows.

1. Human beings are free. They are endowed by God with the capacity for choice and are therefore responsible for their actions. True, in some of its forms, the doctrine of original sin seems to qualify this key premise. Yet, sometimes recognizing the paradox involved, the overwhelming consensus of Christian theology is that however the human will may be blemished or weakened within the actual conditions of history, human beings do have the ability to choose. Otherwise, the call for repentance would be meaningless.

This is not a trivial observation. Jesus' summons to repentance to all who came into earshot—the pious and the reprobate, the weak and the strong, the powerful and the socially marginalized—undercuts any kind of religious, psychological, or sociocultural determinism. The underlying theological anthropology of the call to repentance thus implicitly rejects any notion of karma or kismet that would make God or destiny, or behavior in a past life, or childhood mistreatment responsible for my own sins. It suggests that although there can be mitigating circumstances, neither destiny nor the psychological history of the person can be advanced as the sole reason for his or her conduct. It endows even the most victimized and oppressed peoples with a continuing and genuine responsibility, if only to struggle against whatever deprives them of their personhood. My sins are ultimately mine. The *"cogito ergo sum"* of the Christian view of repentance is *paenitere possum ergo praesto* (I can repent, therefore I am responsible).

2. The words "truly and earnestly" in the classical prayer remind

us that there can be such a thing as unauthentic or even spurious repentance. In our more secularized culture, it is the apology that often takes the place of penitence. But there can be true and false apologies as well, and our public discourse is rife with spurious apologies. Last year, for example, Senator Packwood responded to accusations of sexual harassment by saying, "I'm apologizing for the conduct that it was alleged that I did." A frequent form of failed apology is "I am really sorry that you feel that way" or words to that effect. Perhaps the all-time title for a spurious apology goes to Richard Nixon. In his resignation speech on 8 August 1974, he said, "I regret deeply any injuries that may have been done in the course of events that led to this decision. I would say only that if some of my judgments were wrong, and some were wrong, they were made at the time in what I believed to be the best interest of the nation."

The style and content of these utterances must raise questions about whether they meet the standards of "truly and earnestly" preserved in the Invitation to Communion. For example, in the case of Nixon, the systematic elimination of personal reference and the reliance on the passive voice (injuries . . . may have been done, judgments were made, etc.) suggests a continuing reluctance to accept personal responsibility and raises doubts about the "earnestness," if not the "truth" of these penitential apologies.

3. The words "are in love and charity with your neighbors" mean that the truly penitent person has already taken the first step toward reintegrating him/herself into the human community whose fabric has been torn or weakened by the betrayal of trust that a transgression causes. It is not enough just to vaguely intend to put things right. The word "are" is in the present tense. I must already *be* in love and charity with my neighbors. Here reconciliation between a human being and his/her neighbors and reconciliation with God are firmly linked. During the Days of Awe before Yom Kippur, Jews are reminded that God can forgive those sins that are committed against Him, but that one must seek forgiveness from one's human neighbors as well as from God for the violations enacted against them. In the Christian view, this idea is modified to some extent. All sins, including those against the neighbor, are also sins against God. Since Christians usually retained the moral but not the ritual elements of Torah, it is hard to imagine a sin against God (in a Christian view) that is not also a sin against some neighbor.

4. The phrases "intend to lead a new life" and "walking from henceforth in his holy ways" suggest a determination on the part of

the penitent person not to repeat the destructive conduct. But "intend" also allows for the weakness of human flesh. The Invitation recognizes that we do not always live out even our most earnest intentions. Nonetheless, even though we fall short, we should still *have* those intentions. Further, the "new life" referred to is not one without moral guidelines. "Following the commandments of God" recalls not only the Ten Commandments but also the Golden Rule, which, in many forms of the Communion service, are read just before the Invitation is issued. This reinforces the notion that these biblical principles are not just intended to "convict of sin" as some theologians have said (though that may be one of their functions). They are also intended to provide moral parameters for the "new life" the penitent person now intends to live.

5. Finally, and perhaps most important, it should be remembered that the Invitation is to participation in Communion. It is an invitation to participate in the family of God gathered around the table that symbolizes the whole of humanity. It is the gateway through which one is welcomed back into a fellowship whose trust and confidence one has broken. It is an avenue to the restoration of the multiple relationships without which human life would cease to be human.

This linking of repentance with restoration to community echoes Jesus' linking of the call to repentance with the announcement that the Kingdom of God—the healed and restored human community—was "at hand." The point is enormously central to the Christian view of repentance. Genuine repentance is an integral element in the coming of the reconciled world of justice and peace that God wills for the world. As Karl Barth once remarked, the church should be "the provisional demonstration of God's intention for the whole human race."

In summary, the previous discussion has shown that repentance in the Christian view involves *four* essential components: remorse, resolution, restitution, and restoration.

1. *Remorse* means being genuinely sorry for what one has done. This includes a realistic awareness of the hurt and damage that has been caused to others by my misdeeds. It also encompasses the suffering that is caused by my *failure* to take action as the words "We have done those things which we ought not to have done and we have left undone the things which we ought to have done" suggest. Remorse goes well beyond "recognition" because it implies a degree of empathic pain on the part of the one who has caused the fracture. This dimension is voiced in the line of

the General Confession that says, "The remembrance of them is grievous unto us." The suggestion is that affect as well as cognition is involved in remorse.

2. *Resolution* means being unfeignedly determined not to repeat the transgression another time. It implies a capacity on the part of human beings not only to make free decisions but (with God's help) to change the way they live. It suggests that although the will may be weakened or paralyzed at times, and although habits are hard to overcome, the genuine determination not to repeat the offense is an essential ingredient in any authentic act of repentance. This is a very important point in our current political and cultural climate because it radically questions the fashionable assumption that both victims and their victimizers are caught in an unbreakable and fatalistic spiral of violence and counterviolence.

3. *Restitution* is both concrete evidence that the penitent person has begun to live in a new way and at the same time a modest step toward rebuilding what has been destroyed. It has been suggested recently that our criminal justice system should make much more use of restitution and much less of incarceration, especially for nonviolent offenses. Places of incarceration are often still called "penitentiaries." There is a genuine question, however, about how much remorse they actually induce, and they leave no room at all for restitution.

4. *Restoration* means full reintegration into the human community. In many Christian theologies, the *restoratio humanii* is believed to be no less than the purpose of the Incarnation. Medieval paintings of the crucifixion of Christ often showed the skull of Adam at the base of the cross. The idea is that a new humanity is now taking shape on the spot where the first human being met his tragic denouement. Jesus spends the months of his earthly ministry breaking the social and cultural taboos that had excluded certain types of people (prostitutes, lepers, tax collectors) from table fellowship with many respectable, pious people. For Jesus, this was an act of symbolic restoration. Inclusive table fellowship modeled an inclusive humanity. It prefigured the messianic feast foreseen by the previous prophets. The ultimate feast is unconditionally inclusive.

In order to make this Christian perspective on repentance a bit more tangible let us ask how it might relate to the recent public discussion of whether the United States should apologize to Japan for the atomic bombing of Hiroshima and Nagasaki.

American Repentance

In the same Book of Common Prayer from which the Invitation to Communion was cited above, there follows the "General Confession." It is worth recalling here as we turn to the ongoing discussion in America about the possibility of our nation's apologizing to Japan.

> Almighty God, Father of our Lord Jesus Christ, Maker of all things, Judge of all men; We acknowledge and bewail our manifold sins and wickedness, Which we, from time to time, most grievously have committed, By thought word and deed, Against thy Divine Majesty, Provoking most justly thy wrath and indignation against us. We do *earnestly* repent and are *heartily* sorry for these our misdoings; The remembrance of them is *grievous* unto us; The burden of them is intolerable.

Last year, President Clinton made a public statement that no apology should or will be made to Japan. His statement raises a series of theological questions, of which perhaps the most salient one is: Can *nations* (or their representatives) as well as individuals repent? Can the present generation repent for the misdeeds of a previous one? In his classic *Moral Man and Immoral Society*, the Protestant theologian Reinhold Niebuhr argued very forcefully that behavior that might be expected of individuals should not be expected of collectivities. However, in 1946 that same theologian helped to draft and then signed a long statement entitled "Atomic Warfare and the Christian Faith," a report requested by what was then called the Federal Council of Churches (it was shortly after renamed the National Council of Churches of Christ). Sometimes known as the "Calhoun Report" for its chairman Robert L. Calhoun, then a professor of historical theology at Yale Divinity School, the statement contains the following sentences:

> We would begin with an act of contrition. As American Christians, we are deeply penitent for the irresponsible use already made of the atomic bomb. We are agreed that, whatever one's judgment on the ethics of war in principle, the surprise bombings of Hiroshima and Nagasaki are morally indefensible. . . . Even though the use of the new weapon last August may well have shortened the war, the moral cost was too high. As the power that first used the atomic bomb under these circumstances, we

have sinned grievously against the laws of God and against the people of Japan. Without seeking to apportion blame among individuals, we are compelled to judge our chosen course inexcusable.

This report bears the signature of twenty theologians and church leaders, in addition to Niebuhr and Calhoun, representing the Protestant theological leadership of the era. Admittedly, it does not pretend to represent national sentiment. It was requested by the Federal Council of Churches but was never intended for adoption. In some measure it parallels the statement issued by the Protestant Church of Germany, also after World War II, expressing penitence for its failure to oppose National Socialism with sufficient vigor.

However, there have been instances in which, if not nations or parties, then persons trying to speak *for* those collectivities have repented or apologized. On 29 April 1993, F. W. de Klerk, who was then the president of South Africa, publicly apologized for his National Party's imposition of apartheid on the country. Again, he offered what seemed to him a plausible reason why the policy appeared right to some well-intentioned people at one time, but added, "It was not our intention to deprive people of their rights and to cause misery . . . insofar as that occurred, we deeply regret it."

In July 1995 Pope John Paul II issued a public letter of apology to all women for the suffering and injustice the Catholic church had contributed to causing them over nearly two millennia. Although the pope did not alter his opposition to the priestly ordination of women or contraception as many had hoped, he did commend the efforts of individuals and organizations who work for equality between the sexes. It was, by anyone's reckoning, an extremely unusual and perhaps unprecedented act of what might be called "collective repentance," not just for the sins of an individual but for those of an institution. The problem is that according to Roman Catholic theology the Bishop of Rome *does* have the authority—under certain circumstances—to speak for the whole church. In other institutions, and in nations, the authority is not nearly as clearly delineated.

At about the same time as the pope's statement, the prime minister of Japan officially apologized to the Korean "comfort women," and to the Chinese victims of Japanese wartime atrocities; and President Chirac of France apologized to the Jewish community for the complicity of the French government in the Nazi crimes. Then, as the fiftieth anniversary of the atomic attacks drew near, some church leaders, historians, and others suggested that the time had come for the United

States to apologize to Japan for the atomic bombing of civilian popula-
tions in the closing days of the war. Some have claimed that such an
apology is especially appropriate now that recent evidence indicates
the Japanese were on the brink of surrender in any case, that the entry
of the USSR into the war and not the bombing was a more decisive
factor, and that the sticking point was the status of the emperor who,
after the surrender, was allowed by the United States to continue in his
imperial office, albeit subject to the American occupation authorities.

But the idea of an American apology to Japan never got very far.
The outcry over the text that was to accompany the *Enola Gay* exhibit
in the Smithsonian revealed that the received version of the reason for
using the bomb—allegedly to save millions of American and Japanese
lives—although now historically implausible, still retains a strong hold
on large numbers of people even as its validity is questioned by newly
released documents (see, inter alia, the top secret U.S. Intelligence Report of 30 April 1946 entitled "Use of the Atomic Bomb on Japan"
recently republished in Gar Alperouitz, *Atomic Diplomacy* (London:
Pluto Press, 1994). It was probably in the light of this controversy that
President Clinton went one step further. He not only did not apologize
to Japan, he publicly declared that no apology was appropriate and
none was to be accepted.

Without trying to second-guess President Clinton's reasons for his
decision, we might ask whether any of the essential elements of repentance mentioned above have yet appeared in the collective American
psyche. The answer is that for most Americans the sentiment is quite
mixed.

Polls have shown that about one-half of Americans believe that the
bomb should not have been used the way it was. Still, it is clear that
there is no widespread national feeling of *remorse*. When the suggestion
is made that the United States should apologize for Hiroshima, some
have insisted that this could be considered only after the Japanese have
apologized for Pearl Harbor. The fact that the attack on Hawaii was
directed toward a military target and involved fewer deaths is outweighed in some people's minds by the fact that it was a "sneak attack."
When collectivities are involved, it would appear to be premature to
urge a symbolic figure like the president to apologize (i.e., to engage
in one of the steps in repentance) if there is no national feeling of sorrow
and regret. What would it mean for the president to apologize if the
majority of the population does not support his act? Still, there is such
a thing as "representative repentance," in which a portion of the citizens of a nation assume the responsibility of repenting *for* the totality,
a gesture that is by its nature only partial but hardly insignificant.

Resolution in this case could best take the form of an American pledge never to use nuclear weapons again, or never to be the first to use them. Although this idea has been advanced for many years now, no American president or administration has even been willing to make such a pledge. President Clinton's recent call for a comprehensive ban on all nuclear weapons testing, though not explicitly related to an act of repentance for Hiroshima, would still be a substantive act of resolution and of restoration if it were enacted.

What would the Japanese government and people expect by way of *restitution* if America ever apologized for the atomic raids? Japan hardly needs money. But some imaginative suggestion, perhaps that information on the reality of what nuclear war involves be included in American high school curricula (as treatment of the Holocaust is now in some places), might be an appropriate form of restitution.

As for the *restoration* of relations, at one level that has already begun without the previous three steps. But one sometimes gets the impression that the detente between America and Japan is more fragile than either side wants to admit, that unresolved distrust, resentment, and bitter rivalry still persist, usually but not always just below the surface. These negative currents could become very dangerous if the already strained economic links between the two countries were fractured or other disruptions occurred. Genuine restoration, it seems, awaits a full-orbed repentance by both parties, for Hiroshima *and* for Pearl Harbor. Perhaps one could understand the Calhoun Report as a failed effort to move American public opinion in that direction. But even though that effort did not succeed (one rarely hears about the report today), if its reasoning was sound, then the moral imperative remains in force today.

Is repentance necessarily a specifically "religious" act? I have included in this chapter both insights drawn from the biblical and liturgical resources of the Christian tradition and illustrations from the "secular" world. I have done this to suggest that from a Christian perspective there is no separate and distinct "religious" sphere within which the dynamics of repentance and forgiveness are appropriate while in the "secular world" some other pattern obtains. Quite the opposite. The Christian message is about what God is doing "in, with, and under" the earthly day-to-day world in which we all live. It is not an idealistic message for some other time or some other realm. It is about us, here and now. But it also points to an ultimate fulfillment and consummation of human life and history, something we are permitted to hope for and to taste in anticipation. Therefore, the liturgy for Holy Communion, from which the above excerpts were taken, ends on a note of comfort and joy. After the Invitation and the General Confession, the presiding minister says to the congregation: "Almighty God, our heavenly Father, who of his great mercy hath promised forgiveness of sins to all those who with hearty repentance and true faith turn unto him; Have mercy upon you; pardon and deliver you from all your sins; confirm and strengthen you in all goodness; and bring you to everlasting life; through Jesus Christ our Lord. Amen."

After this, everyone in the congregation—the old and the young, the sick and the healthy, the resident and the sojourner, people of all colors and conditions—gather around the table of bread and wine and partake symbolically in the fully restored human family that God has promised will one day come to pass. The single and sole precondition for their participation in this feast of hope and anticipation is that they have repented and seek to lead a new life.

2

Godly Sorrow, Sorrow of the World: Some Christian Thoughts on Repentance

Harold O. J. Brown

Repentance is not a word that is on everyone's lips in our day. A well-known comedian, referring to a sexual liaison with the adopted daughter of his paramour, simply said, "I screwed up." To admit a "mistake" is about as close as most figures in public life ever come to expressing repentance. Sin, guilt, or fault is not easily acknowledged. Even when the words "I'm sorry" are used, they often imply not an admission of fault, but merely mean that things did not turn out as the speaker might have hoped.[1]

Traditional Christianity—like most of the religions of humanity—regards sin as the fundamental barrier between individual human beings and God; awareness of one's sin is needed in order to repent. Unfortunately, the concept of sin, understood as the transgression of God's Law, as rebellion or covenant breaking, is not an ever-present reality in the minds of most contemporary men and women; indeed, few of us think often about the fact—at least as Christianity sees it—that we live our lives before God.

The Christian concept of repentance presupposes belief in a personal God and an awareness of sin and what it does to human relationships with God. For Christianity, repentance involves more than an internalized awareness of failure or fault, which we might designate as aversion, as turning away from that of which one is ashamed. It also involves adversion, turning to God, to the personal God whose active gift of grace first makes self-understanding and repentance possible, and whose redemptive love then responds to repentance with forgiveness and restoration. The fact that, for the Christian, repentance involves a second party, God, means that in theory and often in practice the one who repents will receive divine aid to shake off the fault, guilt, and sin of the past and to make a new beginning. Thus the Apostle Paul writes, "If anyone is in Christ, he is a new creation: the old has gone; the new has come!"[2] This means that true repentance in the Christian sense should offer hope for a transformed life and changed conduct, for the benefit of those who have been hurt as well as for that of the repentant person himself or herself.

Where there is no awareness of sin, there is no place for repentance in the religious sense. Even where the reality of God is accepted, repentance makes sense only when it is understood that God's love for humankind is love of a special kind, love that is traditionally called covenant life—contrary to the popular tendency to imagine God, if one thinks of him[3] at all, as unconditionally loving. Unconditional love would not require repentance, although perhaps the person who felt unconditionally loved might be moved to repent out of gratitude and self-knowledge.

Repentance and forgiveness in the Christian sense are intensely personal transactions: sin offends the personal God; repentance appeals to God to forgive; restoration makes the forgiven person whole again. Repentance also has a temporal dimension, involving a turning away from the past and an openness to the future. Even a person who has committed a capital crime and is sentenced to death, can, by repentance, be assured of a future beyond the grave.

The God of biblical revelation is indeed a God of love, but his love is no undefined, unconditional love, no promiscuous love, as it were, but rather covenant love, love in the context of a divine covenant between God and man. The biblical concept of covenant differs from a contract or a treaty between equal human partners in that it is freely offered by the divine Sovereign to people of his choice, involving gracious promises on which they can rely, usually with conditions for them to fulfill. God is indeed a God of love (I John 4:8), but this love must be understood in the light of God's fidelity to his own nature and of the reciprocal faithfulness that he expects of us.

God, while being the creator of all things and "King of the Universe," enters into a personal relationship with chosen individuals or an entire people, binds himself by covenant promises to them, and expects covenant loyalty and commitment from them.[4] The Christian concept of repentance is intimately connected with the doctrines of God's covenant love for us and of human sin, which violates that covenant and requires repentance.

Christian repentance involves not merely a turning away from what one has done in the past, but also a rejection of what one has been, and for this reason it does not come easily. It seems to involve self-abasement and humiliation. Although ultimately it brings reconciliation and acceptance, at first it seems to involve a kind of alienation from oneself.

During the Nuremberg war crimes trials, former Reichsminister Hermann Goering expressed contempt for a couple of his fellow prisoners who professed to have been converted and to have repented of their deeds: he found it dishonorable and undignified. For Goering to stand by what he had done and to remain what he was may have been to exhibit a certain kind of heroism, but it also involved a self-destructive rejection of the love of God, a spurning of the divine offer of forgiveness and redemption.

Perhaps the greatest psychological barrier to repentance is the self-love and self-righteousness that consistently refuse to admit fault. Because a proper understanding of human fault is tied to a knowledge of sin, which comes in a clear sense only through the knowledge of the Law of God, Christian repentance is found only in the context of an awareness both of the demands of the Law and of the promises of forgiveness and restoration that are appended to them.

Repentance and Restoration

Repentance in the biblical and Christian sense does not mean opening oneself helplessly to divine wrath. Although God, unlike any human judge or tyrant, is to be feared as "the One who can destroy both body and soul in hell" (Matthew 10:28), he need only be feared when his love is rejected along with his Law. Faith trusts that it will not encounter divine vengeance or indifference, but forgiving love.

Repentance thus involves two parties: the offender and the offended; it differs from mere remorse, which is a solitary thing. Repentance in the biblical and Christian sense is never the act of a single ego, furious with itself for failure, but always means a dialogue, face to face with the God of the Covenant. Repentance figures prominently in both the Hebrew Scriptures and the New Testament. The Gospel of Mark, considered by most scholars to be the first gospel that was written down, begins with summons to repentance by John the Baptist and by Jesus (Mark 1:4, 1:15). While calls to repent and return to God abound in the Hebrew Scriptures, in the New Testament the call is sharper, more central, and more focused.

After a citation from Isaiah, "Prepare ye the way of the Lord, Make straight in the desert a highway for our God" (Isaiah 40:3),[5] John the Baptist began his ministry with a generalized call to repentance, couched in inflammatory language: "O generation of vipers, who has warned you to flee from the wrath to come?" (Matthew 3:7). As the Evangelist Mark puts it, "John did baptize in the wilderness and preach the baptism of repentance for the remission of sins" (Mark 1:4). Jesus began his ministry with the appeal "The time is fulfilled, and the kingdom of God is at hand: repent ye, and believe the gospel" (1:14). The expression "gospel" (Greek *euangelion*, "good news") here is not to be understood as referring to a set of doctrines to be accepted, but rather as a kind of synonym for repentance, for believing the good news that God will receive the sinner who turns away from sin and returns to God.

From a Christian perspective, it is sin, not repentance, that is dishonorable and destructive of personal dignity. For Goering, repentance would have been honorable, not disgraceful. Unfortunately, more people seem to be ashamed of repenting than of sinning, particularly in public life, but also in private. When a convicted prisoner expresses remorse for his misdeed, the cynic sees it as only a ruse to gain more lenient treatment, leaving it to the optimist or the naive to hope that it involves a true change and means that society will be able to count on the prisoner to behave with decency and responsibility in the future.

Counterfeits

Genuine repentance is rare, and sham or expedient repentance is common. True repentance is so valuable that it invites counterfeits, and counterfeit repentance is common enough to make people suspicious of all repentance. The value of repentance depends not on intensity of feeling, but on sincerity and genuineness. History tells us of many "grand penitents," but also bears witness to many hypocrites and frauds. It may not be evident even to the penitent himself or herself whether repentance is truly genuine: the prophet Jeremiah warns, "The heart is deceitful above all things, and desperately wicked: who can know it?" (Jeremiah 17:9). One may have to wait to judge the genuineness of one's own repentance and of that of others to see whether or not it produces "fruits meet for repentance" as John the Baptist demanded (Matthew 3:8). God, however, does not need to wait, as his next word to Jeremiah indicates: "I the Lord search the hearts, I try the reins, even to give to every man according to his ways, and according to the fruit of his doings" (Jeremiah 17:10).

There is such a thing as genuinely transforming repentance; the possibility of counterfeit repentance should not blind us to the vital contribution that true repentance can make in the life of the individual and of society, bringing about fundamental changes of attitude and behavior on which family, friends, and society can place reliance.

Repentance in Action and Thought

The call to repent does not originate in the New Testament; it frequently resounds in the Hebrew Scriptures, naturally enough when falling away and backsliding are cited so often. From the outset, the biblical concept of repentance is accompanied by physical imagery, suggestive of the fact that it means a new direction of life, not merely a new understanding of things. It involves the whole person. The Hebrew word *shub* literally means to "turn back" and implies an almost physical "aversion" as a condition or concomitant of "adversion," of turning to God. One example may stand for many in the Old Testament, namely, God's word to Solomon on the occasion of the dedication of the Temple: "If my people, which are called by my name, shall humble themselves, and pray, and seek my face, and turn from their wicked ways; then will I hear from heaven, and will forgive their sin, and will heal their land" (II Chronicles 7:14).

The people are summoned to both a spiritual change of attitude and a bodily change of posture and orientation. The words "turn" and "ways" may be understood metaphorically, but the implication that true repentance will in some sense be visible is not to be swept aside. Bodily postures, like oral professions, may be feigned; nevertheless, the use of body language does express the idea that true repentance involves the whole person.

Both in the Hebrew Scriptures and in the New Testament, repentance always has the two aspects mentioned above: aversion and adversion, turning from and turning to: turning away from the bondage of sin to the "glorious freedom of the children of God" (Romans 8:21); turning away from bondage to what has been to openness to what can yet be. It also involves turning away from that which is not God, which is impersonal or even unreal, and instead turning to the personal, to the God who is, who knows us and calls us by name.

Turning away from wickedness can be rather impersonal, as one would avert one's face from evil-smelling garbage. The turning toward is always a more personal matter: the repentant person, called by name by God, turns to God in prayer and seeks his face. Repentance thus involves not merely a coming to oneself or to one's senses concerning one's own acts and attitudes in the past, an aversion from such "its," but also an awakening to oneself as an accused, as one standing *"coram Deo,"* before God, *"in foro divino,"* in the divine courtroom.

Upon being accused, that is, upon being directly, personally addressed, the sinner is made to feel personally answerable, that is, to be obliged to respond to the Thou of God. Being obliged to answer for one's acts is to be made responsible. Repentance in this sense of accepting responsibility and consequences is thus to be seen in the context of seeking the face of God, to whom one owes a response.

David committed adultery with Bathsheba and arranged the death of her husband, his own faithful subordinate Uriah. When the prophet Nathan confronted David, saying, "Thou art the man" (II Samuel 12:7), David prayed to God, "Against thee, thee only have I sinned" (Psalm 51:4). This is not a brushing aside of the human dimension of the sins of adultery and murder, but rather a recognition of the fact that one is ultimately answerable to God, with whom forgiveness may be found, and by whom alone new life may be granted.

In the New Testament, repentance involves all that has already been said about turning from sin and turning to God. In addition, the Greek vernacular used in the New Testament adds an element of mental or noetic reorientation: the Greek word *metanoia* means a fundamental change of mind, just as metamorphosis involves a fundamental change in form (*morphe*): the caterpillar becomes a butterfly. Thus repentance in Christian thought is explicitly associated with being "made new," or "born again," as the Greek expressions *anakainosis* and *palingenesis* imply: it implies a certain *"ep' hapax,"* once-and-for-all change.

This has both positive and negative implications. One who repents and is in a realistic sense "regenerate," "born again," should not have to "repent and be converted" more than once. Consequently, repentance in this Christian sense ought to signal a really clear turning and a new beginning, setting the repentant sinner on an entirely new course of conduct.[6] The negative implications become evident when the born-again penitent sins anew—as all or virtually all will do: if repentance really involves a once-and-for-all transformation, a back-slider can hardly expect to be born again another time. One New Testament passage, Hebrews 6:4–6, implies that a second renewal is impossible, a frightening thought for anyone who thinks that he has sinned grievously after being converted.

Roman Catholicism has sought to banish this dread by sacramental means; Protestants sometimes seek to deal with it by redefining sin in their own minds so that it involves only things that they never do. The Hebrew Scriptures too imply that repentance and falling away are not acts that can readily be repeated (see Ezekiel 3:16–21), a conviction that underlies the zeal of the godly Pharisee to keep the Law fully. While the sinner is always invited to repent, there is the underlying suggestion that if one hardens one's heart too often, God will harden it definitively (see Exodus 7:13, 10:1).

The Christian association of repentance with being regenerated, with the new birth, impels some Christians to a kind of Christian Pharisaism, a zealous attempt to fulfill every divine requirement, in order to believe that they are indeed born again. It can delude others into thinking that once they have been "saved," that is, born again through repentance and faith, they no longer need worry about any sins they may subsequently commit and consequently sin with impunity. In what we might call the worst-case scenario, such thinking sees repentance as something that is to be exercised only towards God, and only once, and permits a self-righteous attitude to coexist with a morally defective pattern of life.[7] Although the phenomenon of falling away is also familiar to Jews, the Christian association of repentance with a far-reaching, ideally once-and-for-all *metanoia* exacerbates the familiar human tension between faith and practice.

This "transmindedness" of *metanoia* has two very significant implications for secular life: first, as already suggested, it raises an impersonal sense of defilement to a personal awareness of accountability; second, it changes a preoccupation with the past into an openness to the future, creating the dimension of hope.[8] The significance of repentance in the Christian sense for communities, for society as a whole, lies precisely in this personalization of responsibility, in the fact, or at least the possibility, that it will bring a real, effective transformation of offenders, and permit them a fresh, new departure in life.

Can a profession of repentance actually indicate such an aversion to past evil that one may confidently expect a fundamental change of direction, one sufficient to turn a criminal into a valuable and productive citizen? If repentant, "born-again" Christians really could be depended upon to exhibit the "perseverance of the saints," evangelists could replace judges and prison wardens. Unfortunately, a profession of repentance does not guarantee such a change, but it is accompanied by it with a certain frequency.

While in our secular society we do not put it in the context of Christian repentance, we do use language reminiscent of Christian teaching when dealing with crime and punishment. We do not explicitly challenge offenders to repent, but we place them in a "penitentiary" and speak of "rehabilitation." The term "repentance," with its Christian associations, is seldom used, but sentences are sometimes softened or sharpened as the prisoner expresses or fails to express "remorse."

The introduction of the word "penitentiary" instead of "prison" in the last century reflected the hope that prisoners would become penitents, that is to say, would repent, and would be able to return to society as changed men—and women, though most serious offenders are male—people on whose decency and constancy their fellow citizens can subsequently rely. There was and often still is a religious component to this secular penitential hope. Prisons—or penitentiaries—usually have chaplains, and various ministries operate within them, the best known in recent years being the Prison Fellowship, founded by Chuck Colson.

The approved word today is rehabilitation, not repentance, but prison administrators generally want all of the help that they can get. Without putting full trust in the ability of Christian or other religious ministries[9] to make honest citizens out of convicts, every prison warden can tell stories of prisoners with whom repentance and conversion really "took" and resulted in totally transformed lives—as well as, alas, of prisoners whose profession of repentance proved only a momentary pause in their pursuit of evil.

Christian theology, as already noted, speaks of regeneration, of the new birth, of being born again, of becoming a "new creature" or "new creation." In Christian terms, real repentance must be the beginning of a changed life. The change begins with a declaration of forgiveness in *foro divino* (the divine courtroom), and, at least in Protestant terms, the repentant sinner is said to be justified by faith, "translated" from the power of darkness into the kingdom of Christ the Son.[10] In Christian, or more specifically Protestant, terms, forgiveness is never earned by a reformed life; instead, a reformation of life is made possible by the cleansing of the conscience through forgiveness (Hebrews 9:14).[11] Like the Prodigal Son in the parable, the penitent "comes to himself" (Luke 14:17) and learns to know himself better than he did before repentance, in addition to coming to know the One before whom he repents.

Because repentance involves turning toward as well as turning away from, it directs the mind toward the future in a way that simple remorse, or "worldly sorrow," as Paul put it, cannot do. Repentance implies restitution and restoration, and thus implies a future that is not bound by the habits and vices of the past. A murderer condemned to death can truly repent, like the "Good Thief" dying on the cross, even if his earthly life is almost over. Christianity assures him that his repentance gives him a future that his execution cannot destroy. Jesus said to the dying thief, "Today thou shalt be with me in paradise" (Luke 23:43). The one who is truly repentant in the Christian sense will be liberated from the past and has a new future opened to him, even if death is at his door. It is this aspect of repentance that makes the penitent free, in the words of Hebrews, "to serve the living God" (Hebrews 9:14).

Worldly Sorrow

Repentance follows upon sorrow about the past, but sorrow of a particular kind; hopeful sorrow, if we may put it thus. In the sense in which these words are used here, remorse is not repentance. It, too, involves sorrow, but sorrow of a kind that we may call hopeless sorrow. Remorse is usually bitter; repentance can be hard, but it need not, indeed should not, be bitter. Repentance differs from mere remorse, because by its very nature it implies openness to the future. It is true that to regret or feel sorrow for evil that one has done is morally preferable to indifference or, which is worse, satisfaction with one's evil deeds, but sorrow, as Paul says, can be of two kinds. "Godly sorrow brings repentance that leads to salvation and leaves no regret, but worldly sorrow brings death."[12] In Paul's use of the terms, the sorrow of the world is not based on a sense of personal responsibility or a recognition of one's own guilt, and has no sense of a divine Thou to whom one could confess and from whom one could receive forgiveness. The sorrow of the world is regret for that which is lost, but it does not carry with itself hope for the future. It is the sorrow of Judas at the consequence of his betrayal: "And he cast down the pieces of silver in the temple, and departed, and went and hanged himself."[13]

Judas's sorrow was of the most self-destructive kind, because it did not reckon with divine forgiveness, but made Judas his own judge.

Would God have forgiven even Judas, had he turned to him in repentance? We do not know, for sadly, unlike Peter, Judas did not wait for an answer from God, but exercised vengeance upon himself.

The sorrow of the world takes no account of the fact that we live under the watchful eye of God. It can arise, with similarly sad consequences, for reasons other than remorse for one's own misdeeds, when afflicted by a sense of irreparable loss in an impersonal universe, when there is no sense of a God who ultimately "shall wipe all tears from their eyes" (Revelation 7:17). It is the lament of Aeneas upon beholding a mural portraying the fall of Troy, "*Sunt lacrimae rerum, et mentem mortalia tangunt.*"[14]

In both cases, that of Judas and that of Aeneas, the sorrow of the world weeps, and in Judas's case, rages, before a closed door. Such sorrow will not say, "The past is prologue," for the past is dead. Such sorrow is not Christian repentance, and it leads to death, not to forgiveness and life.

Godly Sorrow

What distinguishes godly sorrow from the sorrow of the world? The world, the present age, is not so much opposed to God as it is ignorant of him and indifferent to him. The sorrow of the world, seen as an impersonal universe, does not reckon with God; godly sorrow does. Cruelty, meaninglessness, and evil will afflict human beings however they may conceive the universe, but sorrow is different in a world where people are unaware of God. In such a world one truly must echo Aeneas, "*Sunt lachrymae rerun, et mentem mortalia tangunt.*"

From a Christian perspective at least, the sorrow that brings the repentance that leads to salvation and leaves no regret is precisely that, namely, sorrow from a Christian perspective. It is the kind of sorrow that is possible in a world that is not of our own making; not the product of a blind universe, of time plus space plus chance, but a world that has a Creator, a world that is God's handiwork.

Conclusion

From this perspective, repentance is the only way for humans to escape from the impasse of fault, sin, and guilt, from bondage to the past, and to enjoy the "glorious liberty of the children of God." It may well be possible for people who do not believe that such a God and such liberty exist to "turn from their wicked way," change direction, be rehabilitated, and lead a different life; we have seen examples. The Christian will nevertheless say, elaborating a bit on the words of Jesus in Matthew 19:26, "With men such things, if not impossible, are hard, but with God all things are possible."

Notes

1. The best-remembered line of Eric Segal's best-selling novella, *Love Story*, is, "Love means never having to say you're sorry." But the love of God for us means precisely that: we do have to say we're sorry.

2. II Corinthians 5:17, New International Version (NIV).

3. It is becoming popular in some circles to introduce "gender neutral" language for God, even to the extent of coining expressions such as "Mother-Father God." Christianity does not attribute maleness or sexuality to the Deity, but inasmuch as the Christian's knowledge of God depends on biblical revelation, because biblical revelation uses masculine pronouns for God, I believe that it is necessary for me to do so as well. We should be able to live with the common linguistic convention of using masculine pronouns in a general, generic sense as well as in a more specific sense for male persons.

4. The doctrine of election is prominent in both the Old Testament and the New and is the subject of many energetic disputes among Jews, Christians, and others as well. It is too complex to be described here. Occasionally God's covenant with an elect individual or group is unconditional: for example, the "Abrahamic covenant" of Genesis 12:3. In other cases, God requires the fulfillment of particular conditions on the part of God's covenant people: see Deuteronomy 28. In general, God's love is not unconditional. Even the best-known Sunday school memory verse, John 3:16, which begins with the words, "God so loved the world," carries the condition, "whosoever believes."

5. Cited from the Authorized (King James) Version. Although the AV is not considered the most exact English translation, it is generally quite reliable; I use it here and elsewhere in this chapter because of its familiarity and the beauty of its language.

6. For this reason, it sometimes happens that criminals who repent and are "converted," becoming in Christian terms a "new creation" (II Corinthians 5:17), expect to be pardoned from the punishment their crimes would otherwise have warranted. From time to time, a court actually accepts this line of thinking and reduces or suspends a sentence.

7. Many readers will be aware of individual Christians who on one hand profess to have been born again and on the other hand transgress the commandments heedlessly and openly. Calvinists, who teach the "perseverance of the saints," will say that such persons were never truly converted; Catholics,

Lutherans, and others will say that they have lost their salvation, and need to repent again (but not: be born again another time).

8. This aspect of guilt has been examined at length by Prof. Paul Ricoeur in *Finitude and Culpability*, vol. 1 of *The Symbolism of Evil* (Boston: Beacon Press, 1969).

9. The Black Muslims, although they espouse a doctrine signally different from Christianity, deserve recognition by Christians for their success in helping African-American prisoners to change their lives, a sort of non-Christian *metanoia*.

10. Colossians 1:13, AV. The AV "translated," like St. Jerome in the Latin Vulgate (*transtulit*, carried over) gives the positional sense of the Greek *metestesen* better than the more contemporary New International Version (NIV): "He has rescued us from the dominion of darkness and brought us into the kingdom of the Son."

11. Readers familiar with the differences between the major Christian confessions know that Roman Catholics and evangelical Protestants differ about whether righteousness or justification is first of all imputed because of saving faith (Protestant) or to be achieved by means of infused grace (Catholic). This difference is not negligible, but it seems fair to say that both Catholics and Protestants intend for repentance to be followed by a life of righteousness.

12. II Corinthians 7:10, NIV. The AV language is more colorful: "Godly sorrow worketh repentance to salvation not to be repented of: but the sorrow of the world worketh death."

13. Matthew 27:5.

14. Virgil, *Aeneid*, Book I: "There are tears for things, and mortal sorrows touch the heart" [lit. "mortal things touch the mind"] (Ann Arbor: University of Michigan Press, 1995), 462.

3

From Sacrifice to Sacrament:
Repentance in a Christian Context

John Lyden

American society does not seem to be one that encourages repentance. Many criminals, politicians, and other public figures seem generally unable to acknowledge, let alone apologize for transgressions. When it is claimed that we live in a society in which morality is declining and values are absent, this is in part an observation of the fact that many people do not acknowledge wrongdoing or turn away from it. Furthermore, there is a general lack of understanding of the nature and process of repentance. Many religious traditions describe repentance as involving a number of steps, including these three: first, one must acknowledge one's sin and be truly sorry for it; second, one must resolve to try to avoid sinning again; and third, one must attempt to make up for the sin by apologizing to those one has offended and compensating them in a fair manner whenever possible. But frequently people have so much trouble with the first two steps they do not even attempt the third. Repentance does "cost" us something—whether in pride, or actual possessions we hand over. The thief has not really repented until and unless he returns the stolen goods. The liar has not made up for her dishonesty until she confesses to those to whom she lied. But this price is too high for those who would rather not place themselves in a position of vulnerability by admitting their own imperfection.

One might attribute this lack of genuine repentance to the nature of humanity and assert that we have always been reluctant to admit our faults and make up for them. While this may be true, such a fatalistic

43

attitude makes it seem as if there is nothing we can or need do to create a population more attentive to repentance. Alternately, one might assume that the allegedly waning influence of religion has led people to neglect repentance to a greater extent in recent decades, and that the solution is to let religious concepts back into the public arena where they can have greater impact on the moral life of society. It is certainly true that religious notions of repentance have often been ignored (regardless of whether or not religious influence is waning). But it is not clear if a "public" religion can do the job of making our society more aware of repentance; we do not have a religiously homogeneous society, but a pluralistic one that guards against the state establishment of any particular religion. We will not become a society that encourages repentance simply by allowing a few religious groups to define morality for all of us.

I would propose, however, that our society could become more attentive to repentance by listening to religious concepts of repentance. This does not mean making one religious concept normative for society or allowing one religious group to dictate society's values, but rather permitting religions to speak out of their traditions to suggest ways in which repentance may be fostered. Those who represent and study various religious traditions may be able to shed some light for all of us on the difficult task of repentance by examining how their own traditions deal with this topic. With this as the model, I will in this chapter critically examine certain aspects of Christian thought and ask what relationship they have to repentance. Specifically, I will consider how Christians and their churches might and should think if they are to be exemplars of repentance. I do not intend to assert that a Christian understanding of repentance is the only or the "best" way of understanding repentance, but rather to show how Christians do or might think about repentance in the context of their own traditions. This in turn may suggest ways in which repentance might be encouraged in our society as a whole.

Christians and Repentance

Christians have not neglected the topic of repentance. Repentance has always been a Christian condition for salvation, and it would seem that this involves the human in the process of appropriating divine salvation. One cannot receive salvation, in other words, unless one is able to freely accept it by turning away from sin and toward God. On the other hand, the significance of the act of repentance has often been belittled as Christians insist that God alone makes this salvation possible. Christians have sometimes had difficulty reconciling the idea that humans are unable to save themselves (and therefore need Christ) with the idea that humans must freely accept this salvation themselves.[1] Are we or are we not responsible for ourselves? Without faith in Christ, his death avails nothing for one. Without repentance for one's sins and acknowledgment of the need for salvation, one will not be able to make the turn from sin to God. But Christians have resisted locating salvation primarily in the human act of faith and repentance, as they insist that salvation comes from God and not from humans. In so doing, Christians run the risk of making it seem as if no moral transformation is needed, for we are saved not by our deeds but by a freely given unmerited gift from God.

There is then a tension within Christian doctrine between God's grace and human freedom. In America today, this tension is often ignored as most churches preach that we freely choose to sin or not, to have faith or not, to do good or not.[2] But even with this emphasis on free will, the tension persists, in that churches proclaim that God will forgive and even has forgiven all sins through a boundless grace that may make the human act that accepts this grace almost irrelevant. If we are forgiven no matter what we do, some might reason, why attempt to reform ourselves? Why seek to become better people who live more in accord with God's will? The answer may lie in the idea that those who know they are forgiven will naturally respond with gratitude to God, desiring to follow God's will to please God. Ideally, this would be the case; but Christians cannot ignore the fact that a focus on God's grace may and sometimes does lead to human irresponsibility, as we conclude that we need do nothing to earn God's favor.

The Christian emphasis on grace consequently creates some problems for a Christian understanding of repentance. The necessity for repentance may be undermined by a confidence in "cheap grace" that is guaranteed no matter what we do. Though churches certainly do not wish to encourage moral laxity through their preaching on God's forgiveness, it may be an unfortunate by-product of Christian doctrine. This makes it all the more pressing to ask, in what ways might repentance be specifically encouraged within a Christian context? To answer this, one needs to look at the Christian view of repentance in relation to the rest of Christian doctrine.

The specifically Christian doctrine of repentance is shaped in large part by the role Christ plays for the Christian. Human repentance must for the Christian somehow be connected with Christ's death, as it is contingent on and participatory in the atonement accomplished by Christ. The Christian knows God's forgiveness through the cross, in that she knows "God so loved the world that He gave his only Son" to die for it (John 3:16). But Christ's atonement cannot remain an act of God that is unrelated to human appropriation of it. Faith in Christ is needed, and this includes repentance, understood as turning from sin to God. The human is not said to make salvation possible (God alone can do that), but without human repentance, the atonement is in a sense incomplete. It is not to be understood that humans add something to God's work; rather, they participate in it, especially by reenacting Christ's sacrifice in such a way that they are made partakers in it. This occurs most visibly in the reception of the sacraments, in particular of the Lord's Supper. Here the salvation of Christ is not only made present, but the recipient actually shares in the sacrifice of Christ. This, the central ritual of Christian worship, actually contains within it the form of Christian repentance based in Christ's atoning act. Participation in the sacraments is in this sense connected with the Christian life and actions that express both the turn from sin and following God.

The Christian understanding of repentance therefore is linked both to an understanding of Christ's death (as that which makes repentance possible) and the celebration of the sacraments (as the ritual means that connect human repentance with God's grace). To develop this specifically Christian understanding of repentance, I will first examine some of the major theories of how Christ atones for human sin with the aim of finding a Christian understanding of atonement that can be the basis for an effective doctrine of repentance. Second, I will examine the role sacraments have played and the role they can play in providing the connection between human repentance and God's grace. The purpose of this is not simply to see what has been said by Christians about repentance, but also to suggest what might be said that could lead to a more effective Christian understanding of repentance.

Christian Views of Atonement

Most theologians have accepted the notion that there are three main types of atonement theories, often referred to (following Gustaf Aulén) as the "satisfaction" or objective-legalist theory; the subjective or "moral influence" theory; and the "classic" theory of Christ's victory

over sin, death, and the devil. In evaluating which view of atonement
is most helpful in developing a Christian doctrine of repentance, I will
suggest that the "classic" view makes repentance almost irrelevant (because God does everything necessary for salvation) and the subjective
view makes Christ's atonement almost irrelevant (as humans do everything necessary for salvation). For this reason, I will propose a variant
of the objective view that seeks to relate human repentance to God's
grace in a more effective way.

The "satisfaction" theory, represented most clearly by Anselm in his
Cur Deus Homo, claims that the death of Christ is required to satisfy the
demands of God's justice that a human pay the debt for human sin. In
part, this is because sin is here understood as a state, a condition in
which humanity finds itself: "original sin," which is more heinous and
deeper than any individual sin. Because of this condition, God cannot
restore humans to paradise "unwashed," that is, simply by a forgiveness that ignores human sin: "Without satisfaction, that is, without voluntary payment of the debt, God can neither pass by the sin
unpunished, nor can the sinner attain that happiness, or happiness
like that, which he had before he sinned."[3] But humans are—precisely
because of sin—unable to pay the debt or to be obedient to God, and
there is also nothing they have of sufficient worth to make the payment. Only God has the ability to pay the debt, and yet humans have
the obligation to pay it.[4] The solution to this dilemma is for God to
become human, so that He who is able to make payment and He who
ought to make payment are the same; "it is necessary that the same
being should be perfect God and perfect man, in order to make this
atonement."[5] The God-man, who is the incarnation of the second person of the Trinity, makes payment with his obedience (unto death) to
the first person of the Trinity, God the Father. This payment merits a
reward for the God-man, who graciously defers this reward and gives
it to the rest of humanity so that we might have eternal life instead of
eternal death.[6]

This view is able to explain why God must become human through
the assumption that someone must make "payment" to God in order
for atonement to occur. Anselm wrote in a medieval world shaped by
the doctrine of penance and the need to make "satisfaction" for sins.
It has been said that this view errs in viewing God as a wrathful tyrant
who is unable to forgive without cause, and in viewing salvation as
something that must be "earned" from the human side (albeit by a
human who also happens to be God). Gustaf Aulén was among the
most significant critics of Anselm in modern times, and he upheld what

he called the "classic" view as a better alternative, to which we must turn to appreciate the critique of the "objective" view.

Aulén believed that prior to Anselm's work in the eleventh century, the standard atonement doctrine did not claim that Christ died to satisfy the demands of God's justice but to free humans from the power of the devil. Because of sin, humans were bound to evil and could not escape.[7] God becomes human to defeat the powers of sin, death, and the devil, through Christ's death and resurrection. Whereas the satisfaction theory stressed how Christ's death pays for human sins, the classic view stresses the victory of Christ over death in His resurrection. Often the church fathers who upheld this view spoke of Christ's death as a "ransom" paid to the devil to free humans from sin; Anselm regarded this as illogical and offensive, for God owes nothing to the devil.[8] And yet as Aulén points out, many of the church fathers did not regard the devil as actually having any "rights" over humanity that had to be satisfied according to some legal demands. Rather, humans are in the devil's power, even if illegitimately, and Christ offers himself to the devil as a means of freeing them.[9] Several of the fathers utilize the idea that the devil was "tricked" in that Christ defeats him by His resurrection, thereby refusing the devil the final victory and revoking payment of the "ransom."[10] Today, we might say God stops payment on the check.

In Aulén's view, the real advantage of all this dualistic imagery that highlights a "cosmic battle" between God and evil is to show that salvation is from God alone. In contrast with Anselm's view, according to which humans must make "payment" to God, Aulén holds that "it is God's love . . . that removes the sentence that rested upon mankind, and creates a new relation between the human race and Himself, a relation which is altogether different from any sort of justification by legal righteousness. The whole dispensation is the work of grace."[11] This is made clear by the fact that "God himself makes the sacrifice" and not any human being.[12] Aulén, who was a bishop of the Lutheran Church of Sweden, rejects Anselm's medieval Roman Catholic assumptions about penance and human satisfaction for sin in favor of the Protestant notion that we do not in any way "merit" salvation. It is solely God's work, and not accomplished by humans.

If Aulén makes salvation solely the work of God and Anselm makes it the work of God and human (in Christ's person), the "subjective" view may make it almost entirely the work of humans. The twelfth-century theologian Peter Abailard is usually cited as the classic representative of this position, although it has enjoyed more popularity since the Enlightenment. According to Abailard, humans are reconciled to God "through this unique act of grace manifested to us—in that his Son has taken upon himself our nature and preserved therein in teaching us by word and example even unto death—he has more fully bound us to himself in love; with the result that our hearts should be enkindled by such a gift of divine grace."[13]

The primary significance of Christ's death is revelation, as it reveals to us God's love for us and so creates a response in us of love for God. "By the faith which we hold concerning Christ love is increased in us, by virtue of the conviction that God in Christ has united our human nature to himself, and, by suffering in that same nature, has demonstrated to us that perfection of love. . . . So we, through his grace, are joined to him as closely as to our neighbor by an indissoluble bond of affection."[14] Christ's death is neither a ransom paid to the devil nor a payment to God's justice. In fact, Abailard identifies God's love with God's justice, so that there is no tension between the two as there is in both of the other theories.[15] God does not need to do anything objectively to the world in order to change His relation to us; God is already the God of love, and the crucifixion only reveals this to us.

If we are to view all three theories in relation to the Christian understanding of repentance, a certain pattern emerges. In the subjective view, the efficacy of atonement seems to be almost entirely dependent on human repentance; it is in the human response to God's love that the atonement occurs, not in God's act. This view has been criticized for eliminating any real need for the death of Christ, as humans are said to be able to repent simply by becoming aware of the loving nature of God. It was in this form that the doctrine found favor in the Enlightenment, a period during which human sin was viewed as no great detriment to moral improvement.[16] Many theologians have found this view inadequate because it seems to make Christ almost irrelevant, and expresses a perhaps unwarranted optimism about human nature. In addition, many theologians have felt that something "objective" must occur in the atonement, and that Christ's death does not simply "reveal" something that was always the case.[17] A new situation comes about as a result of the cross, of which Christians subsequently become aware. If this is the case, a too "subjective" interpretation of the atonement may be an inadequate description of its meaning for Christians, as it de-emphasizes the idea that God acts concretely in the world to make salvation (and therein repentance) possible. Critics of the subjective view could point out that we cannot and do not save ourselves, in the Christian view, and we can only repent knowing that God has done what is necessary.

On the other hand, the "classic" view (especially in the form expressed by Aulén) may move to the opposite extreme. In his concern to point out that God does all and humans do nothing, Aulén marginalizes the role of human repentance in the process of salvation. His major problem with Anselm seems to be that Anselm requires a human savior precisely because repentance must come from a human. In contrast, Aulén claims (with Luther as his authority) that "there is no thought of an offering made to God by Christ simply as man, in his human nature."[18] A more contemporary Lutheran theologian, Gerhard Forde, makes a similar point by claiming that "Christ was sacrificed for us, not for God" because Christ is "not a sacrifice from the human side to God in any way, but rather a gift from God to us."[19] Although such claims do safeguard the Christian emphasis on salvation as the result of God's grace and not human works, they do so potentially at the expense of inclusion of the human in the process of salvation. If the human is entirely passive and God alone is active, how can salvation be appropriated in human life? Even allowing that faith is God's work, it is God's work in the human, who is not simply a passive receptacle of God's grace. Too great a stress on God's action may make human repentance irrelevant or, even worse, impossible in Christian terms.

Anselm's view, for all the criticisms made of it, may point the way to a happy medium between neglecting the role of either God or the human in atonement. By insisting that the savior be both God and human, Anselm was able to unify the roles of both in a single person. Christ can save precisely as one who is God and man, the one who does what God alone can do and what human alone should do. Although Protestants have criticized the fact that Anselm based his view largely on a medieval understanding of the sacrament of penance, it is this sacramental concept that connects the divine and the human acts, and it is sacraments in general that provide the link between Christ's work and human appropriation of it. Through a modern understanding of how sacraments do this, one can develop an understanding of how human repentance is connected with divine grace in Christian terms; it is to this task that I now turn.

Sacraments and Repentance

Baptism

The first sacrament, baptism, is clearly an initiation rite used to bring individuals into the Church. But it has also been understood as conveying God's grace and God's promise of salvation to all who accept Christ's act of atonement for them. As such, it has involved repentance for sins and renunciation of evil as well as acceptance of God's grace and a decision to follow God. At first glance it seems that no clearer example could be found of Christian repentance expressed in ritual form. And yet the situation is complicated by the fact that most Christians regard infant baptism as the norm for membership in the Church. This has reinforced the view that God's grace avails regardless of human repentance and human faith, because infants can neither profess faith nor repent and yet they are baptized. Salvation is again made to seem like something involuntary, created by God regardless of human will.[20]

At the time of the Protestant Reformation, the Roman Catholic practice of infant baptism was rejected by the Anabaptists, and Baptist churches today carry on their view that grace can only be received by a voluntary act of will. The mainline Reformers by and large accepted infant baptism, however, and continue to do so to this day. For this reason, Karl Barth's critique of infant baptism stands out as a strong mainline Protestant voice against the practice.

Although Barth himself was often accused of making it seem as if salvation is "involuntary," or as if all are saved regardless of their attitude to salvation, toward the end of his career his concern to safeguard human freedom led him to reject infant baptism altogether. Barth admitted that "what God does in Jesus Christ through the Holy Spirit is exclusively His action," but we must also remember that "what man can and should do in face of the divine action is wholly his own human action. . . . Our human work has to acknowledge the work of God, to bear witness to it, to confess it, to respond to it."[21] God's action demands a human response, but one that is distinct from God's action as humans and God are distinct. We are to be free partners of God, not puppets of the divine will. To argue that we should baptize infants because God's grace is "independent of all human thought and will, faith and unbelief" is in substance to argue that infant baptism should be required—not only of Christian families but also of whole peoples who might be baptized involuntarily, as was the case during certain periods of history.[22] God's grace will be present whether the sacrament is performed or not, Barth argues; the point of baptism is not to make grace present or repeat God's promises, but to bring into the church those "who are ready to hear and grasp the promise."[23] Infants cannot demonstrate such readiness.

Barth has gone farther than most modern theologians in totally rejecting infant baptism, but others have also come to recognize the need to reform the common understanding of baptism as an involuntary initiation into the Christian community that requires no repentance or faith. Traditionally, churches have defended infant baptism by claiming either that faith is provided by the community or parents who promise to teach the child the faith, or that faith is implicit in the child herself as something to be developed at a later date. But these rationales have often been weak efforts to defend a ritual that is popularly regarded as conferring church membership even in the absence of all faith. As Robert Jenson points out, baptism has largely lost its force because nothing is "renounced" in it, and parents do not take seriously the charge to raise their children in the faith.[24]

That sacraments cannot be regarded as effective without the recipient's faith has been acknowledged for some time. When Luther wrote that a sacrament is "a work that is made use of, that is well pleasing to God not because of what it is in itself but because of your faith and your good use of it," he was reacting against the late medieval view that sacraments convey grace even in the absence of faith.[25] But this late medieval view had not been the view of earlier Catholic theologians, nor is it the view of most contemporary Catholic thinkers. Karl Rahner held that while sacraments are certain offers of God's grace, they are only efficacious "to the extent that they encounter man's openness and freedom" in a response of faith, hope, and love.[26] His stress on human freedom in the process of salvation has guided modern Catholic theology, just as Barth's similar emphasis on freedom has greatly influenced modern Protestant thought. In short, there is a general recognition in modern theology of the need for a conscious act of repentance and faith, but this idea has not always been conveyed at the popular level, where sacraments may still be viewed as "magical" means of redemption.

Penance

One problem may be the lack of an effective sacrament of penance in which the Christian is consciously involved in a ritual act of repentance. Protestants recognize no such sacrament, even though Luther initially did.[27] It is also noteworthy that Luther never abandoned the practice of penance as confession, though he understood it somewhat differently than his Catholic contemporaries. Luther, as well as Calvin, Wesley, Edwards, and other Protestant luminaries, held that public confession of sins was extremely useful and took it for granted as part of Christian life.[28] But today few Protestant churches practice public confession of individual sins, and even in Roman Catholicism this no longer has the centrality it once did.

Why has the practice of penance dwindled over time? Initially it served a situation where a ritual was needed to bring apostate Christians back into the fold; almost all except the Montanists and Donatists acknowledged that Christians will sin, and some sins were regarded as seriously compromising Christian commitment. If the Church is not to rebaptize the repentant every time they sin, there must be a ritual of repentance and readmission to the Church. Penance served this function, practiced as a communal ritual.[29] But in the Middle Ages, penance became an individualistic ritual, detached from the life of the public church and its discipline. Under the influence of Irish monasticism, the distinctively medieval form of penance developed, tied to the imposition of the "works of satisfaction" eschewed by the Protestant Reformers.[30] What had been meant to be a ritual of repentance for major sins became, in the Protestant view, a form of works-righteousness to be rejected. But the demise of communal penance unfortunately meant that there was even less place in the life of the Church for a ritual expression of repentance. In Catholicism, this need has been addressed to some extent with new rites of penance emphasizing the social context of sin, but there can be no denying the fact that penance no longer has the centrality it once did, even for Catholics.[31]

Communion

In the absence of serious contenders, then, the sacrament of communion may be the chief place where repentance is still expressed ritualistically for Christians. There is also here a clear link to Christ's death and resurrection, ritualistically reenacted to make their content visible for Christians. If, as I contend, Christ's death is to be understood not merely as a divine event occurring apart from human involvement (Aulén), nor merely as a divine ratification of what humans can do on their own (Abailard), but as a divine-human process in which people participate in their own redemption, then the sacrament of communion is where this participation is most clearly ritually enacted. Vincent Taylor argued that Christ's "perfect penitence" on our behalf is not meant as a substitute for human repentance, but as that which makes repentance possible for Christians; Christ's repentance is reproduced in them as those who participate in His sacrifice.[32] This participation is concretely enacted in the ritual of communion. "Jesus did not view His suffering as a work accomplished apart from the response of men. The Supper is a means whereby His disciples may participate in the power of His self-offering, since by His word the bread which they are bidden to receive is interpreted by Him as His body, and the wine as His covenant-blood shed for many."[33]

If we view communion as a form of participation in Christ's sacrifice that includes human repentance, this may shed some light on the old Catholic-Protestant controversy regarding the sense in which communion is to be understood as a "sacrifice." The Protestant Reformers claimed that the Catholic Mass was a godless human work that attempted to usurp Christ's role in salvation. The priest, in consecrating the host, seemed to displace Christ as savior by "repeating" His sacrifice. But the Catholic intention was never to make Christ's death irrelevant to the sacrifice of the Mass; rather, it is the basis of the Mass. The Council of Trent, which anathematized the Protestant view, was chiefly concerned to safeguard the notion that the Mass is not merely a commemoration of sacrifice but the actual sacrifice of Christ.[34] As Lucien Deiss explains the Catholic view, the Mass is not a repetition of Christ's sacrifice but an actualization and re-presentation of it: "to actualize does not mean to begin anew, but to render present that which already exists." The Mass does not represent a new sacrifice on Christ's part, but a new participation in it on the part of those who celebrate it.[35] What the priest "offers" in the sacrifice is Christ, simply because "we cannot offer God anything—outside of Christ—which is worthy of his glory." Some might conclude from this that one need not offer anything (because God has Christ already). Deiss rejects this notion as well as the idea that our human offering is a substitute for Christ's offering that makes the latter unnecessary.[36] The Mass is not an addition to Christ's offering on our part, but our own unity with His sacrifice in which our work is united with His.

It is not only Roman Catholics who understand the sacrament of communion as a form of sacrifice. Although Protestants have historically been reluctant to refer to communion as a "sacrifice" lest it be construed as a human rather than a divine "work," Gustaf Aulén commends the effort to bring the notion of sacrifice back into Protestant conceptions of communion.[37] "The real presence and the sacrifice belong together. This sacrifice is present because the living Lord is present." As Christians are united with a "really present" Christ in communion, they are united with His sacrifice, and so are made "partakers of his victory."[38] Aulén is wary of the Catholic or Anglo-Catholic notion that humans offer Christ in communion, but he admits that humans do offer something—thanksgiving, praise, service—in an act in which Christians are included in the sacrifice of Christ.[39] This is not so different from the view of Deiss, that the offering of the Mass is a participation in Christ's sacrifice rather than an addition to it.

Because the sacrament of communion involves human participation, it is not simply a passive reception of grace that entails no human response. The repentance involved in the sacramental act issues in action in the world. Catholic Michael Downey writes that "as the central expression of the church's call and commitment to communion and justice, the eucharist comprises the heart of a Christian morality. . . . To celebrate the eucharist implies that we live our lives motivated by a vision of justice and communion."[40] Presbyterian Arthur Cochrane claims that Christians should understand communion as an act of "agape" (sacrificial love) and "diakonia" (service to others) as the early Christians did. There was no separation between worship and service then, for they literally "served" the poor their food in the act of celebrating communion with them. In Cochrane's view, this act of service did not even require the recipients to be Christians.[41] "What the congregation does in its public gatherings by way of agape and diakonia is to be done in and for the world. It is to carry its service of love by word and deed to all men."[42] In fact, Cochrane believes that the equality of all at the table of communion has radical implications for social ethics. "In the light of the Agape meal, must not a Christian be committed to democracy and socialism?" Any system based in racism, exclusion, or oppression of the poor "is in flagrant contradiction to the Lord's Supper."[43] And Anglican bishop John Robinson claimed that "the test of worship is how far it makes us more sensitive to 'the beyond in our midst,' to the Christ in the hungry, the naked, the homeless, and the prisoner. Only if we are more likely to recognize him there after attending an act of worship is that worship Christian rather than a piece of religiosity in Christian dress."[44]

Conclusions

It can be concluded, then, that repentance in a Christian context will be best understood and best encouraged by churches if it is linked with the doctrines of atonement and the sacraments. God's grace and human responsibility become interconnected for Christians when they understand that Christ's death involves both the divine and the human, and that the two are related in the sacrifice He makes that represents our obligation to God. We are not without responsibility, for even though it is God who makes salvation possible, only humans can realize the benefits of God's grace by their participation in it. The sacraments ritually enact this human participation in salvation that entails repentance, a turning to God in order that the gift of grace might yield fruit in human life. Sacraments also express the communal dimension of sin, repentance, and redemption, so that ritual expression can lead to concrete action. "Repentance" means little if it does not take concrete form as repentance for specific sins that entails specific compensatory action. In a repentant society, which the Christian church might seek to model, members not only confess their sins but also turn away from them by turning to God and to others in love. As noted at the outset of this chapter, repentance must involve at least three steps: sorrow for one's sin, a genuine desire not to repeat it, and action that seeks to redress the wrong that has been done. If Christians always sought to follow through on these steps, there would be less tendency to live by a "cheap grace" that offers forgiveness but does not inspire repentance or real moral action. And these steps of repentance could be found, for Christians, in lives that seek to participate in God's redemption of the world through reenacting and making present atonement—understood by Christians through the death of Christ, as God's own sacrifice made for us.

As noted earlier, the Christian way of understanding repentance is not the only way, nor necessarily the best way. Nor should Christianity be the only resource considered when reflecting on repentance in our society. But, insofar as Christianity is the religion many profess to follow in our society, reflection on the specifically Christian view of repentance (among others) might be instructive and helpful in developing a society more conducive to repentance. That Christians can and ought to repent, according to their own scriptures, is obvious; but whether they will mine the resources of their own traditions to become models of repentance in our society, only time will tell.

Notes

1. In Friedrich Schleiermacher's view, there are two "natural heresies" regarding human appropriation of salvation that are to be avoided: the Pelagian and the Manichaean. Human nature must be defined so that we are both in need of redemption and capable of receiving it. The Pelagian heresy makes it seem as if we can save ourselves, and so are not in need of redemption by

God; and the Manichaean heresy defines human nature in such a way that "the ability to receive redeeming influences is made actually to disappear," and it seems we cannot be saved at all. See Friedrich Schleiermacher, *The Christian Faith*, ed. H. R. MacKintosh and J. S. Stewart (Philadelphia: Fortress Press, 1976), 98.

2. American religion, and American Evangelicalism in particular, has usually accepted the idea that we have the free will to accept God's grace by our own power. This was at least in part due to the influence of preachers like John Wesley who opposed the Calvinist doctrine (upheld in his day by George Whitefield) that God has predetermined who will accept His grace and there is nothing we can do to affect this process. Wesley argued that God would be an unjust tyrant if salvation were based solely on God's arbitrary decision to give or withhold grace from beings who are unfree to respond to God; therefore, it must be not God's decree but our own free decision to follow God that separates the saved from the lost.

3. Anselm of Canterbury, *Saint Anselm: Basic Writings*, trans. S.N. Deane (LaSalle, Ill.: Open Court, 1962), 224–25.

4. Anselm, *Basic Writings*, 245.

5. Anselm, *Basic Writings*, 246.

6. Anselm, *Basic Writings*, 284.

7. Gustaf Aulén, *Christus Victor: An Historical Study of the Three Main Types of the Idea of the Atonement*, trans. A. G. Hebert (New York: Macmillan, 1966), 19–20.

8. Anselm, *Basic Writings*, 187.

9. Gregory of Nazianzen adamantly denied that the devil could have any legitimate rights over humanity, and Irenaeus regarded the devil's dominion over humans as a perversion of the created order (Aulén, *Christus Victor*, 48–50).

10. Gregory of Nyssa claimed that the devil unknowingly "swallows" the divine nature along with the human nature of Christ, just as a fish swallows the hook with the bait; in so doing, he destroys himself. Similarly, Augustine compared Christ to the bait in a mousetrap that catches the devil (Aulén, *Christus Victor*, 52–53).

11. Aulén, *Christus Victor*, 34.

12. Aulén, *Christus Victor*, 31.

13. Peter Abailard, "Exposition of the Epistle to the Romans," in *A Scholastic Miscellany: Anselm to Ockham*, ed. Eugene R. Fairweather (Philadelphia: Westminster, 1956), 283.

14. Abailard, "Romans," 278.

15. Abailard, "Romans," 279.

16. Aulén, *Christus Victor*, 134–35.

17. See, for example, Colin Gunton, *The Actuality of Atonement* (Edinburgh: T. & T. Clark, 1988) or Vernon White, *Atonement and Incarnation* (Cambridge: Cambridge University Press, 1991).

18. Aulén, *Christus Victor*, 108.

19. Gerhard Forde, *Theology Is for Proclamation* (Minneapolis: Fortress, 1990), 174.

20. Gerhard Forde comes close to this when he argues that grace is irresistible (Forde, *Proclamation*, 169–70).

21. Karl Barth, *Church Dogmatics*, vol. 4, part 4, ed. G.W. Bromiley and T. F. Torrance (Edinburgh: T. & T. Clark, 1969), 72.

22. Barth, *Church Dogmatics*, 189–90.

23. Barth, *Church Dogmatics*, 191.

24. Robert W. Jenson, *Visible Words: The Interpretation and Practice of Christian Sacraments* (Philadelphia: Fortress, 1978), 166–67.

25. Martin Luther, "The Blessed Sacrament of the Holy and True Body of Christ, and the Brotherhoods," in *Luther's Works*, vol. 1, *Word and Sacrament*, ed. E. Theodore Bachmann (Philadelphia: Muhlenberg, 1960), 64.

26. Karl Rahner, *Foundations of Christian Faith*, trans. William V. Dych (New York: Crossroad, 1982), 414.

27. See "The Sacrament of Penance" in Luther, *Word and Sacrament*. Luther finally concluded penance was not a sacrament in "The Babylonian Captivity of the Church," written in 1520, and even there he seems unsure (Martin Luther, *Martin Luther: Selections from His Writings*, ed. John Dillenberger [New York: Anchor, 1961], 256, 357).

28. For an impressive selection of Protestant sources promoting public confession of sins, see David Belgum, *Guilt: Where Religion and Psychology Meet* (Englewood Cliffs, N.J.: Prentice-Hall, 1963), 74–94.

29. Jenson, *Visible Words*, 179–80.

30. Jenson, *Visible Words*, 181–82.

31. The Roman Catholic Rite of Penance released in 1973 views sin not as a private matter only of concern to individuals, but as a corporate, social reality to be addressed in a communal context. See Michael Downey, *Clothed in Christ: The Sacraments and Christian Living* (New York: Crossroad, 1987), 99; also James Dallen, *The Reconciling Community: The Rite of Penance* (New York: Pueblo Publishing Co., 1986).

32. Vincent Taylor, *Jesus and His Sacrifice* (New York: St. Martin's Press, 1965), 309.

33. Taylor, *Sacrifice*, 313.

34. J. F. McHugh, "The Sacrifice of the Mass at the Council of Trent," in *Sacrifice and Redemption*, ed. S. W. Sykes (Cambridge: Cambridge University Press, 1991), 174.

35. Lucien Deiss, *It's the Lord's Supper: The Eucharist of Christians*, trans. Edmond Bonin (New York: Paulist Press, 1976), 89.

36. Deiss, *Lord's Supper*, 91–92.

37. Gustaf Aulén, *Eucharist and Sacrifice*, trans. Eric H. Wahlstrom (Philadelphia: Muhlenberg Press, 1958), 185.

38. Aulén, *Eucharist*, 193.

39. Aulén, *Eucharist*, 199–200.
40. Downey, *Clothed in Christ*, 90.
41. Arthur C. Cochrane, *Eating and Drinking with Jesus: An Ethical and Biblical Enquiry* (Philadelphia: Westminster, 1974), 89–91.
42. Cochrane, *Eating*, 93.
43. Cochrane, *Eating*, 100.
44. John A. T. Robinson, *Honest to God* (Philadelphia: Westminster Press, 1963), 90.

4

Repentance in Judaism

Jacob Neusner

Grandsons of Haman studied Torah in Bene Beraq.
Grandsons of Sisera taught children in Jerusalem.
Grandsons of Sennacherib taught Torah in public. And who were
    they? Shemaiah and Abtalion [teachers of Hillel and Shammai].

—Bavli Gittin 57B

Haman then stands for Hitler now. Sisera stands for Petlura, who murdered tens of thousands of Jews in the Ukraine after World War I. Sennacherib represents Nasser, who in 1967 undertook to wipe out the State of Israel. This remarkable statement from the Talmud shows that sin is not indelible either upon one's family or upon oneself. The sinner should be, and is punished; but sin is not indelible. If the sinner repents the sin, atones, and attains reconciliation with God, the sin is wiped off the record, the sinner forgiven, the sinners' successors blameless. The mark of repentance comes to the surface when the one-time sinner gains the chance to repeat the sinful deed but does not do so; then the repentance is complete. To translate into our own times is hardly necessary; indeed, it defies imagination.

For, to understand the power of this statement, we have only to say, "Hitler's grandson teaches Torah in a yeshiva of Bene Beraq," or "Eichmann's grandson sits in a Jerusalem yeshiva, reciting prayers and psalms and learning Talmud." Not only so, but, to go onward with Sennacherib—who can stand for Himmler—and Shemaiah and Abtalion, the greatest authorities of their generation—who can stand for the heads of the great yeshivas and theological courts of the State of Israel—Himmler's grandsons are arbiters of the Torah, that is to say, Judaism, in the State of Israel. The sins of the fathers reach closure

60

with the repentance of the children, their determination to make their own future. But that is what the sinner who repents also does. Such statements represent the outcome of repentance, that is, moral regeneration for oneself, based upon genuine regret, fully realized in deed. They instruct the current generation of Judaism of its moral duties to those of its enemies, in the aftermath of the unique Holocaust, who repent and seek reconciliation. The message declares that sinners who repent are to be forgiven. The nation that repents is to be welcomed back into the company of civilization, as Germany has regained its honor in our day.

The Hebrew word is *teshuvah*, from the root for return, and the concept is generally understood to mean returning to God from a situation of estrangement. It involves not humiliation but reaffirmation of the self in God's image, after God's likeness. It follows that repentance in Judaism forms a theological category encompassing moral issues of action and attitude: wrong action, arrogant attitude, in particular. Repentance forms a step in the path to God that starts with the estrangement represented by sin: doing what I want, instead of what God wants, thus rebellion and arrogance. Sin precipitates punishment, whether personal for individuals or historical for nations; punishment brings about repentance for sin, which in turn leads to atonement for sin and, it follows, reconciliation with God. That sequence of stages in the moral regeneration of sinful humanity, individual or collective, defines the context in which repentance finds its natural home.

True, repentance is a far cry from loving and forgiving one's unrepentant enemy. God forgives sinners who atone and repent, and asks of humanity that same act of grace—but no greater. For forgiveness without a prior act of repentance not only violates the rule of justice but also humiliates the law of mercy, cheapening and trivializing the superhuman act of forgiveness by treating as compulsive what is an act of human, and divine, grace. Sin is to be punished, but repentance is to be responded to with forgiveness, as the written Torah states explicitly: "You shall not bear a grudge nor pursue a dispute beyond reason, nor hate your brother in your heart, but you shall love your neighbor as yourself" (Lev. 19:18). The role of the sinful other is to repent; the task of the sinned-against is to respond to and accept repentance, at which point, loving one's neighbor as oneself becomes the just person's duty, so repentance forms the critical center of the moral transaction in a contentious and willful world.

For Judaism the conception of repentance—regretting sin, determining not to repeat it, seeking forgiveness for it—defines the key to the moral life. No single component of the human condition takes higher priority in establishing the right relationship with God, and none bears more profound implications for this-worldly attitudes and actions. The entire course of a human life, filled as it is with the natural propensity to sin, that is, rebel against God, but comprised also by the compelled requirement of confronting God's response (punishment for sin), takes its direction—finds its critical turning—at the act of repentance, the first step in the regeneration of the human condition as it was meant to be.

The concept takes on specificity when atonement comes to the fore: in the Temple, atonement involved correct offerings for inadvertent sin (deliberate sin was not to be atoned for in that manner); for the prophets, repentance would characterize the entire nation, Israel, coming to its senses in the aftermath of God's punishment. And, as we shall see, in the oral part of that one Torah—revelation—that defines Judaism, repentance takes on a profoundly this-worldly, social sense. But in all statements of the matter, the single trait proves ubiquitous: repentance defines a stage in the relationship of Man and God, inclusive of repentance to one's fellow for sin against him or her.

Let us turn first to the classic statement of repentance and examine the context in the law and theology of Judaism in which the concept takes on concrete and this-worldly form. To understand the context, we recall that God's revelation, the Torah (that is, Judaism), makes its normative statements to holy Israel in two media, one written, the other orally formulated and orally transmitted until being written down long after Sinai. The Hebrew Scriptures (a.k.a., "Old Testament," "Tanakh") set forth the written part of the Torah. The documents that record in writing the originally oral Torah begin with the Mishnah, a late second-century philosophy in the form of a law code, to which over the next four centuries was appended a large and systematic commentary, the Talmud. Alongside, compilations of Scriptural exegeses called Midrashim recorded other components of this same Torah. All together, the two Torahs, oral and written, set forth the full and exhaustive account of God's self-manifestation to humanity through holy Israel, the supernatural community bearing God's blessing from Abraham to the end of time. That formulation of the religious myth, which carries us deep into the world not of history and ethnicity, but of eternity and transcendent, holy community of the faithful, alerts us to the theological framework in which repentance will make its appearance.

For the Torah or Judaism, moving beyond Scripture, we find in

Mishnah the appropriate starting point, in the presentation of the moral dimensions of the Day of Atonement (Yom Kippur):

Mishnah-tractate Yoma 8:8–9

8:8

A. A sin offering and an unconditional guilt offering atone.

B. Death and Day of Atonement atone when joined with repentance.

C. Repentance atones for minor transgressions of positive and negative commandments.

D. And as to serious transgressions, [repentance] suspends the punishment until the Day of Atonement comes along and atones.

8:9

A. He who says, "I shall sin and repent, sin and repent"—

B. they give him no chance to do repentance.

C. [If he said,] "I will sin and the Day of Atonement will atone,"— the Day of Atonement does not atone.

D. For transgressions done between man and the Omnipresent, the Day of Atonement atones.

E. For transgressions between man and man, the Day of Atonement atones, only if the man will regain the good will of his friend.

The process of reconciliation with God—at-one-ment, so to speak— encompasses a number of steps and components, not only repentance; and repentance, for its part, does not reach concrete definition in the formulation of the process. A sin offering in the Temple in Jerusalem, presented for unintentional sin, atones, and therein we find the beginning of the definition of repentance. It lies in the contrast between the sin-offering at A, that is, atonement for unintentional sin, and those things that atone for intentional sin, which are two events: on the one side, the expression of right attitude, *teshuvah*, and, on the other, the return to God. The role of repentance emerges in the contrast with the sin-offering; what one atones for that is inadvertent has no bearing upon what is deliberate. The willful sin can be atoned for only if repentance has taken place, that is to say, genuine regret, a turning away from the sin, after the fact; therefore transforming the sin from one that is deliberate to one that is, if not unintentional beforehand, then at least unintentional afterward. Then death, on the one side, or the Day of Atonement, on the other, work their enchantment.

But that provision for reconciliation even after the fact raises the question of deliberate and willful violation of the law, encompassing repentance—before the fact. And that is the point at which repentance loses its power. If to begin with one has insinuated repentance into the sinful act itself, declaring up front that afterward one will repent, the power of repentance is lost, the act of will denying the post facto possibility altogether. That is the point of 8:9A–C. For, we now observe, the issue of attitude takes over, and it is in the end the fundamental attitude that governs. If to begin with the willful act is joined to an act of will affecting the post facto circumstance, all is lost; one's attitude to begin with nullifies all further possibilities.

Thus far the Mishnah has treated the act of repentance or turning as if it had come to a full and complete definition. But that premise presupposes a rich set of a priori definitions. These come to full articulation in a document that reached closure at the same time as the Talmud of Babylonia, a commentary on Mishnah-tractate *Abot of the Fathers*, called *Abot deRabbi Nathan, the Fathers According to Rabbi Nathan*.

3. A. In Rome R. Matia b. Harash asked R. Eleazar b. Azariah, "Have you heard about the four types of atonement that R. Ishmael expounded?"

B. He said to him, "I heard indeed, but they are three, but with each of them repentance is required.

C. "One verse of Scripture says, 'Return, you backsliding children, says the Lord, I will heal your backsliding' (Jer. 3:22). A second says, 'For on this day shall atonement be made for you to cleanse you' (Lev. 16:30). And a third says, 'Then I will visit their transgression with the rod and their iniquity with strokes' (Ps. 89:33), and a fourth: 'Surely this iniquity shall not be expiated by you until you die' (Is. 22:14).

D. "How so? If someone has violated a religious duty involving an act commission but has repented, he does not move from that spot before he is forgiven forthwith. In this regard it is said, 'Return, you backsliding children, says the Lord, I will heal your backsliding' (Jer. 3:22).

E. "If someone has transgressed a negative commandment but has repented, repentance suspends the punishment and the Day of Atonement atones. In this regard it is said, 'For on this day shall atonement be made for you to cleanse you' (Lev. 16:30).

F. "If someone has transgressed a rule, the penalty of which is extirpation or judicially inflicted capital punishment, but has repented, the repentance and the Day of Atonement suspend the matter, and suffering on the other days of the year effects atonement, and in this regard it is said, 'Then I will visit their transgression with the rod and their iniquity with strokes' (Ps. 89:33).

G. "But one who has profaned the name of heaven—repentance has not got the power to effect suspension of the punishment, nor suffering to wipe it out, nor the Day of Atonement to atone, but repentance and suffering suspend the punishment, and the death will wipe out the sin with them, and in this regard it is said, 'Surely this iniquity shall not be expiated by you until you die' (Is. 22:14)." (*Fathers According to R. Nathan* XXIX:VIII.1)

The issue of repentance now takes concrete form. The secondary articulation takes on a legal aspect as the Mishnah's formulation leads us to anticipate (repentance atones for minor transgressions of positive and negative commandments . . . as to serious transgressions, repentance suspends the punishment until the Day of Atonement comes along and atones). Once the cited distinctions are made, then the exegete will specify how the distinctions work themselves out, thus D, E, F. Here we see how repentance takes its place in the hierarchical process.

The exegesis of the foregoing completed, the Talmud moves, as is its way, from law to theology, deeming each to transmit the same message as the other, the one in the form of norms of behavior, the other, of belief. At the outset, we considered the difficulty that faces secular Jews who, not formed within the theological framework of Judaism, find no basis on which to respond to a genuine act of repentance, which is formed in secular terms but is in conformity to the religious norms that we have examined. That means a statement of regret for the past, and a resolve not to repeat the sins of the past. The impasse to which the public apology brought the Jewish community of Stockholm underscores the pertinence of the rule, as the Talmud expounds the Mishnah's statement, about seeking to regain good will. This is how the Talmud deals with precisely the problem of intransigence on the part of the victim:

VI.1. A. For transgressions done between man and the Omnipresent, the Day of Atonement atones. For transgressions between man and man, the Day of Atonement atones, only if the man will regain the good will of his friend:

2. A. Said R. Isaac, "Whoever offends his fellow, even if through what he says, has to reconcile with him, as it is said, 'My son, if you have become surety for your neighbor, if you have struck your hands for a stranger, you are snared by the words of your mouth . . . do this now, my son, and deliver yourself, seeing you have come into the power of your neighbor, go, humble yourself, and urge your neighbor' (Prov. 6:1–3). If it is a money-claim against you, open the palm of your hand to him [and pay him off], and if not, send a lot of intermediaries to him."

B. Said R. Hisda, "He has to reconcile with him through three sets of three people each: 'He comes before men and says, I have sinned and perverted that which was right and it did not profit me' (Job 33:27)."

C. Said R. Yose bar Hanina, "Whoever seeks reconciliation with his neighbor has to do so only three times: 'Forgive I pray you now . . . and we pray you' (Gen. 50:17).

D. "And if he has died, he brings ten people and sets them up at his grave and says, 'I have sinned against the Lord the God of Israel and against this one, whom I have hurt.'"

The matter has its own limits. Beyond the specified point, the penitent has carried out his obligation as best he can, and nothing more is to be done.

How the canonical literature of Judaism defines the concept of repentance emerges, finally, in a systematic composite of statements on the matter. A sizable abstract allows the Talmud of Babylonia, the final and authoritative statement of the Torah of Sinai, to portray the conception in its usual, systematic way. For, organizing topical presentations on such theological themes, the Talmud makes its statement on the subject in the following terms, a sequence of sayings expressing the main components of the concept:

Babylonian Talmud Tractate Yoma 86A–B

6. A. Said R. Hama bar Hanina, "Great is repentance, which brings healing to the world: 'I will heal their backsliding, I will love them freely' (Hos. 14:5)."

B. *R. Hama bar Hanina contrasted verses*: " 'Return you backsliding children'—*who to begin with were backsliding*. Vs. 'I will heal your backsliding' (Jer. 3:22). *There is no contradiction*: in the one case, the repentance is out of love, in the other, out of fear."

C. *R. Judah contrasted verses*: " 'Return you backsliding children, I will heal your backsliding' (Jer. 3:22). Vs. 'For I am lord to you, and I will take you one of a city and two of a family' (Jer. 3:14)f. *There is no contradiction*: in the one case, the repentance is out of love or fear, in the other, repentance comes as a consequence of suffering."

7. A. Said R. Levi, "Great is repentance, which reaches up to the throne of glory: 'Return, Israel, to the Lord your God' (Hos. 14:2)."

8. A. [86B] Said R. Yohanan, "Great is repentance, for it overrides a negative commandment that is in the Torah: 'If a man put away his wife and she go from him and become another man's wife, may he return to her again? Will not that land be greatly

polluted? But you have played the harlot with many lovers, and would you then return to me, says the Lord' (Jer. 3:1)."

9. A. Said R. Jonathan, "Great is repentance, for it brings redemption near: 'And a redeemer shall come to Zion and to those who return from transgression in Jacob' (Is. 59:20)—how come 'a redeemer shall come to Zion'? Because of 'those who return from transgression in Jacob.' "

10. A. Said R. Simeon b. Laqish, "Great is repentance, for by it sins that were done deliberately are transformed into those that were done inadvertently: 'And when the wicked turns from his wickedness and does that which is lawful and right, he shall live thereby' (Ez. 33:19)—*now 'wickedness' is done deliberately, and yet the prophet calls it stumbling!*"

11. A. Said R. Samuel bar Nahmani to R. Jonathan, "Great is repentance, for it lengthens the years of a person: 'And when the wicked turns from his wickedness . . . he shall live thereby' (Ez. 33:19)."

12. A. *Said R. Isaac, [or] they say in the West in the name of Rabbah bar Mari,* "Come and take note of how the characteristic of the Holy One, blessed be he, is not like the characteristic of mortals. If a mortal insults his fellow by something that he has said, the other may or may not be reconciled with him. And if you say that he is reconciled with him, he may or may not be reconciled by mere words. But with the Holy One, blessed be he, if someone commits a transgression in private, he will be reconciled with him in mere words, as it is said, 'Take with you words and return to the Lord' (Hos. 14:3). And not only so, but [God] credits it to him as goodness: 'and accept that which is good' (Hos. 14:5); and not only so, but Scripture credits it to him as if he had offered up bullocks: 'So will we render for bullocks the offerings of our lips' (Hos. 14:5). Now you might say that reference is made to obligatory bullocks, but Scripture says, 'I will heal their backsliding, I love them freely' (Hos. 14:5)."

13. A. *It has been taught on Tannaite authority:*

B. R. Meir would say, "great is repentance, for on account of a single individual who repents, the whole world is forgiven in its entirety: 'I will heal their backsliding, I will love them freely, for my anger has turned away from him' (Hos. 14:5). What is said is not 'from them' but 'from him.' "

14. A. *How is a person who has repented to be recognized?*

B. Said R. Judah, "For example, if a transgression of the same sort comes to hand once, and a second time, and the one does not repeat what he had done."

C. *R. Judah defined matters more closely:* "With the same woman, at the same season, in the same place."

The act of repentance commences with the sinner, but then compels divine response; the attitude of the penitent governs, the motive— love, fear—making the difference. The power of repentance to win God over, even after recurring sin, forms the leading theme—the leit- motif—of the composite. Israel's own redemption depends upon Isra- el's repentance. The concluding statement proves most concrete. Repentance takes place when the one who has sinned and declares his regret ("in words") faces the opportunity of repeating the sinful action but this time refrains, so No. 14. That we deal with the critical nexus in the relationship between God and humanity emerges in one compo- sition after another, for example, repentance overrides negative com- mandments of the Torah (the more important kind); brings redemption; changes the character of the already-committed sins; lengthens the life of the penitent. Not only so, but the power of repen- tance before the loving god of grace is such that mere words suffice. The upshot is, we deal with a matter of attitude that comes to the sur- face in concrete statements; but as to deeds, since the penitent cannot repeat the sin, and therefore no deed can be required, the penitent has a more difficult task: not to do again what he has done before. The whole complex then draws us deep into an enchanted and transcen- dent universe.

But any discussion of the doctrines of Judaism proves incomplete without attention to the state of opinion among Jewry, for while some of the Jews form a religious community, all of them together constitute an ethnic group. As in the case of any important theological category, therefore, repentance fixes our attention in the case of Judaism upon both religious and theological teachings, on one side, and the moral life of the Jewish people, an ethnic group, encompassing Jews who also are citizens of the State of Israel, on the other. That is because people commonly identify Judaism with the opinions held by Jews, a category- mistake when, as here, a religion appeals to revelation, an ethnic group to public opinion. While the category therefore derives from, and makes sense only in, the setting of a religion that speaks of sin and suffering, atonement, repentance, and forgiveness, it is in the secular setting of the Jews' own immediate experience of absolute evil that the issue of repentance gains acute relevance and demands attention. Can a Nazi repent and find forgiveness? That forms not only a dilemma of theology but a concrete issue debated within the ethnic group. It is why repentance stands for not platitude but profoundly controverted debate: how is such a thing possible?

Now that a clear picture of the meaning and power of repentance in

Judaism has made its impression, we turn to a concrete question: how does the concept of repentance guide Jews in dealing with the moral issues of the age beyond the Holocaust? For, people ask themselves, what response shall we give to the repentant Nazi, and how shall we accord forgiveness to the anti-Semite who wishes to repent? In that secular setting, the issue cuts to the bone—but, as we shall see, brings with it no healing at all. For ethnic Jewishness, like any other ideological ethnicity, bears within itself no resources for responding to repentance, there being no moral imperative in the matter; and absent response, repentance proves an empty act indeed: to whom, for what, not being questions given a response out of the resources of ethnic grievance. Indeed, the natural, this-worldly, and human response to hurt or injury is to nurture the grievance and bear a grudge. Repentance means to compel the response of forgiveness, so in the secular setting the conception carries no compelling logic; there is no impulse to transcend the self implicit in the human condition when formulated in secular terms, by secular Jewishness for example. The conflict between the natural and secular response to sin, repentance, and atonement conveys the more profound and pervasive conflict between what Arthur A. Cohen termed "the natural and supernatural Jew," that is, between the Israel of the here and now, represented by the State of Israel in the Holy Land and the Jewish people or Jewish community abroad, and the holy Israel of which the Torah, the liturgy, and the theology of Judaism speak.

We commence our consideration of the topic with the secular Jewish community, for that is the starting point for any discussion of what the Jews believe, inclusive (so it is thought) of Judaism. That is as it should be, since the Jews form a secular ethnic group, some members of which (in the State of Israel, a great many in fact) happen to practice the religion, Judaism, in one Judaic system or another. Any consideration of the topic of repentance in the case of Judaism, therefore, begins with the Jews, only afterward shading over into the matter of Judaism, to which we shall turn in a systematic way presently. For Jews in the twentieth century, the category, repentance, draws to the surface a deep moral conflict and profound, chronic inner anguish—the pain of memory. For none can address the question of the repentance of the sinner in theological terms, and the criminal in legal terms, without immediately raising the intractable case of the penitent Nazi, who (as a matter of theoretical argument) comes to the Jew to repent and seek forgiveness. In practiced Judaism today, can a Nazi repent?

To set forth in a concrete way the impasse at which secular Jewishness—the shared ethnic sentiments of the Jews as a collectivity ("people")—finds itself, I present a concrete case, which illustrates the intellectual dilemma unresolved—and I think beyond all resolution—within the wholly secular framework of this-worldly, liberal, and humanistic values that govern in organized, wholly ethnic, and mostly atheist Jewry. I take as my illustrative case my own observations of how, in the context of secularity, an organized institutional Jewish community—the Jewish community of Stockholm—found itself unable to respond to an act of repentance of an anti-Semite who wished to retract and repudiate his earlier-expressed views and apologize for them. As it turned out, he found no one to whom to apologize, and no response to his act, which, in theological terms, falls in the category of repentance.

To explain the case very briefly: a professor of history of religion at Uppsala University, whose portfolio included Judaism, Jan Bergman (whom I had known for nearly a quarter-century from the late 1960s), had made a series of scandalous and ignorant, utterly anti-Semitic statements about Judaism. He alleged that "Judaism" says it is a "mitzvah" to "kill goyim." These amazing, libelous statements then were utilized by an Islamic anti-Semitic radio station in Stockholm, which, under Swedish law, was indicted; in the trial, Bergman's statements gave comfort to the Jews' enemy by representing Judaism as a murderous religion (the current conflict in the Middle East then could be explained by appeal to Judaism's insatiable blood lust). When, indignant and scandalized, numerous scholars of Judaism throughout the world protested that an anti-Semite should teach about Judaism in the Uppsala University theological faculty, I participated, with articles in the *National Jewish Post* and the *Encyclopedia Britannica Yearbook* article on Judaism, which I wrote for some decades. So I was a player in the dispute, though not a principal.

But in April 1993, when serving as visiting research professor at Abo Akademi, the Swedish-language university in Finland, I found in the mail a document from Bergman himself, in which he clearly indicated that he did not regard himself as an anti-Semite, did not wish to espouse anti-Semitic opinions, and wanted to retract, and apologize for, statements of an anti-Semitic, anti-Judaic, anti-Zionist, and "Holocaust-revisionist" character that he had made or that had been attributed to him. When I read his statements—in my elementary Swedish it took work—I was reminded of how, in the late 1920s, Henry Ford had apologized for the anti-Semitic character of his *Dearborn Independent* and how, from that time onward, the anti-Semitic character of the boardrooms of American industry was called into question and ultimately (a long time later) delegitimized. It struck me that if Bergman's apology and retraction were to take place, anti-Semitism, anti-Judaism, "Holocaust revisionism," and anti-Zionism would lose legitimacy in the academic world. Here a university figure would find himself compelled to acknowledge the honor of Israel, the Jewish people, the legitimacy and vitality of Judaism, the religion, the facticity of the Holocaust, and the right of the State of Israel to a secure, permanent, and honorable position among the nations of the world. Such a statement would begin that process of the academic delegitimation of anti-Semitism and its companions. As one who practices Judaism, I naturally understood the document as the counterpart, for a gentile, to an act of *teshuvah*, a statement of repentance for wrongs done in the past, and a determination not to repeat such wrongs (a definition we shall meet in the theological setting presently).

When I went to Stockholm in early June 1993, I met with the Stockholm Committee Against Anti-Semitism's leadership and with the president of the Stockholm Jewish community, responsible for the campaign against Bergman, and, securing from them a list of complaints against Bergman, I met with Bergman himself. He drew up a response to every item of the complaint, apologizing for some, denying that he had said others, and repudiating statements made in his name by third parties. At every point he took a position of genuine regret for what he had said and done, and undertook never to repeat these actions and statements that had so disgraced his name. I brought that statement to what I took for granted to be the right address, which was the chief rabbi of Sweden, Morton Narrowe, who wrote out a response that was entirely appropriate: generous and conciliatory. It did not exonerate Bergman for wrongs done in the past but recognized and accepted his statement and offered the renewal of relationships. Narrowe's statement took its spirit from the concept of repentance, even though the transaction was secular and not within the framework of Judaism at all. The two men met at the Hotel Stockholm and embraced. Once friends, they had become friends once more. The documents—Bergman's letter to Narrowe and Narrowe's reply, composed within the weekend and sent on to Bergman—would be delivered to the vice chancellor of Uppsala University, who would publicize them. That, I thought, marked the close of a painful chapter in Swedish life. I was wrong. The organized Jewish community could make no provision for an act that, seen in Judaism, constituted a statement of repentance.

When the next week I returned to Abo, I found the letters from the Committee Against Anti-Semitism and the president of the Stockholm Jewish community, which made it clear that they rejected any possibility of a reconciliation with Bergman based on Bergman's retraction and apology. They could not accord to him that option; they proposed no alternative. In reply I made it clear that Judaism makes provision for the penitence of a sinner, and they denied all possibility that Bergman was ever going to be able to right his relationship with the Jewish community and Judaism. When I introduced the conception of *teshuvah*, repentance, which is a critical moral category of the theology of Judaism; when I pointed out that, on the Day of Atonement, we ask God to forgive us our sins of which we forthrightly repent and which we undertake not to repeat, and that we can do no less in response to Bergman's actions, I found complete incomprehension, indeed, what I regarded as an attitude of disrespect. The leadership acknowledged no authority but their own opinion, no morality but their own feeling of (quite legitimate) outrage.

Here, for the first time in my life, I came face to face with the results of the total secularization of the Jews: their incapacity to respond to the most compelling and insistent teaching of the Torah (that is, of Judaism), their absolute refusal to behave in a concrete circumstance in accord with the morality of *teshuvah* that forms the foundation of our relationship with God. With slight experience within the organized Jewish community in the United States, and only a general knowledge of synagogue life, I was not prepared for the deeply secular—not ignorant, but determinedly hostile—attitude of organized Jewry toward Judaism and its foundation doctrines. So I determined to face the issue head on, and I wrote a letter to Stockholm's Committee Against Anti-Semitism, which frames issues of morality in the setting of the theology of Judaism.

Here is the Judaic theological position addressed to the secular ethnic one, the possibility of forgiveness in the model of God the all-merciful, as against the attitude of enduring ethnic retaliation for unforgivable hurt. The Committee Against Anti-Semitism did not respond; if they could have, they would have. But secular Jewishness, the culture of secular Jews, accords to the Torah no hearing, being unable to make sense of theology's categories for morality. Their ethnicity contained no medium for reconciliation, such as the concepts of repentance, atonement, and, consequently, response through reconciliation, that Judaism sets forth as the moral norm. Here is my letter in which I set forth the theology of repentance for secular Jews:

Shall the affairs of Judaism, the religion, and the Jewish community (Hebrew: *am yisrael*) be conducted in accord with the Torah, revealed by God to Moses at Mount Sinai, or in accord with a secular principle defined, ad hoc, by whom it may concern? That is what is at stake in the matter at hand, and I shall try to explain to you what is at stake.

You clearly do not grasp the facts or the issues at hand, which I set forth here for all concerned. Permit me to instruct you about the religion, Judaism, which governs the attitudes and actions of the faithful in this dispute, and, indeed, in the conduct of the public policy of the Jewish community, so far as that community realizes the religion, Judaism, or, in the native category of Judaism, the Torah. For we are Jews by reason of Judaism, meaning, we frame our actions and faith in response to the commandments of God in the Torah. If you do not share our premises, you of course are free to frame matters by appeal to a different religion or to some secular code, but then you may no longer claim the moral authority of the Torah that, from the perspective of God, defines us as holy Israel. I undertake to instruct you in these matters, since, it is clear to me, you do not grasp what is at stake in the proper conduct of a dispute, including the resolution of this particular dispute, which is now at hand. As a result, you write in a captious and, as I shall explain in detail, disrespectful manner, which is therefore un-Judaic and contrary to the teaching of the Torah.

Anti-Semitism, anti-Judaism, anti-Zionism, "Holocaust revisionism," in all forms, inclusive of systematic delegitimization of the right of the State of Israel to a secure existence, are public issues not mediated by any committee. In the case of Professor Bergman, they also are academic issues, since the focus of protest has been his position at Uppsala University and his (mis)representation of Judaism in that professorship. On that basis was solicited the active involvement of the entire academic world, and on that basis, I took part in the protests from the very start, and in public, and in the press. Many others did too.

The religion, Judaism, rests on the principal commandment, "You shall not bear a grudge nor pursue a dispute beyond reason, nor hate your brother in your heart, but you shall love your neighbor as yourself" (Lev. 19:18). What that means is, it is a religious duty to turn an enemy into a friend, if that is possible. The basis within Judaism for the resolution of disputes, within the commandment of God to Moses in the Torah just now cited, is in the *halakhah* of *teshuvah*, which occurs in the authoritative legal statements of Judaism and which is summarized in Maimonides' *Hilkhot Teshuvah*. To understand the Judaic way of conducting a dispute, however bitter, you must inform yourselves at the very least of the theology and law that governs, with or without the sanction of the Jewish community of Stockholm, by reason of God's commandment. That is what defines public policy in the community of Judaism. If you do not accept these premises, then, of course, no discourse is possible; you will not grasp the actions of those of us who do, and we have no way of communicating with you. The Jewish community—meaning, in Hebrew, *am yisrael*—is in this context not a political entity but a religious body, called into being by God at Sinai through the covenant of the Torah. That is what is always at stake in the public life of Judaism, and that is what governs here.

On that basis, as an action of religious conviction, I both participated in the worldwide expressions of protest against Professor Bergman's anti-Semitic, anti-Judaic, anti-Israel, and "Holocaust-revisionist" statements, but also took note, in the long documentation that ensued, of his insistence that he did not say this, did not mean that, had been misquoted there, and so on and so forth. What this signaled was that, despite public statements and actions to the contrary, he did not wish to be regarded as and was not in his intention anti-Semitic, anti-Judaic, and so on. While the intention does not change the fact, it does recast the situation. What it meant to me, in reading his statements, was, and is, that he wished to retract statements he made that were in fact anti-Semitic, anti-Judaic, and the like, and apologize for them; that he wished to repudiate statements made in his name by others; that he wished to condemn the way in which statements of his have been used, and the like.

I read all of this to indicate that he wished to achieve a reconciliation with the Jewish community (meaning, once more, in Hebrew, *am yisrael* in the theological sense explained above). I saw the possibility of achieving such a reconciliation. In my view, only good could come of what has now come about. Once one party to the dispute wishes to express apology, retraction, and ask for forgiveness, as Mishnah Yoma 9:8 says in so many words, the aggrieved party has the religious obligation to respond appropriately. The Jewish community (*am yisrael*) has no alternative, within Judaism, but to make possible the act of true reconciliation, involving specification of what has been done wrong, for which the offending party explicitly apologizes, and a statement of regret and resolve not to repeat those wrongs. These are matters that are spelled out in the Mishnah, which, beyond the written Torah, is the first document of the Oral Torah and authoritative. I suggest you consult the passage and compare its contents with my account of them. In my judgment Professor Bergman's statement meets the definition just given now.

You cannot defend Judaism if you do not honor the religion yourself and fulfill its requirements as these pertain in context. Each person speaks out of the moral authority, learning, and public record that he or she has written over a lifetime. No one has alleged that you "sanctioned" any one else's engagement, since no one has asked you for such a "sanction." This is a public issue, which all engaged parties have the right to pursue in a public way; there are no monopolies when it comes to anti-

Judaism, anti-Semitism, anti-Zionism, "Holocaust revisionism," and other issues critical to the existence of the Jewish community (transcending the Jewish community of Stockholm). Your letter to me does not suggest you understand that simple fact. That you "sanctioned" no such meeting is therefore irrelevant to the state of the question. No one thought, or said, you did. That you expressed views on the issues, which I recorded and reviewed with you, is the fact. That Professor Bergman's statement does not conclude matters from your perspective certainly is a position you have a right to take, and no one will argue with you about that fact. Nor does anyone doubt you will express yourselves in print in the future as in the past. That is right and proper; everyone will exercise that right.

Bergman has now repented (to use the Judaic theological category) or apologized for the statements he made and repudiated statements imputed to him that he did not make (to use more secular language). This was a *mahloqet leshem shamayim*, a dispute for the sake of Heaven, which is to say, for the honor that we owe to God; but once the action of apology and regret has been offered, by the law of Judaism that governs all of holy Israel, to pursue the matter is no longer a *mahloqet leshem shamayim*. God no longer takes part.

To state the point in as simple and clear language as I can: in Judaism, which is at stake here and always, there is only a religious basis for reconciliation, and many of us do live out our lives, to the best of our abilities, within the Torah. Without that basis, there is no right or wrong, good or evil, let alone moral authority that compels assent and action.

It goes without saying that the matter did not proceed to resolution with the recipients of the letter, those most immediately engaged in the issue. It would carry us far afield to review later stages in the controversy; it suffices to note that, as of this writing, years later, the story continues to unfold in further chapters. The power of an idea sometimes makes itself felt when the idea absents itself; no greater evidence of what is at stake, for Judaism, in the concept of repentance can come before us than the incapacity of Jews who do not practice Judaism to resolve urgent moral complexities in a manner that accommodates both conscience and character. To be human is to sin, to acknowledge and respond to repentance is to exhibit that which, in humanity, is to act like God. So, to summarize that position of Judaism on repentance: it is human to sin, it also is human to repent—an act of humility to wipe out an act of arrogance—and that is why it is divine to respond to repentance with an act of forgiveness, whether the response comes from God or from us.

5

Fire in the Ātman: Repentance in Hinduism

Guy L. Beck

At first glance, the notion of repentance—sorrow for personal sins with the firm resolve to stop sinning—is easily identified with Christianity. Indeed, a major component of the teachings of Jesus was the call to repentance of his followers, along with the Lord's Prayer with its plea for forgiveness of trespasses. And the negative feeling of remorse for sin, if any, in Eastern religions such as Hinduism, Buddhism, or Jainism, seems overshadowed by more visible assortments of self-help measures for positive reparation. As such, an investigation of repentance in Hinduism appears on the surface like just another exercise in foisting Western theological categories upon non-Western traditions. However, more prudent examination is reimbursed by awareness not only of repentance in the Western sense, but of other acutely dramatic strategies of negotiation and response to moral crises, social dilemmas, and other special situations of ambiguity that focus a broader spotlight on the universal human condition.

Repentance in the West has involved both ritualistic restoration and the cleansing power of grace. In biblical terms, sin was a violation of divine law in thought, word, and deed; in more developed thought, sin was the rupture of an interpersonal bond with God that brought in its wake the threat of severance from God and the holy covenant community.[1] As certain extreme forms of sin were considered "unrepentable" (unforgivable), a distinction between intentional and unintentional sin was ascertained among the ancient Israelites so that some of these sins could be pardoned only if committed unintentionally.[2]

During New Testament times, repentance was central to the preaching of both John the Baptist and Jesus Christ.[3] The early church fathers came to recognize the qualities of repentance and faith as mutually dependent: repentance as the turning away from sin, and faith as the turning toward God out of love. In later Roman Catholicism, the concept of contrition developed in order to include these two categories. Contrition leading to repentance had previously referred to the sorrow that arose in the soul due to sin, but a distinction was made at the Council of Trent in 1546 regarding the motive behind the act of repentance: imperfect contrition indicated sorrow and a turning away from sin due to servile fear of hell or punishment for sin, while perfect contrition necessarily involved the pure motive of turning toward God out of pure love.[4] This classification is useful in approaching the complex though lesser-understood Hindu traditions of expiation and repentance.

Repentance in the Vedas and Classical Hinduism

Evidence for humble repentance in Hinduism, including even imperfect contrition, is found to be much earlier than both the Israelite and Christian records, going as far back as the Vedic period (6000–2000 B.C.E.) in India. Of the approximately twelve hymns to the Vedic deity Varuṇa found in the *Rig-Veda*, there are several good examples of prayers of repentance and forgiveness. In fact, there is no hymn to Varuṇa in which some reference to a plea for forgiveness of sin does not occur. Varuṇa, a mighty regent sitting on his throne within a palace in the highest heaven, has a face, eyes, arms, hands, and feet, and is said to move his arms, walk, drive a chariot, sit, and even eat and drink. He sits upon a great throne within his golden mansion in heaven, firm with a thousand columns and accessible through a thousand doors. The eye of Varuṇa is the sun that watches over all the actions of humankind. The all-seeing sun rises from its own abode and visits the dwellings of Varuṇa and Mitra (his partner) to report the deeds of men and women. According to the Brāhmaṇa literature, Varuṇa sits in the midst of heaven yet is able to view the agonies of sinners in their places of punishment. Varuṇa's spies, related to the spies of the Iranian Mithra, and perhaps represented by the stars, cast their eyes across the entire world. "Around Varuṇa sat his scouts, or spies [*spas*], who flew all over the world, and brought back reports on the conduct of mortals."[5]

Both Varuna and Mitra are described as lords of order (*rita*) who by means of order are upholders of order. Rita, encompassing all of creation and providing a framework for the gods, was the cosmic blueprint according to which everything operated—the seasons, night and day, earth's rotation, and so on. Varuna as the guardian of Rita was able to free humans from bondage resulting from activities that were a disturbance to this order. Since Rita was the cosmic order represented by Varuna, any activity that was false or "out-of-line" with Rita was termed *anrita* (chaos) and thus was punishable. Varuna in his majestic power and status as the punisher of *anrita* was a moral governor far above any other Vedic deity. His fiery wrath was roused by sin, the infringement of his ordinances. Together with Mitra, Varuna was the dispeller, hater, and severe punisher of many types of transgressions, but especially of falsehood. The fetters (*pāśa*, a term unique to Varuna in the Veda but later associated with Lord Śiva as his noose of mercy) with which he bound sinners were cast either sevenfold or threefold, ensnaring the persons who told lies and bypassing those who spoke the truth.

Beside ritual errors and falsehood, sin in Vedic times included other kinds of moral transgressions: "Varuna was so pure and holy that the mere performance of sacrifice would not ensure his favor, for he abhorred sin, or that which was not conformable to Rita. The idea of sin included many purely ritual sins and breaches of taboo, but it also certainly included lying, which Varuna and Mitra particularly loathed, and evil deeds prompted by anger, drink, gambling, and the influence of wicked men." The principal punishment that Varuna inflicted upon the sinner was the condition of dropsy, an abnormal accumulation of fluid in body tissues or cavities: "He [Varuna] caught and bound evildoers in his snares, so that they became diseased, especially with dropsy."[6]

When understood within the entire context of the Vedic cosmos, sin was a break with the balance of order that must be repaired, much like what would have been a rupture of the covenant among the Israelites. The result was not only disorder (*anrita*), but a debt that had to be repaid in full: "Man's transgression is a debt (*rina*) which he contracts at the hands of the guardians of Rita—whatever moral transgressions men commit are considered sins against the gods—a debt which man must pay in order to reestablish the balance he has upset."[7]

Varuna was gracious to those who repented. For them he untied the fetters like a rope and removed all the sins committed by individuals as well as those committed by their fathers. He spared the suppliant who daily transgressed his laws and was merciful to those who broke his laws by thoughtlessness. Varuṇa is said to have had hundreds of remedies for the humbled sinner, and drove away death as well as forgave those who repented. As the wise guardian of immortality, he could take away or prolong life, and the righteous hoped to see him in the next world reigning in bliss.

An example of a prayer for forgiveness from one of the earliest portions of the *Rig-Veda* (7.89), the original Vedic text, is as follows:

> Let me not yet, King Varuṇa, enter into the House of Clay: Have mercy, spare me, Mighty Lord. When Thunderer! I move along tremulous like a wind-blown skin, Have Mercy, spare me, Mighty Lord. O Bright and Powerful God, through want of strength I erred and went astray: Have mercy, spare me, Mighty Lord. Thirst found thy worshipper though he stood in the midst of water-floods: Have mercy, spare me, Mighty Lord. O Varuṇa, whatever the offence may be which we as men commit against the heavenly host, When through our want of thought we violate thy laws, punish us not, O God, for that iniquity.[8]

The Vedic afterlife for sinners known as the "House of Clay" may have been like the old Israelite underworld: "and when they died they descended to the 'House of Clay,' apparently a sort of gloomy subterranean Sheol, very different from the cheerful 'World of the Fathers,' the Āryan heaven."[9]

Another example from *Rig-Veda* (I.24.14–15) suggests a direct plea for release from the bondage of sin: "With bending down, oblations, sacrifices, O Varuṇa, we deprecate thine anger: Wise Asura, thou King of wide dominion, loosen the bonds of sin by us committed. Loosen the bonds, O Varuṇa, that hold me, loosen the bonds above, between, and under."[10] Since the overriding motive behind these two prayers appears to be fear of punishment more than pure love of God, they might be viewed as archaic examples of imperfect contrition.

Petitions to Varuṇa found in the pre-Buddhist *Mahānārāyaṇa-Upaniṣad* (1.55–56) suggest a growing tendency toward attitudes of remorse for past sins coupled with affection for the deity: "I take refuge in Varuṇa who is of golden luster or who has a golden diadem. O Varuṇa, being entreated by me, grant me the saving grace. For I have enjoyed what belongs to bad people and accepted gifts from sinners. May Indra, Varuṇa, Bṛhaspati, and Sāvitrī completely destroy that sin committed by me and my people in thought, word, and act."[11] The inclusion of other deities who may alleviate sin is a trend in the enveloping notion of divine grace in the theistic traditions.

Scholars have suggested a possible Semitic influence on the theistic features of Varuṇa, who was otherwise equated with Uranos of classical Roman religion. But Varuṇa goes back to the Indo-Iranian period, and represents one of the earliest sky-gods of antiquity. Ahura-Mazda of the Zoroastrian Avesta resembles Varuṇa in character if not in name, since he was an Āryan deity of the earlier Asura class of Vedic gods, as was Varuṇa. Recognizing the general Zoroastrian influence on Judaism, there is the added possibility of the influence of Vedic notions of deity on Semitic theology via Zoroastrianism.

These issues notwithstanding, similarities between Varuṇa and Yahweh are quite apparent, as noted by A. L. Basham:

> Not only did Varuṇa punish the sins of the individual but, like the Yahweh of the Old Testament, he visited the sins of his ancestors upon him [cf. the legacy of original sin in the West], and his ubiquity ensured that there was no escape for the sinner. . . . So humble was the worshipper in Varuṇa's presence, so conscious of weakness, guilt and shortcoming, that on reading the hymns to Varuṇa one is inevitably reminded of the penitential psalms of the Old Testament.[12]

In addition, a closer look at the texts reveals that the features of fiery wrath and vengeance against sin are also shared by the biblical Yahweh and Varuṇa.

While the early Vedic culture reflected a relatively optimistic worldview in which proper performance of ritual sacrifices virtually guaranteed entrance into a permanent heaven, the authors of the Upanishads spoke fatalistically about the future course of events. Instead of positing a nearly automatic immortality with the gods in heaven upon completing a life of Vedic ritual and sacrifice, they laid down an inexorable law proclaiming that the results of all actions, good or evil, must be experienced and that a person's actions and behavior determined the character of the next birth. Thus, at the time of death, the accumulated balance of moral or immoral acts decided the outcome of the next life, good or bad. The only exception was the person who had realized the immutable Brahman.

This theodicy was a moral system meant to come to terms with the presence of evil and injustice in the world, yet immediately fostered two opposing viewpoints among the Hindu theoreticians. According to the strict law of karma, there was no scope for expiation or repentance, since everyone had to experience the consequences of sinful activities in order for the sins to be destroyed. On the other hand, since there is ample evidence of expiatory measures regarding mishaps and irregularities in the performance of Vedic rites, the opposing view was immediately introduced in favor of expiatory measures, particularly for accidental or unintentional sins, transgressions committed unknowingly. This view was mooted in the early Dharma-Śāstras (lawbooks), particularly the *Gautama-Dharma-Sūtra*, probably the earliest discourse on expiations for sins. Thus the doctrine of *prayaścitta* (expiation) was developed as a more flexible means of confronting moral causation and social justice.

Accordingly, many of the Dharma-Śāstras written during the classical period of Hinduism discuss various sins and moral transgressions along with their respective atonements, which became the basis of early Hindu law governing the four castes (*varṇa*) and stages of life (*āśrama*). The *Manu-Saṃhitā* (ca. 500 B.C.E.–200 C.E.), said to be composed by the ancient lawgiver Manu, is the most important of these texts. The many penances enumerated there formed the core of the ancient Indian criminal code representing a unique congruence of canon and civil law. In fact, these specific atonements had been a major part of traditional jurisprudence in India before the modern period. These expiations consisted of acts of charity and purification, vows of fasting and continence, and performance of rituals and recitations, with subsequent societal acceptance of such acts. As stated in *Manu-Saṃhitā* 11.44, "A man who fails to perform a prescribed act, or commits a disapproved act, or becomes addicted to sensory objects, should perform a restoration (both unintentional and intentional)."[13]

Repeated references to Varuṇa in the lawbook of Manu affirm a continuity with the earlier Vedic understanding of sin and repentance. In *Manu-Saṃhitā* 9.245, "Varuṇa is the lord of punishment, for he holds the rod of punishment over kings."[14] Varuṇa becomes a divine exemplar for earthly kings in the admonition of Manu in 9.309: "He [the King] should seize evil men just as Varuṇa is seen to bind people with his ropes, for in this he behaves like Varuṇa."[15] In 11.253, Manu advises continuous chanting for one year of the two aforementioned Vedic hymns to Varuṇa in order to "dispel gross or subtle errors."[16] The Vedic severity of punishment for falsehood is reiterated in Manu 8.82: "Anyone who tells lies in testifying is helplessly bound fast by Varuṇa's ropes for a hundred rebirths; therefore one should speak the truth in testifying."[17]

The *Manu-Saṃhitā* accepted the prevailing notion that the effects of sins from previous births would become manifest in certain physical characteristics during one's present lifetime. According to *Manu-Saṃhitā* 11.48–53:

Some evil-hearted men undergo a reverse transformation of their form because of evil practices here (in this life), and some because of those committed in a former life. A man who steals gold has mangled finger-nails; a man who drinks liquor has discolored teeth; a priest-killer suffers from consumption; and a man who violates his guru's marriage-bed has a diseased skin. A slanderer has a putrid nose; an informer, a putrid mouth; a man who steals grain lacks a part of his body, but an adulterator of grain has a superfluity (of parts of his body). A thief of food has indiges-tion; a thief of words is a mute; a man who steals clothing has white lep-rosy; and a horse-thief is lame. A man who steals lamps becomes blind, and a man who extinguishes lamps, one-eyed; a sadist is always sick, and an adulterer is rheumatic. Thus, because of the particular effects of their past actions, men who are despised by good people are born idiotic, mute, blind, deaf, and deformed. [54] Because, a restoration should al-ways be performed for cleansing, since men who have not paid for their guilt are reborn with distinguishing marks that make them the object of reproach.[18]

This discussion of the effects of sin served to accentuate the need for the expiatory rites prescribed in the Dharma-Śāstras, as these rites guaranteed the protection of the sinner from future consequences.

Sin in classical Hinduism is defined by Benjamin Walker as "the taint resulting from the wilful or unknowing transgression of Dharma, the moral or spiritual law," and termed either *doṣa*, "mistake or fault," or *pāpa*, "sin."[19] The current stock of sins in any particular human being was derived from any or all of three possible sources: individual sins carried over from previous lifetimes, mental and physical deformities inherited from ancestors due to their sins, and sins committed in the present lifetime under the normal influence of ignorance accompany-ing the embodied state.

While sin according to the stringent law of karma of the earlier Upanishads was not transferable and had to be borne out by the sinner in future lifetimes, the evolving notion according to the Dharma-Śās-tras was that sin was a kind of "substance" that could be transferred to others by physical contact, speech, or thought. This explains a ten-dency among Hindus to avoid the company of sinners as one avoids a beggar with sores. While sins could be transferred, the reverse was true. Virtue (*puṇya*) acted as a purifying agent and could be conveyed to others by association. Hence the importance of seeing the deity or guru, hearing the discourses of saints, and associating with virtuous people on the assumption that some of the virtue, or merit, will "rub off." Sin in classical Hinduism was thus not an original flaw or defect in the human race or ancestors but was closer to the notion of a personal contamination or defilement that could be "wiped off" according to the will of the sinner. While the gods and other angelic beings were not exempt from committing sin, they were generally considered to be on a more purified level of existence due to their accumulated penances, austerities, and sacrifices.

Two principal divisions of sins are generally given in the Dharma-Śāstras and Manu: the *Mahāpātaka*, or major sins, and the *Upapātaka*, or minor sins. With some modification, these may be compared with the division of mortal and venial sins of Catholicism, with some attention also paid to whether the sin was deliberate or unintentional. Confession of sins to a priest or other individual, as in Catholicism, is normally not an option for Hindus, though public confession and restitution for sins has been practiced by Buddhists and Jains in India.

Realizing that certain sinful acts may be unpardonable or "unrepentable," a distinction was made in Hinduism, as in ancient Israel, between intentional and unintentional sin. *Manu-Saṁhitā* 11.46 states, "An evil committed unintentionally is cleansed by reciting the Veda, but one committed intentionally, in confusion, is cleansed by different sorts of particular restorations."[20] The words "in confusion" might be compared to today's legal plea of "temporary insanity" but does not excuse one from the consequences of intentionally committing one of the five major sins listed below.

According to *Manu-Saṁhitā* 11.55,[21] the *Mahāpātaka* sins are five, including the killing of a brāhmaṇa, drinking liquor, stealing, sexual intercourse with the wife of one's guru or spiritual mentor, and associating with someone who has committed any of these.[22] Abortion is equated with these in Manu but not listed as such.[23] Since the brāhmaṇa, or priestly class, was regarded as the repository of Dharma, and thus the spiritual "head" of society, the intentional killing of a member of this class constituted the most heinous crime. Drinking liquor was thought to be an abominable act, as alcohol was considered one of the most polluting substances, classed along with feces, urine, and menstrual fluids. And the mentor's wife was equivalent to one's own mother, with whom any improper relation was unthinkable.

Forgiveness of, or expiation for, any or all of the five major sins was impossible during a human lifetime, as the normal rituals for purification and expiation could not have the cumulative effect to remove the effect of these sins before death. Thus, a more radical application of pain and suffering was demanded whereby these sins would be expunged or "burned off" only after several reincarnations in the body

of a lower animal, or by being tortured in hell. Though there are at
least seven different hellish worlds in Hinduism with punishments that
make the Western hell look tame by comparison, hell in the Hindu
worldview is purgatorial and generally not a permanent situation, only
a severe measure of restitution for the otherwise unforgivable sinner.

During the lifetime of any particularly highly placed individual such
as a king, the deliberate commission of any of the above great sins
was tantamount to excommunication from the community of Hindus,
bearing some resemblance both to the penalty for willful sin in the
Bible, and, in previous ages, to that of mortal sin in Catholicism. Upon
advising a course of action for a king in the event of the major transgressions being committed, Manu 9.238–242 states, "These miserable
men, whom no one should eat with, no one should sacrifice for, no
one should read to, and no one should marry—must wander the earth,
excommunicated from all religion."[24]

The *Upapātaka*, or lesser sins (Manu 11.60–67),[25] are morally degrading yet could be expiated through penances. The sins include killing a cow; sacrificing for those unfit for the sacrifice; selling one's self;
abandoning one's guru, mother, father, or son, and (abandoning) the
private study (of the Veda) and the (domestic sacrificial) fire; allowing
one's younger brother to marry before one; marrying before one's
older brother; giving a daughter to either of those, or sacrificing for
them; corrupting a virgin; practicing usury; breaking a vow; selling a
pool, a pleasure garden, a wife, or a child; living as an outlaw; abandoning a relative; learning (the Veda) for pay or teaching (the Veda)
for pay; selling things that should not be marketed; committing adultery; lying; or killing a person of low caste.

Following a rather sophisticated casuistry that further classified
major and minor sins, Manu describes their atonement (*prayaścitta*)
through assorted penances or vows (*vrata*). In common parlance, *prayaścitta* referred to a kind of post facto response that cleared away the
consequences of already committed sinful acts, whereas *vrata* is closer
to a conditional promise to perform future penitential acts, as in "if
you give me a son or protect me from diseases, I will worship you
through various rituals and on pilgrimages." But in Manu these two
terms are used interchangeably. Prescriptions are given for each of the
Upapātakas, and for the five *Mahāpātakas* if only committed unintentionally. For example, "A priest-killer should build a hut in the forest
and live there for twelve years to purify himself, eating food that he
has begged for and using the skull of a corpse. . . . Or he may walk a
thousand miles to dispel the priest-killing, reciting one of the Vedas,

eating little, and restraining his sensory powers" (*Manu-Saṁhitā* 11.73, 76).[26]

A series of vows are defined and prescribed as atonements of the respective sins as follows: (1) Painful Vow: eat in the morning for three days, then in the evening for three days, for three days he should eat food that he has not asked for, and for the next three days he should not eat; (2) Painful Heating Vow: ingest cow's urine, cow dung, milk, yogurt, melted butter, water infused with sacrificial grass, then fast for one night; (3) Extra-Painful Vow: same as above except only one mouthful at each meal; (4) Hot-Painful Vow: drink, for three days each, hot water, hot milk, hot clarified butter, and hot air, and bathe once with a concentrated mind; (5) Moon-course Vow: decrease food by one ball every day of the dark lunar fortnight, and increase it during the bright lunar fortnight, and wash at sunrise, noon, and sunset. The above penances, either performed singularly, in combination, or in variation accompanied by recitation of selected Vedic hymns and mantras, were also recommended by Manu for purification from multiple varieties of defilement and pollution.[27]

Despite the overall emphasis on self-restitution in the *Manu-Saṁhitā* and in other classical Hindu lawbooks, repentance was esteemed in Dharma-Śāstra works as helping to make the repentant person fit for receiving expiatory rites. Accordingly, Manu mentions repentance by the sinner as a necessary constituent for restoration to purity. In *Manu-Saṁhitā* 11.228–231:

> An evil-doer is freed from his evil by declaring (the act), by remorse [*anu-tāpa*], by inner heat [*tāpas*], by recitation (of the Veda), and, in extremity, by giving gifts. The more a man of his own accord declares the wrong that he has done, the more he is freed from that wrong, like a snake from its skin. The more his mind-and-heart despises the evil action that he has committed, the more his body is freed from that wrong. For a man who has done evil and felt remorse is set free from that evil, but he is purified by ceasing (to do it, with the resolution), I will not do that again.[28]

The word for remorse in the above passage, *anutāpa*, "following-heat" or "following-pain," became the most prevalent term for repentance and contrition in classical Hinduism. Other related words in Sanskrit include *paścatāpa*, "after-fire," that is, sorrow, regret, and repentance. The presence of the root word, *tāpas* ("fire," "inner heat"), in the above terms is important. The earlier Vedic and Upanishadic notions of *tāpas* as the fire of ritual and the "inner heat" produced by asceticism were extended in Manu (11.242) to signify the fire of purificatory penance within the mind and heart: "Whatever guilt people incur in mind-and-heart, speech, or action, they quickly burn all that away with inner heat [*tāpas*] alone, for inner heat [*tāpas*] is their wealth."[29]

While the purifying fire of Vedic asceticism was already equated in Manu with penance and atonement for sin, it was just one more step to assimilate the concept of fire (*tāpas*) with the sorrow and pain of contrition felt within the self (*ātman*) leading to repentance. Thus, the feeling of remorse was itself a form of atonement since the "burning sensation" of interior guilt was equated with the purificatory fire of sacrifice to the Vedic gods such as Varuṇa. The metaphor of burning is significant here, as it also bridges with the motif of substance wherein sin is something independent that could be burned off from one's person as it also could be rubbed off upon others.

Repentance, and especially the feeling of contrition, in Hinduism continued to actuate purification of sin, and, as a concept in itself, contributed significantly to the literature of the emerging Bhakti movements in medieval India. In the vernacular literatures associated with these groups, we find the use of the word *tāpa* to signify penances and austerities in general along with the word for sin, *pāpa*, to represent the meaning of repentance, thus the term *pāpa-tāpa* with the double entendre of the burning fire of sin coupled with the fire of penance—repentance.

Repentance in Theistic Hinduism and the Bhakti Traditions

Over and beyond the expiatory rites mentioned in the Dharma-Śāstras, the sectarian Purāṇas recommended worship of one of the great lords such as Śiva or Vishnu, who, if appeased, forgives almost any transgression. Consequently, forgiveness of sin due to grace in Vaiṣṇava and Śaiva traditions virtually eclipsed the earlier focus on self-atonement, though a continuous thread going back to the prayers for Varuṇa's mercy can be traced. While sin could result from the influence of demons (as well as from personal bad karma), divine grace (*kripā*, *dayā*, *karuṇā*, *prasād*, etc.) and forgiveness were now awarded directly by the intervention of personal deities and avatāras such as Vishnu, Rāma, Krishna, Śiva, Durgā, and so on, who would always triumph over evil. As such, the attitude of "perfect contrition" as well as a kind of "sin/grace dialectic" clearly emerged here within Hindu-ism. Moreover, the literary expression of contrition became profuse within the theistic traditions, as a clearer and more profound reliance on divine grace was reached.

The analysis of sin in theistic Hinduism includes a list of offensive states-of-mind that cause defilement and often lead to sinful acts.[30] Accordingly, these Hindu "capital sins" include hatred, jealousy, enmity, envy, impatience, anger, wrath, complaining, slandering, egoism, desire, greed, self-righteousness, arrogance, sensuality, lust for women, concupiscence, and gluttony.[31] In *Bhagavad-Gītā* 16.21, lust, anger, and greed bring degradation to the soul and are known as three gates that ultimately lead to hell. All of the above states have to be curbed in order to prevent the commission of more serious or mortal sins. As such, some of the forms of penance that are listed in the Purāṇas include charity to brahmanas (as well as to beggars and cripples), fasting on certain days or for prescribed lengths of time, and pilgrimage to holy places that have the power to remove sin. Many persons would repair directly to sacred places in order to die, removing all fear of punishment in the happy prospect of a celestial afterlife. Also on many lists of penances are singing, dancing, making music, clapping the hands, drinking deity and guru foot-wash, eating food sacraments, and recitation of mantras and prayers. Whereas the availability of the expiatory rites prescribed in the Dharma-Śāstras was mostly limited to twice-born males, these devotional practices seeking divine grace were open to all people regardless of race, gender, social status, or occupation. That had been vouchsafed by texts such as the *Bhagavad-Gītā* and *Bhāgavata-Purāṇa*.

While a recitation of the Veda was certainly effective in removing ritual errors in times past, the recitation of Sanskrit hymns (*stotra*) and the repetition of divine names performed on a rosary (*japa*) gradually became the most popular means of wiping out the above states-of-mind and paving the way for eternal salvation. Klaus Klostermaier observes, "*Japa* may be the most common and widespread means of atonement for Hindus today."[32] This idea squares with the more general pronouncements found in the Purāṇas and other literatures about the present age of Kali-Yuga, which represents the fourth and final age within the Hindu time cycle, an age marked by irreligion and vice. Eschewing all other forms of religiosity and penance, scores of important saints in the Bhakti tradition had advocated the practice of *japa* or *nām-kīrtan* (chanting of God's names) as the only means of forgiveness and repentance in this present age, since the expiatory rites and vows prescribed in the Dharma-Śāstras were no longer feasible due to the deterioration of human society.

The salvational power of mantras containing divine names had certainly been established in the Purāṇas themselves. For example, the *Viṣṇu-Purāṇa* states that those who contemplate upon the mantra of twelve letters (*oṁ namo bhagavate vāsudevāya*) containing the name of Vāsudeva (Krishna) are freed from the cycle of births and deaths. The *Nṛsiṁha-Purāṇa* proclaims, "what is the use of many mantras and the performance of many *vratas*, when the mantra *oṁ namo nārāyaṇāya* ['I surrender to Nārāyaṇa,' another name of Vishnu] is capable of securing all desired objects." And the mantra of five letters, *namaḥ śivāya*, discussed at length in the *Liṅga-Purāṇa* (I.85), removes all sin and bestows all blessings including permanent association with Lord Śiva.

In addition to removing sin and obtaining release, the recitation of divine names was said to contribute toward the development of pure love of God if performed in the proper demeanor of submission. Among the great Hindu saints, Śrī Caitanya Mahāprabhu of sixteenth-century Bengal described the proper attitude for reciting the name of God, providing a model for thousands of practitioners: "One should chant the holy name of the Lord in a humble state of mind, thinking oneself lower than the straw in the street; one should be more tolerant than a tree, devoid of all sense of false prestige and should be ready to offer all respects to others. In such a state of mind one can chant the holy name of the Lord constantly."[33]

More than a mere ritual specialist, the initiating guru in theistic Hinduism served as a spiritual guide who imparted the particular divine mantras or names to be used by individual religious practitioners in their quest for devotion and release. While there was no formal confession of sins to another human being as in the Catholic tradition, contrite persons in Hinduism confessed transgressions, either verbally or mentally, directly to God in their private devotions while praying, chanting on the rosary, or reciting hymns in front of their favorite deity.

Among saints and holy persons, this mien of seeking divine grace and forgiveness of sin from a personal deity was frequently accompanied by a mood of radical self-deprecation (*akiñcanyā*). Evidence of *akiñcanyā* tendered by a human being became an occasion and even a condition for the deity to demonstrate unlimited compassion and grace. An early example of this notion, as well as the idea of confessing directly to the Lord, is contained in a prayer from the *Padma-Purāṇa:* "My dear Lord, there is no sinful living entity who is more of a sinner than myself. Nor is there a greater offender than myself. I am so greatly sinful and offensive that when I come to confess my sinful activities before you, I am ashamed."[34]

Akiñcanyā soon found its way into the vernacular devotional literature, and became a device that was wielded by many poetic saints to express attitudes of surrender and helplessness. Several examples will now be cited in order to demonstrate the manner in which this genre of penitential prayer developed from the medieval period onward. Beginning with early South Indian Vaiṣṇavism (devotion to Vishnu or his avatāras), the great saint Yamunācārya (918–1040 c.e.), the predecessor of Śrī Rāmānuja of the Śrī Vaiṣṇava Sampradāya, expressed feelings of lowliness and self-recrimination in "The Jewel" (47, 48, 58):

> Shame on me, an impure, immodest, cruel creature! With avarice I long, my Lord, to be your servant, a state that is beyond the reach of even the greatest of yogīs—Brahmā, Śiva, and Sanaka. . . . I have committed thousands of sins. I am helpless and come for refuge to your sacred feet. By your grace, make me yours. . . . Though I am lowly and beastly, the abode of enormous, inescapable sins without beginning. O ocean of compassion [*dayā sindho*], O friend, O sea of boundless affection [*vātsalya*], I pray to you, for my fear vanishes when I think of your attributes.[35]

Kurattalvan (twelfth century), the principal successor of Śrī Rāmānuja in Śrī Rangam, meditated on his lowliness with perhaps the most poignant language in Śrī Vaiṣṇava literature. While many saints have expressed feelings of worthlessness and reproached themselves for their sins, Kurattalvan's verses make his fallenness the very basis for seeking the lord's compassion and forgiveness. In his "Vaikuṇṭha-Stava" (84, 89), he says,

> Alas, alas! Woe is me! There is no redemption! I am wicked; I fall, I fall. . . . What hope have I to talk to you? What right have I, a worthless, stained person, to even think of you, who are full of auspicious qualities! . . . What is the use of my ranting? I have done every deed that can be called sin—big and small, both consciously and unwittingly. Please forgive me through your grace (*kripā*).[36]

In the tradition of South Indian Śaivism (devotion to Śiva), there are a number of humble petitions to Lord Śiva from the massive *Tevaram* collection in Tamil. This particular example exhibits a not uncommon contempt for the seductive nature of women as a cause of his fallenness (154):

Why was I born, I who cared only for my pride, I who was caught in women's snares, I who failed to think of my dear kinsman, my ambrosia, the world's beginning and end, my Lord whose form bright as the sunset sky lay buried within my heart. Once, a slave of past karma, I failed to remember my Lord. Now, having gone mad, I babble like a fool. I cannot hold in my heart the god who is all the goodness that dwells in me. Why was I born? (160.7) Like carrion crows alighting on a carcass, evil deeds from the past swarm upon me, delude me, silence my words of praise for you. O Lord of the universe, give me right knowledge, so that I may shed this putrid, loathsome form, oozing with pus, this wound ridden with foul disease.[37]

One of the famous Nayanmar devotees of Lord Śiva in South India, Appar (around the seventh to ninth centuries), voiced a profound sense of sin and remorse for his inescapable predicament: "Wicked is my race, and wicked my character and ways; so great is my sin that I sin even in doing good. Wicked am I and foolish not to unite myself with the good. No animal am I, yet I cannot help behaving like an animal. I can preach at men to hate what is wrong, but such a miserable sinner am I that I can only beg and never give."[38]

While there are numerous examples from many poets in North India such as Kabir,[39] Sūr Dās, Tulasī Dās, and so on, sensations of maximum remorse and self-deprecation in North Indian Vaiṣṇavism are found in the collection of Bengali poems of Narottam Dās (seventeenth century) known as *Prārthanā*.[40] Two recently published selections from poems 43 and 45 are cited below.

[43] O Lord Hari! How attached I am to my work! I have a cunning frame of mind regarding worldly possessions, and I have no attraction for the company of saintly devotees. How am I going to get out of this predicament? . . . So now what is the use of this body to do any work? It is just a heavy burden for me to pull around. . . . What a sad thing to say! This life has gone by with so many pains for nothing and in such a groaning manner! So Narottam Dās tells himself, What a disgrace! Shame on me!

[45] O Vaiṣṇavas! I, who am of very bad character, am making this offering unto you. I have sunken fatefully into the unbearable ocean of material suffering, and ask that you simply pull me out by the hair. Fate is so strong that, being unable to hear about religious knowledge, I am constantly bound by my own fruitive activities (karma). I cannot find any deliverance from this miserable condition and thus, being helpless and afflicted, am crying out to you. I am being yanked around by lust, anger, greed, illusion, madness, and false pride. As such, I am like a blind man

who knows neither the right path nor the wrong path. Neglecting good advice, my mind is absorbed in illusion. I have not desired to take your feet. Narottam Dās says, "seeing this condition, I am afraid. As soon as possible, please take me by your side."

An attitude of total helplessness and surrender to God permeate many of Narottam's poems. Despite frequent allusions to being afraid, he is firmly placed, along with the others, in the category of perfect contrition; his fear is less a fear of punishment and physical suffering than an existential dread of loneliness, of separation from, and of offending the Lord he once knew, being bound up in the impersonal network of his own fruitive work. A comparable attitude is expressed in Christianity as follows: "It is in discovering the greatness of God's love that our heart is shaken by the horror and weight of sin and begins to fear offending God by sin and being separated from him."[41]

Lastly, a modern example of repentance from the nineteenth-century Hindu renaissance, reveals ways in which European patterns of education and erudition flooded the intelligentsia of India. A Vaiṣṇava poet and saint of Bengal, Śrīla Bhaktivinoda Ṭhākura (1838–1914), regretfully wasted his time in ordinary academic pursuits and the reading of too many books. He finally sought the shelter of Lord Krishna in his song "Vidyāra Vilāse" (In the Pastimes of Scholarship):

Once I spent long, long hours in the pastimes of scholarship. I never took to service of Your Feet as I do now. Reading on and on, never finding satiation, I felt that knowledge would be the highest goal. That hope was false and fruitless—that knowledge was ignorance. Materialistic studies are the glare of Māyā only, for they are an obstacle to spiritual progress. . . . When they are stretched out over a long period of time, one loses all energy and is sapped of all power to enjoy. By the time old age comes, nothing in the world is tasteful. Now at the end of life I realize that all my academic study is ignorance. Realization of this fact is burning like a piercing dart. . . . Reflecting upon my materialistic studies, I now surrender to Your Feet.[42]

While modern in context, it is reminiscent of the call of previous Indian saints to wipe clean the blackboard of the mind of all book knowledge and materialistic learning in order to receive divine wisdom.

Overall, repentance in the developing Hindu devotional tradition strikes one with the forceful theme of utter dependence on grace alone for remission of sin, leaving aside completely all self-restorative rituals and penances. As we have seen, these poets, sailing into uncharted sacred waters, frequently indulged in magnified self-deprecation to the extent of proclaiming themselves the worst of sinners, the most fallen, the most wicked, almost as if extreme degradation was an advantage on the route to salvation. Here there is very little, if any, fear of hell or punishment of sins that are openly admitted and, in some cases, even flaunted. Several poets even desire the pains of hell, a place of constant remembrance of their beloved Lord who would then be obligated to save them, as if deliberate sin and transgression guaranteed the receipt of grace. In Indian mythology, the notorious demons who sinned against God were released into heaven simply because they concentrated on the Lord in anger or were killed by him personally. According to medieval Hindu theology, then, complete reliance on the saving grace of God can only be assured if all other options, including self-help rituals and restorations, are entirely incapable of removing the enormity of accumulated sins. Since the highest levels of devotion compel a complete and total surrender to God, the lowliest sinners seem to have an edge in that they have painted themselves into a corner, which, if God's grace is what it purports to be, prompts immediate attention by the Lord who is deemed all-merciful. They thus stand naked before God in an attitude of what could even be dubbed as "ultra-perfect" contrition. This principle was well realized by the articulate poet-saints who, judging by historical accounts, were certainly not in fact the worst sinners on earth. Rather, such statements and others comprised an enlarging stock of poetic devices that expressed a certain frame of mind that was becoming normalized, expected, and even preferable within the emerging Hindu devotional tradition.

Such posturing eventually became the standard for nearly all Hindu practice, centering on humility before the greatness of God and creation as a prerequisite for Bhakti (love of God), leading to *prapatti* (full surrender). In contrast to the self-expiation prescribed by the classical Dharma-Śāstras, the burning fire of sin in the ātman was extinguished in devotional Hinduism, not by the deeds of the repentant practitioner, but by the unpredictable flood of divine mercy from above.

Notes

1. In the Torah (Pentateuch) we find both sin offerings and guilt offerings as expiatory measures for specific kinds of sin, especially ritual errors. These offerings comprised simple animal sacrifices performed according to Levitical

regulations, with the removal of sin represented by a priest smearing sacrificial blood on the altar horns. After the guilt for the worshiper's sin was transferred to the animal by the laying on of hands by the priest, spiritual death, the otherwise human penalty for sin previously awarded to Adam, was vicariously inflicted on the sacrificial animal (see Leviticus 4:5–13, 6:24–30). A variant of this is the notion of the scapegoat, wherein the sins of the entire community were transferred to a goat who was thereupon set free.

2. As stated in Numbers 15:29–31,

> You shall have one law for him who does anything unwittingly, for him who is native among the people of Israel, and for the stranger who sojourns among them. But the person who does anything with a high hand, whether he is native or a sojourner, reviles the Lord, and that person shall be cut off from among his people. Because he has despised the word of the Lord, and has broken his commandment, that person shall be utterly cut off; his [the Lord's] iniquity shall be upon him.

The threat of being severed from the holy community generated the most poignant fear among the people. This peril was also taken very seriously in Islam, wherein vigorous debates have ensued regarding the status and fate of sinners and apostate Muslims.

The archetypal prayer for repentance (*shuv* in Hebrew) in the Bible is Psalm 51. King David, after being accused by Nathan the Prophet, repents for his sin (*het* in Hebrew) of arranging for the killing of Uriah and committing adultery with Uriah's wife, Bathsheba: "Have mercy on me, O God, according to thy steadfast love; according to thy abundant mercy blot out my transgressions, wash me thoroughly from my iniquity, and cleanse me from my sin! For I know my transgressions, and my sin is ever before me." David feels intense guilt for this act and fully surrenders himself to the Lord's mercy, which, using the metaphor of the cleansing agent hyssop used for lepers, can purify him of his transgression of the law of God regarding murder and adultery. The implication here is that only God can "unsin" the sinner who is otherwise perpetually confronted with guilt.

3. As stated in Matthew 3:2, "In those days came John the Baptist, preaching in the wilderness of Judea, 'Repent, for the Kingdom of Heaven is at hand.' Judea and the Jordan region were baptized by him, confessing their sins." Accordingly, Jesus preached a message of repentance, as in Matthew 4:17: "From that time Jesus began to preach, saying 'Repent, for the Kingdom of Heaven is at hand.' " Jesus further warned in Luke 13:3, 5, "Unless you repent, you will all likewise perish." And while the Christian church developed into larger ecclesiastical structures, the horror of severance from the community continued, as in the recurring threatening pronouncement, "outside the church there is no salvation."

4. Both imperfect and perfect contrition, according to Christian theology, must arise from God's grace and should not be viewed as attributable to

human capacities alone. According to Catholic theologian Karl Rahner, contrition means "the conversion of a sinner to God in faith, hope and love in response (under the impulse of grace) to God's merciful willingness to forgive him" (Karl Rahner and Herbert Vorgrimler, *Theological Dictionary* [New York: Herder & Herder, 1965], 100). Grace was necessary to seek and obtain forgiveness, and also to initiate a direct and voluntary rejection of the previous life. While the documents of the Council of Trent included conditions for contrition as "sorrow of heart and detestation for sin committed, with the resolution not to sin again" (see Karl Rahner, ed., *Encyclopedia of Theology: A Concise Sacramentum Mundi* [New York: Seabury Press, 1975], 288), this was not a repression but an acknowledgment and assumption of responsibility for past sins, with the understanding that the instigation for repentance must arise from divine initiative. The two complementary components, aversion from sin and reversion to God, or, in other words, repentance for past sins, such as those committed after baptism and remitted during the sacrament known as penance, and faith in the cleansing power of God's grace, have functioned together in what theologian Stephen J. Duffy has currently revealed to be a continuous, co-dependent, dialectic throughout Christian history. See his *Dynamics of Grace: Perspectives in Theological Anthropology* (Collegeville, Minn.: The Liturgical Press, 1993), 362–65. This notion is intriguing, as a comparable kind of dialectical system also operates within the Hindu tradition, as we shall see.

5. A. L. Basham, *The Wonder That Was India* (New York: Grove Press, 1954), 236.

6. Basham, *The Wonder*, 237.

7. Jeanine Miller, *The Vision of Cosmic Order in the Vedas* (London: Routledge & Kegan Paul, 1985), 142.

8. Ralph T. H. Griffith, trans., *The Hymns of the Rig-Veda* (Delhi: Motilal Banarsidass, 1973 reprint), 378.

9. Basham, *The Wonder*, 237.

10. Griffith, *The Hymns*, 15.

11. Swami Vimalananda, trans., *Mahānārāyaṇa-Upanishad* (Madras: Sri Ramakrishna Math, 1979), 75–77.

12. Basham, *The Wonder*, 237.

13. Wendy Doniger and Brian K. Smith, trans., *The Laws of Manu* (New Delhi: Penguin Books, 1991), 255.

14. Doniger and Smith, *The Laws*, 224.

15. Doniger and Smith, *The Laws*, 230.

16. Doniger and Smith, *The Laws*, 230.

17. Doniger and Smith, *The Laws*, 160.

18. Doniger and Smith, *The Laws*, 255–56.

19. Benjamin Walker, *The Hindu World: An Encyclopedic Survey of Hinduism* (New Delhi: Munshiram Manoharlal Publishers Pvt. Ltd., 1983 reprint), vol. 2, 400.

20. Doniger and Smith, *The Laws*, 255.

21. Doniger and Smith, *The Laws*, 256.

22. *Śiśuhatya*, or the destruction of an unborn child, willfully causing an abortion, is mentioned as one of the five by the Catholic missionary Abbe J. A. Dubois in his *Hindu Manners, Customs, and Ceremonies* (New Delhi: Asian Educational Services: 1990), 197, as well as by Benjamin Walker in *Hindu World*, vol. 2, 401.

23. Doniger and Smith, *The Laws*, 259.

24. Doniger and Smith, *The Laws*, 224.

25. Doniger and Smith, *The Laws*, 257.

26. Doniger and Smith, *The Laws*, 258.

27. Doniger and Smith, *The Laws*, 262–72.

28. Doniger and Smith, *The Laws*, 273.

29. Doniger and Smith, *The Laws*, 274. Comparison could be made with the purifying fire of Catholic purgatory, wherein remaining sins of transgressors are burned off by high-temperature flames.

30. These are comparable as a class to the seven capital sins in Catholicism, namely pride, avarice, envy, wrath, lust, gluttony, and sloth or acedia, which are called "capital" because they engender other sins and vices.

31. Walker, *Hindu World*, 401.

32. Klaus K. Klostermaier, *A Survey of Hinduism* (Albany, New York: SUNY Press, 1989), 171.

33. *Songs of the Vaiṣṇava Ācāryas* (Culver City, Calif.: BBT Publishing, 1974), 25.

34. Quoted in A. C. Bhaktivedanta Swami, *The Nectar of Devotion* (Los Angeles, Calif.: BBT Publishing, 1970), 81.

35. Vasudha Narayanan, *The Way and the Goal: Expressions of Devotion in the Early Śrī Vaiṣṇava Tradition* (Washington, D.C.: Institute for Vaishnava Studies and Center for the Study of World Religions, Harvard University, 1987), 66.

36. Narayanan, *The Way*, 97–98.

37. Indira Viswanathan Peterson, *Poems to Śiva: The Hymns of the Tamil Saints* (Princeton, N.J.: Princeton University Press, 1989), 224–25, 227.

38. Quoted in J. L. Brockington, *Sacred Thread: A Short History of Hinduism* (Delhi: Oxford University Press, 1992 reprint), 131.

39. Early North Indian devotional traditions in Hindi include this submissive petition by Kabir (ca. 1370–1450): "Kabir, I searched the whole world, but I found none (so) bad: Kabir is the worst of all, none is worse than Kabir! . . . Kabir, the Creator is perfect in all, in Him, there is no blemish: If I search my own heart, (I see) all defects in myself!" (Charlotte Vaudeville, *Kabir* [Oxford: Clarendon Press, 1974], 190–91).

40. This work has been translated in full by myself as part of the article "An Introduction to the Poetry of Narottam Dās," in *Journal of Vaiṣṇava Studies* 4.4 (Fall 1996): 17–52.

41. Libreria Editrice Vaticana, *Catechism of the Catholic Church* (Liguori, Mo.: Liguori Publications, 1994), 360.

42. *Songs of the Vaiṣṇava Ācāryas*, 54.

6

Repentance in the Islamic Tradition

Mahmoud Ayoub

Repentance may be regarded as the cornerstone of the religious life of both the individual and society. For the pious of any religious community, repentance is an outward manifestation of faith and a link between the divine and the heart and soul of the person of faith. Repentance is a means of salvation through expiation and contrition, an expression of humility before the awesome presence of divine majesty, and an inexhaustible source of divine mercy. Even for the nonreligious humanist, remorseful repentance may be an act of moral discipline. Repentance can also be the voice of moral conscience in society.

Although these general characteristics of repentance can be fruitfully studied as common elements in the devotional practices of the theistic, and particularly monotheistic religious traditions, the present chapter is concerned with the place of repentance in Muslim faith and piety. We shall first examine the lexical meanings of the Arabic word *tawbah* and other important terms in the rich vocabulary of repentance in the Islamic tradition. Repentance is an essential element of the Qur'anic worldview. We shall therefore begin our investigation of repentance in Muslim law and piety with the Qur'ān. Next in importance to the Qur'ān as a primary source of moral and spiritual guidance is the life-example (*sunnah*) of the Prophet Muḥammad. His sayings (*ḥadīths*) contain many pietistic moral and legal injunctions that amplify the Qur'anic view of repentance both as an ideal and actual practice in Muslim society.

Following this preliminary examination of the meaning and significance of repentance in the Qur'ān and prophetic tradition, we shall examine its actual function in Islamic jurisprudence. A point of special concern in this regard will be the role of repentance in mitigating punishments for major offenses (*ḥudūd*) as enshrined in the Qur'ān and prophetic tradition, and codified by the legal schools.

From its inception, Islam saw itself as a faith-tradition continuous with those of ancient prophets and their divine messages to humanity. In particular, biblical personages such as Adam, Noah, Abraham, Moses, David, and others provide living models of repentance for pious Muslims. Next to the prophets in moral and spiritual perfection are their immediate disciples. A few examples of the repentance of ancient prophets, as well as the repentance of some of the companions (*ṣaḥābah*) of the Prophet Muḥammad, will serve as a good point of transition to our discussion of repentance in Muslim mystical or Sufi devotions. This will be followed by a brief discussion of repentance in Shi'ite thought and piety. Finally a few general remarks about the philosophy of repentance and its possible significance to contemporary society will conclude this study.

The Terminology of Repentance

The primary term in the Qur'anic vocabulary of repentance is *tawbah*, a feminine noun derived from the trilateral root *t/w/b*. It generally means "frequently returning to," or "turning toward someone, or some place."[1] The word *tawbah* with all its derivatives and rich and subtle nuances of meaning points to a long history of Arabic usage, but also to broader and perhaps more ancient Semitic roots.[2]

Two other terms generally related to the word *tawbah* in both meaning and signification are *awbah* and *inābah*. While the word *tawbah* has come to mean penitently turning to God with contrition for a sin or offense intentionally committed, *awbah* has retained the broader meaning of frequent returning to God with humility, devotion, and praise. In its verbal form, *awbah* is used in the Qur'ān to mean constant praise or glorification of God, as in the command: "O mountains, glorify often [*awwibī*] with him [i.e., David]."[3] As a verbal noun (*iyāb*), the term signifies the ultimate return of all human beings to God for the final judgment.[4]

The term *inābah* signifies turning to God for help in total submission to His will. The Qur'ān enjoins the faithful: "Turn [*anībū*] to your Lord and submit to Him before chastisement comes upon you, and you will be helped" (Q. 39:54). *Inābah* has the sense of turning to God for help with resolute faith and obedience.[5] Thus, *inābah* is in a certain sense equivalent to *islām*, and the one who so turns to God (*munīb*) is a true *muslim* (submitter) to God.

Like the Hebrew *teshuvah* and the Greek *metanoia*, the word *tawbah* means "oft turning" to God. From the point of view of the sacred law, *tawbah* signifies an act of conscious turning to God with a penitent and contrite heart. The active participle *tawwāb* implies an attitude of constant turning. Yet *tawwāb* is one of the beautiful names of God in the Qur'ān. Thus, God is oft turning (*tawwāb*) toward His servant with infinite grace and mercy, while the servant ought to be oft turning (*tawwāb*) to God with humble repentance (*tawbah*).

Tawbah, as we have seen, basically means oft turning. While legally it signifies turning to God for forgiveness of a sin or act of disobedience, its primary sense of turning to God as a personal act of love and devotion, and not necessarily from a state of sin, is a more exalted and deeper level of repentance. Thus, the Prophet Muḥammad, who is believed by Muslims to have been protected (*maʿṣūm*) by God from sin and error, is said to have declared: "I turn to God every day seventy times."[6] It is this personal attitude of constantly turning to God with sincere love and devotion that characterizes the language of repentance in the Qur'ān and prophetic tradition.

Repentance in the Qur'ān and Prophetic Tradition

It should be clear from the above discussion that repentance is one of the fundamental principles of Qur'anic theology and worldview. Its central importance is clearly indicated by the fact that the word *tawbah* with all its derivatives occurs eighty-seven times in the Qur'ān.[7] Most of these, moreover, belong to the Madinan period of revelation—when Muḥammad the prophet was also the founder and head of a religio-political and social commonwealth. This fact clearly signifies the social importance of repentance.

Repentance is not a metaphysical or theological concept, but rather a practical attitude or state of moral and religious consciousness. Among the basic elements of this state or attitude are the following: awe in the presence of the Holy, awareness of sin and genuine remorse for it, regret over lost opportunities, sincere contrition and the resolve to mend one's ways.[8] Yet the Qur'ān insists that this change of heart, or reorientation of one's life toward God through repentance can only

be achieved through divine succor. True repentance is therefore ultimately a gift of grace for which the penitent must be thankful. Thus,
the Qur'ān enjoins every human being to care for his parents and to
be thankful for God's bounties toward him and them. He should then
declare repentance in total submission to God.[9] Based on this and similar Qur'anic texts and pious prophetic *ḥadīths*, as will be demonstrated
later in this discussion, turning to God in sincere repentance (*tawbah*
or *inābah*) and gratitude (*shukr*) for the grace of repentance became the
first stations on the spiritual journey to God in Sufi piety.

The Qur'ān presents divine mercy as an important corollary to
human repentance. As a just and moral sovereign Lord, God is "severe
in punishment," but He is also the All-forgiving (*ghafūr*), All-merciful
(*raḥīm*) God.[10] In this same vein, the Qur'ān frequently correlates
God's infinite mercy with the deep human proclivity to sin. God is
ready to forgive all sins, even the unforgivable sin of association (*shirk*)
of other things with Him,[11] if the sinner turns sincerely to God with
faith in Him alone.[12] Furthermore, despair of God's infinite mercy and
forgiveness is itself a grave sin. God says, "O my servants who have
been extravagantly severe with themselves,[13] despair not of the mercy
of God, for surely God forgives all sins" (Q. 39:53).

Qur'anic theology is a theology of absolute transcendence. This implies not only the absolute transcendence of God over all His creation,
but His absolute freedom from all limitations and constraints in His
relations with His creatures. Yet God commands Muḥammad that if
those who believe in God's revelations come to him, he should say
to them: " 'Peace be upon you!' Your Lord has prescribed mercy for
Himself—Surely if any of you does evil in ignorance, but thereafter
repents and mends [his conduct], surely God is All-forgiving, All-merciful."[14] It is noteworthy that this is the only obligation that God imposed upon Himself in the Qur'ān.

It must be further observed that the term *tawbah* when applied to
God implies a divine pledge or covenant of mercy and forgiveness
toward those who sincerely repent, however often they may ignorantly
violate their side of the covenant. The Qur'ān asserts, "Surely *tawbah*
is incumbent upon God towards those who do evil in ignorance, then
soon thereafter repent. Those God shall turn towards them, for God
is All-knowing, All-wise." But, the Qur'ān insists, repentance will not
be accepted from anyone who, when faced by death would say, "Now
I repent," nor from those who die as rejecters of faith (Q. 4:17–18).

There is no doctrine of atonement or redemption in Islam. Expiation may, however, be attained by means of certain acts of penance

and restitution. We will examine the juristic aspects of expiation in the next section. But here it must be observed that, like repentance, expiation is ultimately a divine gift of grace and forgiveness, and not a human act.

The Qur'anic term for expiation, *takfīr*, is derived from the trilateral root *k/f/r*, which means "to hide" or "cover up." It is the same root from which the word *kufr* (rejection, or covering up of faith) is derived. Hence, when applied to human acts, the term means either to reject faith, or to expiate a grave offense toward God or society. But when applied to God, the term means to cover up, pardon, or efface human sin and its consequences. It is in fact to change the sins or evil deeds of a sincere penitent into good ones:

> Those who do not call upon another god beside God, do not slay a soul which God has forbidden except for a just cause, nor commit fornication—for whoever does that will incur great guilt, his torment will be multiplied on the day of Resurrection; in it he shall dwell forever disgraced, except for those who repent and do good, their evil deed shall be changed into good deeds. God is surely All-forgiving, All-merciful. (Q. 25:68–70)

Divine pardon, however, cannot be taken for granted. Therefore, the person of faith must always live between hope in God's mercy and fear of His punishment. This attitude of uncertainty is meant to strengthen the resolve of the pious to strive constantly to earn God's mercy and rich reward in the hereafter through sincere repentance: "O you who have faith, turn to God with sincere repentance, that perhaps your Lord may expiate for you your evil deeds and make you enter into gardens [of paradise] beneath which rivers flow" (Q. 66:8).

These conditional Qur'anic invitations for the pious to turn to God with sincere repentance in order that He may turn toward them with mercy and forgiveness are warmly echoed in the prophetic tradition. Here the emphasis is less on human action and divine response, and more on God's initiative. His infinite mercy and forgiveness are readily offered to the penitent sinner no matter how grave and frequent are his sins.

The Qur'anic assertion that God prescribed mercy for Himself is dramatically and concretely reiterated in a prophetic *ḥadīth*, thus: "When God created the creation, He prescribed with His own hand for Himself, 'my mercy shall overcome my wrath.' "[15]

In tone and purport, this pious literature resembles the books of the biblical prophets. In both, God seeks the sinner and rejoices at his repentance. This recurrent theme is often graphically presented in terms of the desert life of early Muslim Arab society.

In one typical hyperbolic tradition of this genre we are told:

> God is more joyful at the repentance of His servant when he returns to Him than one of you would be if he were upon his she-camel with his food and drink in an arid desert. She runs away from him, and he despairs of ever finding her. In desperation, he falls asleep in the shade of a tree. But when he awakes, he finds her standing beside him. With exceeding joy, he rushes to take her by the rope, exclaiming: "O God, you are my servant and I am your lord"; he erred from joy.[16]

An even more dramatic *hadīth* asserts: "God is more joyful at the repentance of His servant than a sterile man or woman who begets a child, an erring person who finds the right path, and a thirsty person who accidently comes upon a source of refreshing water."[17]

Beside the Qur'ān—which Muslims believe to have been directly and verbally revealed by God to Muḥammad—and the Prophet's own inspired sayings, there is a considerable body of pious divine logia known as *hadīth qudsi*. These logia are, for the most part, expressions of divine compassion toward the penitent, and even obdurate sinner. In one such divine *hadīth*, God says,

> O child of Adam, so long as you call upon me and hope in me, I will forgive all your sins, and I do not care. O child of Adam, even if your sins were to reach the zenith of heaven, and yet you beg my forgiveness I will forgive you, and I do not care. O child of Adam, if you were to come to me with enough sins to fill the entire earth, but you meet me not associating anything with me, I will meet you with its full measure of forgiveness.[18]

This divine *hadīth* echoes the Qur'anic assertion that God's mercy encompasses all things.[19] Furthermore, this reassurance of divine mercy is used in both the Qur'ān and prophetic tradition as a means of encouragement for the sinner to repent and turn to God for forgiveness. God will, according to a well-attested prophetic tradition, "accept the repentance of His servant so long as he had not breathed his last."[20]

God's infinite mercy encompasses not only space, but time as well. The Prophet is said to have asserted that God stretches out His hand during the night for those who had sinned by day to repent, and He stretches it during the day for the sinners of the night to do likewise. This He will do until the sun shall rise from the west, that is, until the day of Resurrection.[21] According to yet another tradition, there is a door of divine mercy in the place of the setting of the sun whose width is the distance of a seventy-year journey. This door will remain open until the sun shall rise from its direction. Then, "the faith of any person will avail him nothing, unless he had believed beforehand and through his faith had earned some good."[22]

Divine mercy and compassion toward a repentant sinner must not be taken as a license to sin and rely on God's mercy. Sincere intention therefore to turn to God with true repentance and the resolve not to repeat the same offense are necessary conditions for true repentance. But since inner thoughts and intentions are known to God alone, sincere repentance must be demonstrated through outward behavior. To this end, jurists and Sufi masters instituted many rules and techniques for penitents to follow in their struggle to obey God's law and sincerely turn to Him.

The first of these rules is remorse or contrition (*nadam*). In a widely accepted *ḥadīth*, the Prophet is reported to have said, "Contrition (*nadam*) is repentance (*tawbah*)." He also said, "The expiation of a sin is contrition."[23] From this it follows that a person who truly repents from a sin is as though he had no sin.[24] But a person who habitually sins and repents without any serious intention to reform his character through the discipline of repentance is in reality deceiving himself and God. It is thus reported that the Prophet said: He who begs God's forgiveness for a sin but still persists in it is like one who mocks his Lord.[25]

There are sins against God and sins against other human beings. A second important rule is therefore that a person should repent in secret, between himself and God for sins against God, such as evil thoughts or neglect of obligatory acts of worship. As for the sins against others, they include wrongdoing, slander, willful deception, treachery, and any physical or moral injury. Repentance in such cases should be accompanied by restitution and a humble request for forgiveness from the victim. If forgiveness and restitution are not earnestly sought here, they will have to be exacted on the day of judgment, when no material restitution is possible.[26] A well-known companion, Muʿādh b. Jabal, asked the Prophet for pious advice. The Prophet answered, "Fear God to the best of your ability and remember Him always. Whenever you commit an evil deed, perform for it an act of repentance, the secret ones in secret and the public ones in public."[27]

The best expiation for a public offense is to confess it publicly and accept its consequences. A woman who had committed adultery is said to have come to the Prophet, confessed her offense, and asked that she be duly punished for it. Since adultery is a major offense (*ḥadd*), its punishment is death by stoning. The woman was pregnant. The Prophet sent her away and told her to wait until she delivered. When she returned with the child in her arms, and again asked for her punishment, the Prophet sent her away a second time to nurse the child. Finally she returned leading the child by the hand with a piece of bread in his mouth.

Had the woman not returned and simply repented, she would have escaped punishment. But since she wished to expiate her sin with her own blood, the Prophet ordered that she be stoned to death. Afterwards he prayed over her and gave her an honorable burial. 'Umar b. al-Khaṭṭāb, the second caliph, protested, "You pray over her even though she had committed adultery!" The Prophet answered, "But she had performed such a sincere act of repentance which, if it were divided among seventy inhabitants of Madīnah, it would suffice them. Is there anything nobler than her offering her life freely to God?"[28] This and similar traditions became the basis for an elaborate jurisprudence of repentance, to which we shall now turn.

Repentance and the Sacred Law

Traditional Islam has no concept of human rights as defined in the United Nations 1945 Declaration and generally understood in the West. Rather, there are rights of God and rights of human beings. God's rights consist of His commands and prohibitions, while those of His human servants are expressed in their attitude of absolute submission (*islām*) to His will and obedience to His law.

Islam rests on certain divinely instituted obligations (*farā'iḍ*) corresponding to fundamental human and divine rights. These obligations are categorized as acts of worship (*'ibādāt*) and human interrelations or transactions (*mu'āmalāt*). They are two-dimensional relations, between the individual and God, and between the individual and society.

Most offenses that call for repentance are violations of either the rights of God or those of His human creatures. But inasmuch as most human rights are legislated by God, they are considered as His rights as well. Often, therefore, violating "the rights of the servants" is tantamount to violating "the rights of God."

The pillars or fundamentals of Islam, such as the canonical prayers, almsgiving, the fast of Ramaḍān, and the *ḥajj* pilgrimage, are absolute obligations, which all Muslims must fulfill, barring extreme circumstances. Willful neglect of any of these obligations constitutes an offense against God, which can be forgiven only after contrite and sincere repentance. Other obligations, like armed struggle (*jihād*) in God's cause, are relative obligations that can become absolute only under special circumstances. But inner striving, or the "greater *jihād*" of the soul, is an absolute and universal obligation incumbent on every believer at all times.

Sincere repentance or turning to God is a form of inner *jihād*, and hence an absolute obligation. This is the opinion of the great jurist, theologian, philosopher, and mystic al-Ghazālī (d. 1111), who says, "Repentance is an absolute and universal obligation (*fard 'ayn*) incumbent upon every person, and therefore no human being is without need of it."[29] Ghazālī further argues that repentance is necessary at all times because human beings are always prone to sin either of the body or of the heart. Since, moreover, religious obligations are ultimately expressions of faith, which is the work of both the heart and the body, then violating or neglecting any one of them requires an act of both inward and outward repentance.

It will not be possible within the scope of this chapter to examine the minutiae of legal discussions of repentance in relation to the different offenses and their punishments. It is important to note, however, the tension between repentance as a moral and devotional ideal depicted in the Qur'ān and *ḥadīth* tradition and the speculative and often purely scholastic treatment of this ideal by the jurists. The reason for that is perhaps that the primary concern of the law is outward probity and justice, as well as the proper observance of religious obligations. The law cannot legislate for good and evil as such, or the inner feelings and intentions of the heart. A few examples of the juristic treatment of major offenses and the effect of repentance on them will suffice to illustrate this point.

Among the most strictly and repeatedly enjoined obligations in the Qur'ān is the regular observance of the five daily prayers. Hence, willfully abandoning or neglecting this important ritual is regarded as a grave infraction of one of the fundamental rights of God. Understandably, therefore, repentance of such a grave sin has been a subject of much debate among jurists.

According to conservative and literalist jurists, such as the well-known medieval savant Ibn Taymīyah (d. 1328), a person who knows that it is unlawful to neglect the prayers, yet intentionally does so, must humbly repent and regularly perform them. He cannot, however, make up for past prayers because one of the primary conditions for the validity of the prayers is punctuality. Since the time for the proper performance of these prayers would be irrecoverably lost, so too would the opportunity to make amends by making them up. According to this view, such a person is actually an apostate, and his resumption of prayers is tantamount to his return to Islam. His past sins will be forgiven in accordance with the divine promise, "Say to those who have rejected faith, if they desist their past shall be forgiven them" (Q. 8:38).[30]

More liberal jurists, including the founders of the four Sunni legal schools, hold that the repentance of one who abandons the prayers should be clearly manifested in sincere contrition. The sincerity of his repentance must be shown in the zealous performance of all divine obligations including the prayers, both those neglected in the past and those required in the present. They base their argument for the necessity to make up missed prayers on the prophetic injunction: "Anyone who misses his prayer because of sleep or forgetfulness, let him perform it when he remembers it." The Prophet also said: "If I command you to do something, do as much of it as you are able to."[31] Consonant with these injunctions, it has been argued that the permission to make up missed prayers is a gracious act of divine leniency, similar to the permission for a sick person to perform the prayers sitting or lying down. By analogy, therefore, it is lawful to perform prayers outside their proper time.[32]

Neglect or violation of any of God's rights or the rights of His servants is in reality a crime against God or human beings. Since God promised forgiveness to those who sincerely repent, regardless of the gravity of their sin, then crimes against God alone fall outside the purview of the sacred law. Two such offenses (*ḥudūd*) are neglect of the prayers out of laziness and apostasy. An outward show of repentance is enough to satisfy the law, for punishment or forgiveness for these two offenses will only be manifested on the day of judgment. If punishment for such offenses is carried out here on earth, it is meant to bring the apostate or recalcitrant person back to the community and to make of him an example for others. The only requirement of the law is that a repentant person who had neglected the prayers out of laziness rather than disbelief should make up what he missed.[33]

In contrast with the five daily prayers, which are solely God's rights, wronging others through cheating in trade or wages, or in any way usurping the wealth or property of others is a violation of a human right. Yet, because God forbade wrongdoing, such transgressions constitute an offense (*ḥadd*) against God.[34] The first requirement that a repentant wrongdoer should fulfill is to redress those he wronged by compensating them for their losses.

Jurists have disagreed concerning the case of a usurper who dies before being able to restore the wealth he usurped to its rightful owners or to their heirs. According to some, the repentance of such a person will be invalid unless he gives back the usurped wealth. If this is not possible, then requital will be exacted from him on the day of Resurrection through his balance of good and evil deeds. Either his good deeds will be discounted from his balance and accounted for those he had wronged, or their evil deeds will be laid upon him, and thus he would be consigned to Hell. The only thing such a transgressing repentant could do in this life is to endure wrong and hurt patiently, and to constantly beg God's forgiveness.

As for his illicit wealth, it should be set aside as unlawful to use in any way, or it should be turned over to the religious/legal authority (*imām*) who would keep it for its rightful owners. It would then be legally treated as lost property until it is claimed.

Others argued that the door of repentance will always be open for such a wrongdoer, for God would never shut the door of repentance in the face of any penitent sinner. He should therefore give that unlawful wealth in alms on behalf of its owners. On the day of Resurrection, they would either concur with him, and thus the merit of this good deed would be theirs, or if they did not, then he would be rewarded and they would have of the merit of his good deeds a reward commensurate with the wrong they suffered.[35]

Punishable offenses (*ḥudūd*) are acts of public rebellion against the sacred law. Therefore, guilt must be publicly established through morally upright witnesses or public confession, and publicly punished. From this it follows that if the guilty person repents of his offense before he is apprehended and punished, then his repentance must be accepted.

The case of the adulterous woman discussed above is one of several cases where the guilty man or woman chooses public punishment rather than private repentance as the only means of expiating guilt. In one case, that of a man called Māʿiz, as the stones began to be hurled at him, he ran away. But he was caught and stoned to death. When the Prophet heard of Māʿiz's attempted escape, he said: "Should you not have let him go, so that he may turn to God in repentance and that God may turn towards him?"[36]

It was observed above that all major offenses that God has prohibited are transgressions against His rights. It has therefore been argued that they all are capable of forgiveness through repentance. This view has been supported by the Qur'anic verse "Say to those who have rejected faith, if they desist their past will be forgiven them" (Q. 8:38). Nevertheless, jurists have disagreed as to whether repentance alone is sufficient in annulling punishment, or whether—if the offense is against human beings, such as theft, drunkenness, and adultery—punishment must in any case be carried out.

There is general agreement among jurists that if an offender repents after suffering punishment for his offense, he will be surely forgiven. This is based on the Prophet's saying: "If a thief repents after committing theft [and his hand is cut off], his hand shall precede him to Paradise. But if he does not repent, his hand shall precede him to the Fire."[37] Jurists have disagreed, however, regarding the effect of repentance before punishment is meted out.

Most Ḥanbalite jurists have argued on the basis of the Qur'ān and *ḥadīth* tradition that repentance annuls all punishments both legally and in fact. This means that no punishment should be inflicted after repentance. Others held the opposite view, namely that repentance has no effect on the punishment of a person who violates the rights of individual human beings. Still others, including Ibn Taymīyah, held that both repentance and punishment are expiatory acts that cleanse the offender from the consequences of sin. While either would be sufficient in obtaining divine forgiveness, it is of greater merit to endure punishment along with the harsh discipline of repentance.[38]

It was argued above that juristic discussions of repentance in relation to human and divine rights, and their offenses and punishments, have been at best theoretical and speculative. It must be added here that since most Muslim countries today apply some form of Western criminal law, the opinions of the jurists are of interest only to students of Islamic and comparative law. Yet the tension between piety and law, or between a humanistic and legal *islām* remains. Traditionally this tension was between Sufis and jurists. Now it is between those who wish to apply the letter of the *sharī'ah* law in Muslim society and those who wish to live by its spirit. But repentance is a dynamic spiritual relationship between God and His pious servants, and it is this relationship that will concern us for the rest of this discussion.

Degrees of Repentance

It was observed above that there is no doctrine of redemption in Islam. This means that there is no doctrine of original sin either. Rather, every human being is capable of sin and righteousness, and therefore is alone answerable for his own actions. The Qur'ān categorically states: "No soul shall bear the burden of another soul" (Q. 35:18). But since human beings are by nature subject to greed, lust, heedlessness, and other vices, they cannot attain eternal felicity or salvation through their effort alone. Rather, salvation is ultimately a divine gift of grace and mercy for those who constantly turn to God in sincere repentance.

It may be argued that the innate human tendency to sin in Islam is somewhat akin to original sin in Christianity. Likewise, true repentance, at least in its expiatory effect, is analogous to redemption. But there is no savior in Islam, and this makes repentance—and its corollary, divine forgiveness—the cornerstone of Islamic faith, law, and piety.

Adam, the first human being, was according to Islam both the first prophet, "the elect of God," but also the first sinner. Adam, the Qur'ān asserts, "disobeyed his Lord and transgressed. But then his Lord elected him, turned towards him, and guided him" (Q. 20:21–22). The pious traditionist Ḥasan al-Baṣrī is said to have related that when God turned toward Adam, the angels congratulated him. The archangels Gabriel and Michael came down to him and said, "O Adam, may you be well comforted with God's turning towards you!" He said, "[This is in deed a great favor]. But if beyond this there is anything to pray for, then where shall my station be?" God revealed to him: "O Adam, you have forever given your descendants hardship and toil, but you have also given them repentance. Therefore whosoever among them calls upon me, I shall promptly answer him as I have answered you. If anyone of them begs my forgiveness, I shall not be miserly towards him, for I am near, answering prayers."[39]

Like Judaism and Christianity, Islam regards human history as the story of God's dealing with humanity. But Islam specifically holds that God made His will for humankind known through revelation to a long series of prophets beginning with Adam and ending with Muḥammad. Thus, human history is prophetic history. Prophets are the nearest of God's creatures to Him; they are His true representatives on earth. Their mission is to guide humanity to the worship of God alone, and their personal lives serve as models for the faithful to emulate.

While the Qur'ān recounts minor shortcomings of some prophets in order to emphasize their humanity, later tradition makes of these shortcomings examples of sorrowful repentance for the pious to imitate. Adam's sin, for instance, was an act of disobedience committed in weakness, not in insolent defiance of God's command. It was not an offense (*hadd*) against God. Yet he wept for a hundred years in repentance of his sin. He wept so bitterly that the earth sprouted grass and trees on the spot where his tears fell. It was only then that God taught him "certain words, and He relented towards him" (Q. 2:37). Tradition even reports Adam's prayer for forgiveness for the pious to use: "O God, there is no God except you, all glory and praise be to you. I have wronged myself and done evil. Forgive me, for you are All-forgiving, All-merciful."[40]

Noah's sin was that he argued with God regarding his son who sought protection from the flood in a mountain and refused to enter the ark.[41] Still, Noah penitently wept for three hundred years before God would forgive and bless him. The sin of which Moses had to repent was that he asked to see God with his own eyes.[42]

Prophets are protected by God from major sins, such as associating other things with God or violating any of His rights. Therefore, the offenses of David and Solomon, who are prophets according to the Islamic tradition, have presented a serious problem for Muslim traditionists and theologians. The Qur'ān vaguely alludes to David's lustful and murderous episode with Uriah and his wife.[43] According to later tradition, however, David's sin was one of conceit rather than adultery and murder. As he secluded himself for his daily worship, he thought that he could commit no sin. A beautiful bird flew into his prayer chamber, and David interrupted his worship and ran after the bird. The bird flew into a garden where David saw Uriah's wife bathing. He fell in love with her, arranged for her husband to be killed in battle, and married her. Thus, his sin was not one of adultery; therefore it was not a major offense (*hadd*) against God. It was not a prophet like him who reminded him of his sin and reproached him for it but two angels. David prostrated himself in humble repentance before God for forty days, weeping and begging forgiveness.[44]

The sin of his son, King Solomon, was that he allowed one of his wives to worship an idol in his house. As a punishment, Solomon lost his royal ring, and hence his kingdom, to one of the evil spirits of the jinn who were subject to him. He was thus humiliated for forty days before God accepted his repentance, forgave him, and restored him to his throne. The account of Solomon's repentance is clearly legendary, having neither biblical nor Qur'anic basis. It is meant to explicate the following brief Qur'anic allusion: "We had indeed tempted Solomon and placed on his throne the form of a body, then he humbly returned to God" (Q. 38:34).[45]

The nearest to the prophets in moral character and piety are their immediate disciples. This has been the case with the Prophet Muḥammad's companions. While the accounts of the repentance of some appear to be hagiographical, the repentance of three men is especially interesting. Their repentance is alluded to in general terms in the Qur'ān.

They were three men of the Helpers (*anṣār*) of Madīnah who stayed behind and did not join the expedition for the battle of Tabūk against the Byzantines.[46] They were shunned by the whole community, including their own wives. They were filled with remorse for disobeying the Prophet, until finally God turned toward them and forgave them.[47]

One of them, Ka'b b. Mālik, gave most of his wealth in alms and pledged never to utter a falsehood. Another, Abū Lubābah, tied himself to a pillar where he stayed without food for seven days. Finally, he was told that God had forgiven him; still he refused to free himself until the Prophet came and untied him with his own hand. As a sign of his repentance, he pledged to desert the home in which he committed this grave sin and give all his wealth in alms "to God and His messenger." But the Prophet counseled, "One third will be sufficient ransom for you."[48]

The prophets and their disciples or close companions represent a special class of repenters. But the actual types of penitents are, according to Ghazālī, four. They are so categorized in accordance with the stations attained by their souls on their mystical journey to God. The first are those who live in a constant state of repentance to the end of their lives. This is the perfect repentance of the prophets. Theirs is the "sincere or pure (*naṣūḥ*) repentance" to which the Qur'ān calls the true believers.[49] The tranquil soul of such people is called in the Qur'ān "the contented (*muṭma'innah*) soul."[50]

The second are those who obey God in all things. They are free from grave sins, but are tried with minor sins. Yet even these, they do not commit intentionally. They live in a continuous state of remorse for every sin they commit and always resolve never to return to it again. The soul of such people is known as "the reproaching (*lawwāmah*) soul."[51] The Prophet said, "All the children of Adam are sinners, and the best sinners are the penitents who constantly beg God's forgiveness."[52]

The third type of repenters are those who confess their sins and repent of them to the best of their ability. But these are people whose carnal souls always tempt them to evil. Thus they procrastinate with their repentance day after day. This kind of soul is known as "the tempting (*musawwilah*) soul." These people mix good with evil deeds.[53] The final destiny of these people is with God. He may in His mercy cause them to die in a state of repentance, or if they are predestined for perdition, then they die in a state of sin.

The fourth type are people who turn to God for some time, but then they turn away without any serious intention to repent. These are known as "the persisters (*muṣirrīn*) in evil." The soul of such a person is known as "the soul enjoining evil (*al-ammārah bil-sū'*)."[54] The end of these people is uncertain, and their fate is in God's hand. If they die having faith in the oneness of God, they may be saved. Ghazālī, however, comments, "It is not impossible that God's infinite forgiveness may embrace such a person for a reason hidden from us."[55] Ghazālī sums up: "Human beings are all deprived except the people of knowledge. The people of knowledge are all deprived except those who are active [in good works]. But they too are deprived except those who are sincere, for the status of these people is great in deed."[56]

These are the people of God, the Sufis. They live in God, strive in God, and die in God. Their journey from this nether world (*dunya*) of material existence to the higher realm of the Truth[57] begins in repentance and ends in the annihilation of their ego in the divine I, and their attributes in God's attributes. It will not be possible to follow this long and arduous journey of the soul, but only to witness their psychological preparation for their travel toward God, who is the goal and end of their journey.

Repentance in Sufi Piety

The mystical life is a journey from God to the world of created things and back to God the creator of all things. Outwardly, this journey consists of acts of obedience and worship of God, and the struggle (*jihād*) against the carnal soul and its many ruses and allurements. Inwardly, it is the journey of the heart from the temple of the idols of multiplicity to the *ka'bah* of unity, from the ignorance of "there is no god" to the knowledge of "except God."[58]

Turning to God in total and sincere repentance constitutes the preparation, vehicle, and first step of this journey. As water is necessary for the outward purity without which worship would be invalid, so is repentance necessary for the inner purity of the heart before one can truly love God. In the view of the famous Persian Sufi master and theoretician Hujwiri (d. ca. 1077), repentance (*tawbah*) is the first station of the traveler (*sālik*) on the way to the truth. Like ritual purification, sincere repentance is the first step of those who desire to serve God.[59]

Repentance in Sufi piety is an ongoing battle against the carnal soul. The earliest Sufi psychologist of repentance, al-Muḥāsibī (d. 857) presents an elaborate program of ascetic and spiritual exercises for disciplining and ultimately subduing the soul and raising it to the station of contentment with God. Every human being, the Prophet is said to have asserted, has his own satan within himself, which is his soul. This enemy within must be overcome by subjecting it to the privation of food and sleep, as well as pleasant human company. The difficult task of subduing the soul must be attempted through long periods of silence and harsh admonition, reminding the soul of the evil of its deeds.[60]

For Muḥāsibī and Sufi psychology in general, the soul—or more accurately the self (*nafs*)—is not an abstract power or faculty in the body, but a person within the person, with its own inner life and will. It is, as we saw above, instinctively cunning and wicked, but potentially righteous and good. To realize this potential, the soul must be disciplined, refined, and encouraged or even compelled to turn to God. Muḥāsibī's small but important treatise on repentance is in fact a manual of discipline of the soul.

With proper ascetic discipline and rigorous spiritual exercises, the soul would ultimately return to God and abandon the vices that had initially separated it from Him. But the soul always longs for social preeminence, and thus will seek the praise of others for its seemingly righteous conduct. There should therefore be a constant warning against seeking by acts of obedience to God nearness to anything other than God.

There are certain innate tendencies or characteristics that turn the soul away from God, and that should be strongly resisted. These are hypocrisy, self-conceit, arrogance, and love of power.[61] As these evil traits are overcome, the signs of true repentance appear. These are striving for obedience to God in all things, renunciation of the world, illumination of the heart with the light of certainty, fear of God and hope in Him.

When the heart and soul of the penitent are finally cleansed of everything other than God, he would shun anything that turns him away from his Lord and the pleasure of His company and love of Him. These efforts, moreover, result in the states of sorrow, longing, and fear of separation of the lover from his beloved. Muḥāsibī describes these psychological states thus: "One moment the penitent is seized by trembling and palpitation of the heart. Another moment he bursts out weeping with copious tears. Still another moment he is overcome by deep sighs, and another moment he loses his mind. Anyone who sees him, unaware of his inner state, would think him mad." In these states, the penitent would not care whether people shun him or seek his company.[62]

Muḥāsibī asserts that repentance is a divine gift of grace, and that the servant would not turn to God truly unless God first turns toward him with the light of His noble countenance. As for the true penitent, Muḥāsibī says the following: "If you ask him, you would find him well acquainted with the way to God. If he answers you, he would describe a way which he himself had traversed, hardships which he had experienced and repudiated, a struggle which he had engaged in and high stations of nearness to God which he had reached."[63]

Classical Sufis held diverse opinions regarding the nature and essential characteristics of repentance. The well-known shaykh and thinker Sahl b. 'Abd Allāh al-Tustarī (d. 896) and his followers held that repentance consists in not forgetting one's sins and always regretting them. He argued that one must not feel happy because of any good deeds that one may perform, for sincere remorse is superior to good works. Furthermore, true contrition is the best antidote for self-conceit.

His equally famous contemporary, Junayd of Baghdad (d. 910), and his disciples held the opposite view, namely, that true repentance consists in forgetting one's sins. Their argument is that a sincere penitent is a lover of God, and is therefore in constant contemplation of God. In the state of contemplation, one must not think of sin, for the recollection of sin is a veil between God and those who contemplate Him. Hujwiri comments, "Those who hold the penitent to be self-dependent regard his forgetfulness of sin as heedlessness, while those who hold that he is dependent on God, deem his remembrance of sin to be polytheism."[64]

Others held that repentance is of three kinds: turning from what is wrong to what is right, from what is right to what is of even greater rectitude, and from selfhood to God. The first is the repentance of ordinary people, the second is of the elect, and the third belongs to those who have attained true love of God.[65] With regard to the elect, they are free of sin; therefore it is impossible for them to repent of any transgression. As for the lovers of God, they are not conscious of any sin or repentance, but of God alone. This is the station of annihilation (*fanā'*) that is reserved for the elect of the elect.

It is to this station that the following definitions of repentance by some of the great shaykhs of early Sufism point. Ruwaym (d. 915) said, "The meaning of repentance is that you should repent of repentance."[66] The great woman saint Rābiʻah al-ʻAdawīyah (d. 801) said, "I asked pardon of God for my little sincerity in saying I ask pardon of God."[67] Another shaykh, Ibrahim al-Daqqāq (d. 1015 or 1021), said, "Repentance means that you should be to God a face without a back even as you have formerly been unto him a back without a face."[68]

Repentance in Shīʻī Thought and Piety

Shīʻī faith and piety are based on a deep ethos of psychological longing and sorrow, repentance, and martyrdom. In contrast with mainstream Sunni Islam, Shīʻī devotions are highly liturgical in both tone and content. In tone, they express a deep yearning for "a perfect dominion" under the messianic rule of God's vicegerency (*walī*) and proof (*hujjah*) over His creatures, the hidden Imām, whose reappearance the faithful await with emotional expectation. In content, beside the canonical worship common to all Muslim legal schools, Shīʻī devotions include highly mystical and somewhat metaphysical prayers attributed to one or another of the Twelve Shīʻī Imāms, as well as symbolic liturgical pilgrimages to their sacred shrines.

This messianic worldview is based on a pessimistic assessment of human society, which contrasts sharply with the seeming success story of early Islam. It implies the belief that sin is a primary cause of imperfection in the world, natural calamities, and human tribulations. This idea gives repentance redemptive significance and a uniquely liturgical character.

The causal connection between sin and general human evil is characterized by a contemporary Shīʻī thinker as follows: "It has been scientifically proven that anything that God has prohibited is a source of evil for both the individual and society."[69] The fifth Imām, Muhammad al-Bāqir, is reported to have declared: "No calamity befalls a servant except as punishment for a sin he has committed."[70] Sin, according to the Imām, sullies the heart and repentance purifies it. But if a person persists in sin, then his heart becomes hard and completely enveloped by the stain of sin, so that he could never hope for any good. The Imām continued, "This is the meaning of God's saying, 'Rather that which they have earned has tarnished their hearts.' "[71]

More specifically, sin may deprive the sinner of worldly riches, divine bounty, and even the ability to offer proper worship.[72] In fact, human conduct is directly related to divine preordination of human happiness or wretchedness. According to the Shī'ī doctrine of *badā'*, God may decree something, then alter it as a result of a person's righteous or evil deeds.[73] Thus, the sixth Imām, Ja'far al-Ṣādiq, is reported to have said, "Those who die due to their sins are more than those who die because they had fulfilled their decreed term of life. And there are more of those who live long because of their goodness than those who live according to their decreed lifespan."[74]

This cosmic view of sin demands a concomitant view of repentance. Although the legal treatment of sin and repentance in Shī'ī jurisprudence is essentially the same as that of other legal schools, the question of whether repentance is a legal or rational obligation has been the subject of much debate. Interestingly, the majority view is that repentance is a rational necessity that depends not only on the force of law, but on reason and moral guidance as well.[75]

This view of repentance is consonant with the Shī'ī theological view that good and evil are not only divinely preordained and legislated as such, but also rationally knowable. Therefore, repentance, like all human actions, is a matter of human choice and divine assistance, rather than inexorable divine predestination. It also means that it is the obligation of every Muslim to admonish, and even if necessary compel, a transgressor to repent.[76]

As a liturgical act of penance, repentance must be publicly shown through special rituals. The Imām Ja'far al-Ṣādiq was asked what pure or sincere (*naṣūḥ*) repentance is, and he defined it ritualistically as fasting Wednesday, Thursday, and Friday of every week. The practice of sincere repentance involves three rituals: a complete body wash, or ritualistic purification (*ghusl*), the three-day fast, and the prayer (*ṣalāt*) of repentance. This prayer consists of four cycles (*rak'ahs*); in each, specific passages from the Qur'ān should be recited. The prayer also includes the supplication (*du'ā'*) of repentance of the Imām Zayn al-'Ābidīn, 'Alī, son of the martyred Imām Ḥusayn.[77]

Sin and repentance are both individual and social phenomena. Public sin is any act of transgression whose consequences are harmful to society, regardless of whether it is committed by the whole society or only a few individuals. The Qur'ān declares, "When We wish to destroy a town, We send a command to those of its inhabitants who are extravagantly wasteful, and so they commit abomination in it. Thus is judgment passed against it, and We devastate it utterly" (Q. 17:16).

According to a tradition attributed to Imām 'Alī, God would not punish society for the sin of some of its members if these few sinned in secret without the knowledge of the majority. But if they commit public transgressions, and the majority does not restrain them, then both groups incur God's chastisement.[78] This is because public reprehensible or indecent behavior, even of the few, may, if left unchecked, infect the whole society. It is therefore the moral duty of every Muslim, according to the Qur'ān, to "enjoin good or decent (*ma'rūf*) behavior" and "dissuade from indecent or reprehensible (*munkar*) conduct."[79]

It was observed earlier that repentance is the expiation of sin and that the best expiation is the sacrifice of life. The first movement of expiatory repentance in Islam arose in the city of Kūfah in Iraq. After the tragic massacre of Ḥusayn b. 'Alī, the Prophet's grandson, in Karbalā' in 680—less than fifty years after the Prophet's death—many of the supporters (*shī'ah*) of 'Alī and his descendants were filled with deep remorse for having betrayed their Imām. They formed a small and ill-prepared army of penitents to avenge the blood of Ḥusayn, and thus expiate their sin. They first made pilgrimage to his tomb, where they declared their repentance during a night and a day of weeping and prayers for forgiveness. Their leader, Sulaymān b. Ṣurad al-Khuzā'ī, described their ill-fated penitential mission in these words:

> O people, anyone desiring by this uprising God's face and the hereafter, is one of us, and God's mercy may be upon him, alive or dead. But for anyone who desires this world, by God, he will receive neither booty nor reward, save God's good pleasure. For we have neither gold and silver, nor any goods, but only our swords on our shoulders.[80]

This ethos of remorse and martyrdom continues to this day to dominate Shī'ī piety, art, and even politics. The movement of penitents lives on in every commemorative observance of the sufferings and martyrdom of Imām Ḥusayn, his family, and small band of followers. Where it is no longer possible to express repentance, the faithful express deep regret and disappointment for not being part of the Imām's small band of fighters, or among those who died avenging his blood.

Conclusion

We have seen in the foregoing discussion that repentance is a devotional act of worship, a moral commitment to good and just conduct, and an ongoing exercise of spiritual and psychological discipline. We also saw that repentance can serve as a legal/moral framework of social morality and good order.

One important question remains: What has repentance as a religious and moral phenomenon to offer to today's world? The question is especially relevant to the current global order of advanced technology, high finance, rapid communication, and the consequent social disintegration and rampant civil and international conflict. To even attempt an answer to this question is far beyond the scope of this chapter. Nonetheless, a few general reflections from the Islamic point of view may be useful to the general purpose of this volume.

The Qur'ān addresses all those who have faith: "turn to God altogether that you may prosper" (Q. 24:31). Muslims have taken prosperity to mean success in both this world and the next. But prosperity even in this world does not simply mean the quest for wealth and political power; it must also include social and international harmony and cooperation. In this quest, turning to God and human decency in having the moral courage to remorsefully admit wrong and seek to right it, may guide the human family to true world peace and prosperity.

In today's world, more than ever, repentance is needed as a source of moral and spiritual discipline and a cure for the all-too-human tendency to love power and material possessions. It is also needed as a means of directing both the individual and society toward higher values. In our technologized, yet lonely world, repentance may be psychologically cathartic and therapeutic. Its catharsis lies in its power to transform the soul and purge it of the dross of selfishness, anger, and fear. Its healing or therapeutic power is its ability to liberate human beings from guilt and despair through faith and hope. Ultimately, the feeling of guilt without the liberation of repentance can be a prison that suffocates the human spirit.

Notes

1. Abū al-Qāsim Maḥmūd b. 'Umar al-Zamakhsharī, *Asās al-Balāghah*, ed. 'Abd al-Raḥīm Maḥmūd (Cairo: Maṭba'at Awlād Urvand, 1953), 40.

2. Arthur Jeffery, *The Foreign Vocabulary of the Qur'ān* (Lahore: al-Biruni, 1977), 87 and 95. Jeffery argues that the term *tawbah* may go back to Aramaic or even Akkadian roots.

3. Q. 34:10. All Qur'anic and other Arabic text citations are my own translations. The mountains are here commanded to repeat again and again with the great psalmist his hymns of glory to God. See for a good lexical discussion

of this term, Abū al-Faḍl Jamāl al-Dīn Muḥammad b. Makram b. Manẓūr, *Lisān al-'Arab*, 15 vols. (Beirut: Dār Ṣādir, n.d.), vol. 1, 217–21.

4. See for example Q. 88:25–26. See also Ibn Manẓūr, *Lisān*, 217 ff.

5. Ibid., 475.

6. 'Alī Dawūd Muḥammad Jaffāl, *al-Tawbah wa-atharuhā fi isqāṭ al-ḥudūd fī al-fiqh al-islāmī* (Beirut: Dār al-Nahḍah al-'Arabīyah lil-ṭibā'ah wal-nashr 1409/1989), 25–26.

7. Frederick M. Denny, "The Qur'anic Vocabulary of Repentance: Orientations and Attitudes," *Journal of the American Academy of Religion* 47, 4 (December 1980): 650.

8. Ibid.

9. See Q. 46:15; and on the relationship of these two concepts, see Toshihiko Izutsu, *Ethico Religious Concepts in the Qur'ān* (Montreal: McGill University Press, 1966), 110.

10. These three divine attributes are frequently invoked, as in this verse: "God is severe in punishment, and He is All-forgiving, All-merciful" (5:98).

11. The Qur'ān states, "God will not forgive that associates be ascribed to Him, but other than this, He forgives whomsoever He will" (4:48).

12. See Izutsu, *Ethico Religious Concepts*, 10–11.

13. The word *asrafū* (being extravagantly severe) could also mean being extravagantly wasteful. The well-known Qur'ān lexicographer al-Rāghib al-Iṣfahānī explains the word as generally meaning to "transgress the limit" in any action, although in general usage it refers to wasteful spending. See his *Mufradāt alfāẓ al-Qur'ān*, ed. Nadīm Mar'ashlī (Cairo: Dār al-Kātib al-'Arabī, 1392/1972), 236.

14. Q. 6:54; see also vol. 12. The address to the believers with the salutation of peace conveys a sense of calm but confident elation with the glad tidings of divine mercy and forgiveness.

15. 'Alā' al-Dīn 'Alī al-Muttaqī b. Ḥusām al-Dīn al-Hindī, *Kanz al-'ummāl fī sunan al-aqwāl wal-af'āl*, 16 vols. (Beirut: Mu'assasat al-Risālah, 1399/1979), vol. 4, 249.

16. Shams al-Dīn Abū 'Abd Allāh Muḥammad b. Abī Bakr ibn Qayyim al-Jawzīyah, *Kitāb al-Tawbah*, ed. Ṣābir al-Baṭāwī (Beirut: Dār al-Jīl, 1412/1992), 24; and Hindī, *Kanz*, 203–4.

17. Hindī, *Kanz*, 205.

18. Ibid., 214.

19. Q. 7:156 and 40:7.

20. Jaffāl, *Tawbah*, 36; and Hindī, *Kanz*, 210.

21. Jaffāl, *Tawbah*, 209.

22. Q. 6:158; Hindī, *Kanz*, 211.

23. Jaffāl, *Tawbah*, 39, and Hindī, *Kanz*, 215.

24. Jaffāl, *Tawbah*, 38.

25. Hindī, *Kanz*, 208.

26. See Hindī, *Kanz*, 206.

27. Jaffāl, *Tawbah*, 38.
28. Ibid.
29. Abū Ḥāmid Muḥammad b. Muḥammad al-Ghazālī, *Iḥyā' 'ulūm al-dīn*, 4 vols. (Beirut: Dār al-Ma'rifah, n.d.), vol. 4, *Kitāb al-Tawbah*, 9. This important section of al-Ghazālī's magnum opus is available in English: M. S. Stern, *Al-Ghazālī on Repentance* (New Delhi: Sterling Publishers, 1990).
30. Jaffāl, *Tawbah*, 44.
31. Ibid., 45.
32. For a comprehensive discussion of this issue, see Jawzīyah, *Tawbah*, 204–15.
33. Jaffāl, *Tawbah*, 201–2.
34. Ghazālī, *Iḥyā'*, 37.
35. Jaffāl, *Tawbah*, 48–49.
36. Ibid., 184.
37. Ibid., 183.
38. Ibid., 185–96.
39. Ghazālī, *Iḥyā'*, 5.
40. Abū Muḥammad 'Abd Allāh b. Qudāmāh al-Maqdisī, *Kitāb al-Tawwābīn*, ed. 'Abd al-Qādir al-Arna'ūṭ (Beirut: Dār al-Kutub al-'ilmīyah, 1394/1974), 10–11.
41. This episode is told in the Qur'ān but not in Genesis. See Q. 11:42–48.
42. This episode differs significantly in the Qur'ān from the biblical account. See Q. 7:143 ff.
43. See II Sam. 11–12 and Q. 38: 21–25.
44. Qudāmāh, *Tawwābīn*, 16–20.
45. Ibid., 21–26.
46. This expedition was sent by the Prophet in 631 shortly before his death. It was perhaps meant to test the ability of the nascent Muslim state to face a major power in Syria, not far from Arabia proper. The battle was a failure and several prominent companions were killed. This, of course, lent greater gravity to the sin of the three men.
47. See Q. 9:117–18.
48. Qudāmāh, *Tawwābīn*, 202; see also 92–102.
49. "O you who have faith, turn to God with pure repentance" (Q. 66:8).
50. God addresses this soul thus: "O you contented soul, return to your Lord pleased [with Him] and pleasing [to Him]. Enter into the company of my servant; enter into my Paradise" (89:27–28).
51. This term is used in the Qur'ān in connection with the day of Resurrection; see 75:2. For a description of these people, see Q. 25:68 and 42:37.
52. Ghazālī, *Iḥyā'*, 44.
53. For a description of such people see Q. 12:18 and 12:83.
54. For a description of this soul, see Q. 12:53.
55. Ghazālī, *Iḥyā'*, 45.
56. Ibid.

57. *al-Ḥagg* (the Truth) is one of the beautiful names of God.

58. *"lā ilaha illā Allāh"* (there is no god except God) is the *shahādah*, or profession of faith of *islām*. When uttered with the intention of accepting Islam, it signifies that person's entry into the Muslim community. Contemplating it inwardly means negating, or breaking the idols of the heart in the same way that Muḥammad broke the idols of the Ka'bah, thus consecrating it for the worship of God alone.

59. 'Alī b. 'Uthmān al-Julabi al-Hujwiri, *Kashf al-Maḥjūb*, trans. R. A. Nicholson (London: Luzac, 1966), 294.

60. Al-Ḥārith b. Asad al-Muḥāsibī, *Kitāb al-Tawbah*, ed. 'Abd al-Qādir Aḥmad 'aṭā (Cairo: Dār al-I'tiṣām, 1982), 25; see also 21 ff.

61. Muḥāsibī, *Tawbah*, 34. For Ghazālī, these four innate characteristics are lordly, satanic, animal, and bestial traits; they are the roots of all evil in the human personality. See Ghazālī, *Iḥīyā'*, 16–17.

62. Muḥāsibī, *Tawbah*, 36–37.

63. Ibid., 39.

64. Hujwiri, *Kashf*, 296–97.

65. Ibid., 297.

66. Abū Bakr al-Kalābādhī, *Kitāb al-Ta'arruf ilā madhhab ahl al-taṣawwuf*, trans. A. J. Arberry, "Doctrine of the Sufis" (reprint of Cambridge University Press, Sh. Muḥammad Ashraf, Lahore, 1966), 91.

67. Ibid., 92.

68. Ibid., 92 [language was changed to modern usage].

69. Mahdī al-Fatlāwī, *al-Tawbah wa-al-Tā'ibūn* (Beirut: Mu'assasat al-A'lamī, 1405/1985), 23.

70. Muḥammad b. Ya'qūb b. Isḥāq al-Kulaynī, *al-Kāfī, Kitāb al-īmān wa-al-kufr, Bāb al-dhunūb, ḥadīth* #4; see also *ḥadīth* #3.

71. Ibid., *ḥadīth* #20; Q. 83:14.

72. Fatlāwī, *Tawbah*, 30–31. See also Q. 8:52–53.

73. The word *badā'* is derived from the trilateral root *b/d/ū*, which means "to appear or seem." See M. Ayoub, "Divine Preordination and Human Hope: A Study of the Concept of *Badā'* in Shī'ī Tradition," *Journal of the American Oriental Society* 106, no.4 (1986): 623–32.

74. Fatlāwī, *Tawbah*, 34.

75. Ibid., 102–3. For additional arguments concerning this point, see Ni'mat Allāh al-Mūsawī al-Jazā'irī, *al-Anwār al-Ni'mānīyah*, 4 vols. (Tabrīz: Maṭba'at Shirkat-i Chāp, n.d.), vol. 3, 147.

76. Fatlāwī, *Tawbah*, 103.

77. Ibid., 158–61. This moving supplication is one (no. 12) of the popular collection of prayers of the Imām entitled *al-Ṣaḥīfah al-kāmilah al-Sajjādīyah*, translated with the Arabic text by William C. Chittick under the title *The Psalms of Islam* (London: Muḥammadi Trust, 1988), 44–48. See also no. 69, "Whispered Prayers," 232–34.

78. Muḥammad ibn al-Ḥasan al-Ḥurr al-Āmilī, *Wasā'il al-Shī'ah*, ed. 'Abd al-

Raḥīm al-Rabbānī al-Shīrāzī, 20 vols. (Beirut: Dār Iḥīyā' al-Turāth al-'Arabī, n.d.), vol. 11, 407.

79. The Qur'ān states, "You are the best community brought forth for humankind; you enjoin the good, dissuade from the bad, and have faith in God" (3:110). This verse lays down moral conduct as a condition for true faith in God.

80. Fatlāwī, *Tawbah*, 221–22; see also 218–25.

7

A Buddhist Approach to Repentance

Malcolm David Eckel

It is hard to introduce a Buddhist voice into a conversation on repentance and not be struck by the deep differences that separate Buddhism from the religious traditions of the West. To a Christian, Jewish, or Islamic ear, the word "repentance" suggests judgment, sin, and guilt. The word moves in the shadow, if not in the presence, of a God who calls human beings to "return" to a new relationship with the absolute, personal source of life. From a purely Western religious perspective, it is tempting to argue that the concept of repentance is so closely tied to the concept of God that repentance without God is a moral and spiritual impossibility. Buddhists raise a quiet voice against this theistic assumption. The gods have a role in Buddhist visions of the cosmos, but they play little role in the great Buddhist struggle for release from the cycle of birth and death. "Think of the gods," someone said, "as friends in the town hall, very helpful for building permits, but no help when it comes to the great matters of birth and rebirth."[1] For guidance on the way to nirvana, a person turns not to God or the gods but to the teaching and example of the Buddha.

It would be wrong to let the theistic echoes in the concept of repentance drown out the Buddhist voice, not only because of the injustice this would do to the Buddhists themselves, but because it would rob the conversation of one of its most eloquent participants. Buddhists may make little room for God, but they are deeply concerned about practices of self-examination, feelings of remorse, the renunciation of unwholesome patterns of life, and the possibility of radical moral change. Stories of Buddhist saints abound with examples of malefactors who recognize the error of their ways, confess their faults, and reform their lives. Even the story of the Buddha contains a crucial element of self-scrutiny and moral transformation. One has much to learn from these accounts, not merely to enrich the vocabulary of repentance and probe some of its basic assumptions, but to reflect on the significance of the boundaries that seem to separate the Buddhist ethical tradition from the West. As Edward Said recently remarked, the time for the naive separation of "West" and "East" is rapidly passing, if it is not already gone.[2] Buddhist attitudes toward moral transformation help us look more closely not only at what we mean by "repentance" but at what we mean by "we."

To scrutinize the relationship between Buddhist views of repentance and the views that are present in the theistic traditions of the West, I will proceed in a style that is, in some respects, dialogical. I will set a series of Buddhist sources side by side with comparable sources from the Western tradition, not to suggest that the two traditions are entirely the same or entirely different, but to strike one tradition against the other, as if I were striking flint against steel, to see if the sparks they set off can illuminate both traditions. Let me begin with a view of repentance that has already struck sparks in the discussion of America's most significant recent intervention in the Buddhist world, the war in Vietnam.

When Robert S. McNamara's book about the lessons of Vietnam was published in the spring of 1995, it provoked a flurry of controversy about the nature of repentance.[3] Commentators asked whether his confession of misjudgments was truly convincing. Did he really acknowledge his most serious mistakes, and did he withhold his confession so long that it came at no personal cost and involved little possibility of making amends? Writing in the *New York Times* (17 April 1995), Anthony Lewis faulted McNamara for failing to speak the truth when it really mattered. In McNamara's defense, Theodore Draper argued that McNamara's criticism of the Vietnam War had been known for years.[4] Draper went on to say that the main interest of the book lay not in its revelations about American policy but in its expressions of regret and remorse: he felt that McNamara deserved credit for his attempt to express regret and make amends. These commentators drew their readers into a secular drama of remorse, confession, and amendment of life that could have been drawn from the words of the English prayer book: Did McNamara "truly and earnestly repent of his sins"? Was he "in love and charity with his neighbors"? Did he "intend to lead a new life"?

The religious echoes were not simply the creation of the book's reviewers. McNamara presented his own book as the result of a process of deep self-examination. He said that political leaders were now being treated with such cynicism and contempt that he felt compelled to break years of silence and express his regret about the role he played in forming American policy toward Vietnam. He framed his regret in a metaphor of retrospective vision: looking back on the events of the war, he searched his heart and pored over the written record to make its lessons applicable to a new generation. Near the end of the book, after he had laid out the lessons he hoped to draw from his retrospective vision, he invoked the name of God: "These are the lessons of Vietnam. Pray God we learn them" (p. 332). His book did not have the same inner-directed intensity or the same devotional focus as Augustine's *Confessions*, but it is not difficult to see in it a reflection of the tradition of Christian confession that has governed so many acts of Christian self-scrutiny and moral reformation.

Buddhists also have a tradition of public self-scrutiny, a tradition that is evident today in the writings of the two Buddhist leaders who have recently been awarded the Nobel Prize for Peace. Tenzin Gyatso, the Fourteenth Dalai Lama, and Aung San Suu Kyi of Burma have both written forcefully about the relationship between Buddhist ethical values and political action, and both are associated with political movements of protest and reform. The Dalai Lama has served as the focus of resistance to the Chinese occupation of Tibet, and Aung San Suu Kyi has been the focus of resistance to the Burmese military government. Both advocate an inner, personal transformation as an essential feature of political reform, and both insist on a transformation that is distinctively Buddhist. While these two figures represent different branches of the Buddhist tradition (the Dalai Lama represents the Mahāyāna tradition that is found in Tibet, China, Japan, Korea, and Vietnam and Aung San Suu Kyi the Theravāda that is found throughout the countries of Southeast Asia), their political discourse taps some of the most ancient and venerable themes in the Buddhist analysis of action and personal reform.

In an essay that was released to mark her receipt of the Sakharov Prize for Freedom of Thought in 1990, Aung San Suu Kyi wrote the following:

> The quintessential revolution is that of the spirit, born of an intellectual conviction of the need for change in those mental attitudes and values which shape the course of a nation's development. A revolution which

aims merely at changing official policies and institutions with a view to an improvement in material conditions has little chance of genuine success. . . . There has to be a united determination to persevere in the struggle, to make sacrifices in the name of enduring truths, to resist the corrupting influences of desire, ill will, ignorance, and fear.[5]

The Dalai Lama ended his recent autobiography on a similar note when he said:

I believe that this suffering is caused by ignorance, and that people inflict pain on others in pursuit of their own happiness or satisfaction. Yet true happiness comes from a sense of inner peace and contentment, which in turn must be achieved through cultivation of altruism, of love, of compassion, and through the elimination of anger, selfishness, and greed.[6]

Aung San Suu Kyi and the Dalai Lama share a concern for truth; both seek to avoid the so-called three poisons, desire, hatred, and ignorance; and both cultivate a quality of self-understanding that might be described, in the Dalai Lama's words, as "contentment" and "inner peace," or simply, in the words of Aung San Suu Kyi, as "freedom from fear." While these are not unfamiliar concepts (it is hard to imagine a religious tradition that would not affirm them in one form or another), they are deeply rooted Buddhist attitudes toward life.

It is not uncommon for these attitudes to be given public, political expression. The words of the Dalai Lama and Aung San Suu Kyi stand in a tradition of Buddhist political discourse that goes back at least as far as the emperor Asoka in the third century B.C.E. The legend of Asoka's life describes him as a cruel king, bent on conquest and domination. After a particularly bloody campaign to conquer the kingdom of Kalinga, Asoka was overcome by remorse and decided to adopt the Buddha's teaching as a program for action in his kingdom. His rock edicts speak of his sorrow about the suffering caused by his campaigns: "The Beloved of the Gods, conqueror of the Kalingas, is moved to remorse now. For he has felt profound sorrow and regret because the conquest of a people previously unconquered involves slaughter, death and deportation."[7] The edicts also speak of his determination to promote "conquest by morality" (*dhamma-vijaya*) rather than conquest by force of arms. Asoka's moral transformation has been a model for Buddhist leadership throughout the Buddhist world, and it contains not just the remorse and amendment of life that one associates with the Christian model of repentance but also an act of public confession, in this case expressed in the form of a public edict.

The political context, of course, is not crucial for the act of repentance. The Buddhist tradition has many other remarkable stories of repentance that apply to people in more mundane conditions of life. We read, for example, in the Pali Canon of a man named Aṅgulimāla who was born into a brahmin family in Kosala.[8] As a young man he achieved great success as a student and was much favored by his teacher. Fellow students became jealous and attempted to poison his relationship with the teacher by accusing him of sleeping with the teacher's wife. The teacher became enraged and vowed to kill him. To make his revenge more devious, the teacher demanded that Aṅgulimāla make, as the final payment for his teaching, a gift of a thousand human fingers. Aṅgulimāla, ever the dutiful student, hid himself in a forest and began to kill travelers and unsuspecting villagers in order to steal their fingers. To number his victims, he strung the fingers together in a garland and wore the garland around his neck (hence the name Aṅgulimāla, "Garland of Fingers"). When word about Aṅgulimāla began to spread, the king sent out a detachment of armed men to track him down and kill him. Aṅgulimāla's mother heard about the plan and set out into the forest to warn him. The Buddha saw the events unfolding and realized that, if he did not intervene, Aṅgulimāla's mother would become another of Aṅgulimāla's victims. Meanwhile Aṅgulimāla was waiting eagerly in the forest for his last victim to reach the number of a thousand fingers.

To save the king, the mother, and, not incidentally, Aṅgulimāla himself, the Buddha took a leisurely walk in Aṅgulimāla's forest. Aṅgulimāla saw him and gave chase, and the Buddha managed, with every leisurely step, to stretch out the distance between them. Aṅgulimāla shouted at him to stop. The Buddha turned and said, "I have stopped, why haven't you?" Aṅgulimāla said, "How can you, who speak the truth, claim that you have stopped, when the distance between us grows bigger and bigger?" The Buddha said, "I have stopped forever bringing harm to living beings, and, if you do not stop now, you will be stopped by rebirth in hell." Aṅgulimāla drew closer, threw himself down at the Buddha's feet, told him that he would give up his violent ways, and begged to be ordained a monk. The Buddha pronounced the phrases of ordination over him and made him a member of the monastic order.

Aṅgulimāla prospered in his discipline and practice, becoming one of the elders of the monastic community, but constantly ran into difficulties when he entered villages begging for alms. The villagers remembered what he had done, and they attacked him whenever he came near. One particular day he was out on his begging rounds and saw a woman struggling in childbirth. He realized that he struck such terror in the woman's heart that there was nothing he could do to help. Back in the monastery, he asked the Buddha how the situation could be changed. The Buddha told him to go to the village and perform an "act of truth" (*saccakiriyā*) in which he said, "As I have never willfully taken the life of any creature since the day I was born, thereby may peace be unto thee and to thy womb!"[9] Aṅgulimāla told the Buddha that this was impossible: the words were simply untrue. The Buddha told him that they bore the force of truth if Aṅgulimāla measured his life "from the moment of his birth as a member of the Elect." Aṅgulimāla went back to the village, made his "act of truth," and the pain of the woman's childbirth was relieved. In the Sinhalese communities where this story is told and elaborated, the words of Aṅgulimāla's "act of truth" continue to be used as a charm to ward off the dangers of childbirth.

The most striking feature in the stories of Asoka and Aṅgulimāla is not merely their mapping of the movements of remorse, confession, and moral reformation, but their affirmation of the possibility that a person can make a radical break with the past. Before they change their ways, Aṅgulimāla and Asoka are images of consummate evil: their crimes represent grisly and brutal violations of the Buddhist prohibition against murder. But both murderers are capable of making a radical break with their evil deeds and going through (in the words applied to Aṅgulimāla) a new "birth." This new birth carries with it a sense of conviction and moral power. In Asoka's case, this is the power to promulgate a new kind of conquest based on the Buddha's teaching. In the case of Aṅgulimāla, it is the power to speak words of healing. Each, in his own way, is a paradigm of Buddhist repentance. But the model of radical moral transformation lies even more deeply in the tradition, in the story of another figure who cast aside the role of a warrior and assumed a new identity. This is the story of Siddhārtha Gautama, the man who became the Buddha.

Traditional accounts of the Buddha's life begin with his birth in a princely family in a part of India that is now located in southern Nepal.[10] He is said to have been raised in a palace and, because of predictions made at the time of his birth, protected from seeing evidence of human suffering that might inspire him to give up his duties as a prince and enter a life of renunciation. The restrictions did not work. The young man saw "four sights"—an old person, a sick person, a corpse, and a renunciant—and the sights are said to have shaken him deeply. One account explains that his "passion" (the word can also mean "intoxication") for youthful pleasures disappeared; another says that his heart was "agitated." He went back to the palace to plan the moment when he could escape and seek an end to human suffering. When the moment came, he gave up his possessions and, with the help of his charioteer, cut off his hair, left the palace, and took up the life of a wandering beggar. He passed through various stages of study and practice until he finally became the "Awakened One," or the Buddha. After his awakening, he lived a long and productive monastic life before passing definitively beyond the realm of suffering and rebirth in an event that is known in Buddhist tradition as his parinirvana. Of all the significant events in his life, the great "going forth" (*pravrajyā*) from the palace may be the one that most shapes the lives of ordinary Buddhists. It is the event that marks his decisive turn away from the pleasures of princely life and toward the pursuit of nirvana. No matter how remote nirvana may be as an actual goal for most Buddhists, it is still possible to experience the ideal of the Buddha's "going forth." In many Buddhist countries in Southeast Asia, the "going forth" is ritually reenacted as a coming of age ceremony for young Buddhist males.

As with many of the stories of the Buddha's life, the historical events of the Buddha's renunciation are difficult to extract from the accretions of legend. Partial accounts of the "going forth" are scattered through a variety of sources and must be pieced together to provide even the skeletal account I have given here. But the stories give a glimpse of the way Buddhist communities came to view the critical change of heart that sets a person on the path to nirvana. First, there is an implicit *analysis* of the problems of the human condition, symbolized by the vision of old age, sickness, and death. This analysis notes two important things: life is painful (*dukkha*), and life involves a process of impermanence or change (*anicca*). Second, the stories suggest the possibility of a *solution:* they show that a person can give up attachment to the pleasures of the world and face old age and death with equanimity and peace. Finally, there is an implicit message about the importance of *perception* and *awareness*. The young man sees four sights. He does not hear about them from someone else or read about them in a book. He sees them directly, and his vision brings about a profound cognitive and emotional change. He conceives of himself differently, his former pleasures no longer satisfy him, and he reforms his actions in a radical way.

If we use the Buddha's story like flint against steel, how could we strike some Christian sparks? One way might be to scrutinize the word that names the Christian act of repentance itself. We read in Kittel's *Theological Dictionary of the New Testament* that the word most often translated as "repentance" (*metanoia*) unites two linguistic and theological traditions.[11] Its Greek antecedents suggest that repentance is an "afterthought" (*meta-noia*) or change of mind, with the implication that this afterthought brings a feeling of regret and remorse. The Hebrew antecedent of the word suggests a "turning" or "returning," as in the appeal by the Hebrew prophets for the people of Israel to "turn away" from their wickedness and return to a life of obedience to God. The Hebrew Bible indicates that this "turn" can be expressed in a ritual of public repentance, involving fasting, the rending of clothing, and rituals of mourning, but the Bible also contains a strong prophetic tradition that rejects public displays of contrition in favor of an inward movement of the heart, as in the book of Joel: "And yet, the Lord says, even now turn back to me with your whole heart, fast, and weep, and beat your breasts. Rend your hearts and not your garments; turn back to the Lord your God; for he is gracious and compassionate, long-suffering and ever constant, ever ready to repent of the threatened evil."[12]

The complexity of the Greek and Hebrew traditions makes it difficult to give a single, univocal interpretation of the phrase that begins the account of Jesus' ministry in the Gospel of Mark: "Repent (*meta-noeite*), and believe the Gospel." The word "repent!" can be heard four different ways.[13] It can ask for a change of awareness ("Change your mind!"). It can call for remorse ("Feel sorry!"). It can advocate an act of contrition ("Do penance!"). Or it can call for a change in relationship with God ("Return to God!"). The tension and ambiguity that surround these four interpretations seem to stem from two basic issues in the concept of repentance itself. Is repentance primarily a change of feeling or a change of mind? And does repentance have to do mainly with a person's actions (as in a public act of contrition) or a person's inner state?

The Buddhist story about the Buddha's conversion works in a comparable way with the tension of thought and feeling. On one level, the key to the story is clearly a new form of *insight* or *awareness*. When the Buddha sees the four sights, he looks at himself in a new way. This is a cognitive transformation, like the "afterthought" suggested by the root meaning of the word *metanoia*. Buddhist sources often say that a person who understands the meaning of suffering already has taken the most important step on the path to awakening. To know that living beings experience "suffering" is to know not just that some experiences are painful, but that the pleasures of life are impermanent (*an-icca*) and insubstantial (*anattā*). This sense of insubstantiality, or "no self," applies not just to the pleasures that a person experiences but also to the person who experiences the pleasures. Different schools of Buddhist philosophy have given different interpretations of what it means to say that things (and people) have no self, but they seldom disagree about the importance of this doctrine. It would be impossible to pursue nirvana without plumbing the significance of this basic insight into the nature of human life.

It is also true to say, however, that the story of the four sights implies a change of emotional orientation. One canonical account of the four sights says that the young man, Siddhārtha Gautama, lost his "passion" or "intoxication" for youthful pleasures, another that his heart was "agitated." What does this loss of intoxication mean? There clearly is a sense that a person who begins to see things as they are (as impermanent and insubstantial) will lose the feelings of desire and hatred that the Dalai Lama and Aung San Suu Kyi saw as the root of personal and communal suffering. In traditional Buddhist literature, this feeling of detachment is sometimes depicted in the image of a saint who sits alone on top of a mountain and gazes dispassionately on the people below.

When the wise one by awareness expels unawareness,
Having ascended the palace of wisdom,
He, free from sorrow, steadfast,
The sorrowing folk observes, the childish,
As one standing on a mountain
[Observes] those standing on the ground below.[14]

In this verse from the Theravāda scriptures, the saint's vision carries with it a sense of detachment, equanimity, and peace. In Mahāyāna literature it can be associated with strong emotional sensitivity, as in the verses that speak of a saint who no longer grieves for himself but looks back toward the valley and weeps tears of compassion for those who have been left behind.[15] When the Dalai Lama speaks of cultivating altruism, love, and compassion, he speaks from this Mahāyāna tradition of emotional sensitivity in the midst of detachment.

The most intriguing emotional element in the story of the four sights, however, is the feeling of "agitation." How can someone be agitated and detached at the same time? There is a possible answer to this question in an article by Ananda Coomaraswamy, the great historian of Indian art, on the concept of "aesthetic shock."[16] Buddhist texts refer to sights that have the ability to induce a state of "shock" (*saṃvega*) in the viewer. Coomaraswamy associates this shock particularly with experiences of holy places and works of Buddhist art, hence the term "aesthetic shock." The word can also be used, however, to refer to an experience in which people see something that suddenly casts their lives in a new light. There are scriptural accounts of the Buddha's ability to manifest visions of hell to shock the gods into an awareness of suffering. This sense of shock is associated particularly with a vision of the cycle of transmigration (*saṃsāra*) that lies at the foundation of Indian Buddhist attitudes toward the world. When one comes face to face with the prospect of endless death and rebirth, one realizes that the pleasures of this life are fleeting and cannot bring lasting satisfaction.

A vivid example of shock at the vision of death and rebirth is found in a story from the *Brahmavaivarta Purāṇa* told by Heinrich Zimmer in his *Myths and Symbols of Indian Art and Civilization*.[17] In the story, Indra, the king of the gods, has won a great victory and in celebration decides to build a magnificent palace. He commissions Viśvakarman, the divine architect, to begin the construction. Viśvakarman builds and builds, but nothing satisfies Indra's ambition. Finally, Viśvakarman grows weary and goes to the god Brahmā for help. Brahmā approaches Viṣṇu, and Viṣṇu promises to bring Viśvakarman relief. The next day a brahmin boy appears at the gates of Indra's palace. Indra ushers him inside, and the boy begins to question him about the building. How long will it take to finish? How much more will Viśvakarman be asked to build? Indra asks why the boy is so curious, and the boy tells him that no previous Indra has ever succeeded in completing such a palace. The boy goes on to instruct him about the cosmic cycles of creation and dissolution. Suddenly the boy looks down and smiles as he sees a line of ants crawling across the palace floor. Indra is puzzled and asks him why. The boy says that each of the ants has been an Indra in a previous life, and each one has fallen down through the cycle of death and rebirth and been born as an ant. The implication of the vision is clear: "You too, Indra, through the cycle of death and rebirth, will be like one of these ants."

The story goes on to describe the appearance of a holy man, a manifestation of the god Śiva, who tempts Indra to leave his palace and take up the life of a wandering sage. Indra's wife then intervenes and keeps him from giving up his status as a warrior. The important point, however, is not the end of the narrative, since such narratives seem to go on almost without end. The point lies in the moment of insight when Indra sees the line of ants and understands that someday he will be like them. This is the moment of shock that Buddhists name by the word *saṃvega*. It is aesthetic in that it involves the senses, particularly the sense of sight, but it would be more accurate to call it a form of cognitive shock. It is a sight that brings a radical change in Indra's awareness of himself. Zimmer describes this change by saying that Indra, "for all his celestial splendor, had been reduced in his own regard to insignificance." This realization has emotional force. Indra is shocked, and the shock changes his emotional orientation not only toward the palace but toward all the great symbols of his pride and accomplishment. Here we see the same combination of agitation and detachment that characterized the conversion stories of the future Buddha. The agitation shakes loose mistaken concepts of the self and allows both of these two princes to become detached from the bonds that bind them, each to his own particular palace.

What, then, about the tension between repentance as an external action and repentance as an inner state? The Buddhist conversion stories suggest the presence of a connection between changes of heart and changes of action. It was the agitation of the four sights that provoked the future Buddha to renounce his life in the palace and go forth as a mendicant. This act of renunciation continues to be enacted in the contemporary ritual of Buddhist ordination. Are there other rituals that cultivate and perpetuate an attitude of repentance? The answer is yes, and some of these rituals shed important light on the role of repentance in the maintenance of collective discipline in Buddhist communities.

In Theravāda monasticism, the rules of the monastic code are recited twice a month, on the days of the new and the full moon, and monks are expected to confess any violations and accept the appropriate penalties. A recent account of the monastic code by Thanissaro Bhikkhu makes it clear that the purpose of confession is not to wipe away guilt or eliminate the effects of bad action.[18] Good and bad actions (*kamma*), merit (*puñña*) and sin (*pāpa*), have to be worked out in their own way in the cycle of death and rebirth. Confession is useful, however, "to strengthen one's resolve to refrain from such behavior in the future, and to reassure other bhikkhus that one is still serious about the training."[19] The most serious penalty for violations of the rules is complete ostracism from the monastic community. This penalty applies to murder, major theft, and acts of sexual intercourse. For lesser offenses, a six-day period of penance is imposed in which the offending monk loses some of his privileges.[20] For example, he cannot live in the same room with a full-fledged monk; he has to live in a monastery with at least four full-fledged monks; and he has to tell the monks in the monastery every day that he is observing penance and tell them of the precise nature of his offense. When the period of penance is over, his status in the monastery is restored.

While the process of penance has a public dimension, the focus still lies on the mind and heart of the individual monk. Thanissaro Bhikkhu points out that the act of confession functions as a form of meditation.[21] It focuses the mind on the nature of the offense and helps a monk to develop the discipline and restraint that will help him avoid the offense in the future. Sometimes a monk is asked to forfeit things that have been inappropriately gained. This forfeit is said to function as a meditation on simplicity. The threat of ostracism serves as a reminder that the monk risks losing all of the spiritual gains that were made possible by his presence in the monastery. The external acts of confession and penance, as powerful as they may be in healing the breaches that divide the community, have an essential inward focus: they function as meditative devices to advance the internal development of the offending monk.

The same relationship between external action and internal development is apparent in a Mahāyāna text known as *The Introduction to the Practice of Enlightenment (Bodhicaryāvatāra)*. The *Introduction* was written in India around the seventh century by a monk named Śāntideva, and is much revered by the Buddhists of Tibet, including the Dalai Lama. The text has been treated as a doctrinal summary of the practices that lead to enlightenment, but its form and function are essentially liturgical. It announces its purpose in the first chapter by praising what it calls the "mind of enlightenment" (*bodhicitta*), or the aspiration to become a Buddha, then it moves through an elaborate confession of sins, a meditation on various states of vigilance in the practice of the path, and a presentation of the no-self doctrine (in the form of Emptiness). It ends with a "transfer of merit" in which the practitioner expresses the hope that the benefits of the text will be used for the welfare of all sentient beings. The issue of repentance is introduced by "the confession of sins" (*pāpa-deśanā*) in chapter two.

The chapter starts with a series of verses that seem to describe the standard act of worship (*pūjā*) as a metaphor for a spiritual transformation. The first verse gives a traditional act of homage to the "three jewels": "In order to grasp this mind [of enlightenment], I worship the Buddhas, the spotless jewel of the Dharma, and the children of the

Buddha, with their oceans of virtues." Then the text elaborates this worship in a way that seems, at least initially, to be nothing more than an act of the imagination. The worshiper offers as many flowers, fruits, medicinal herbs, jewels, and beautiful waters as there are in the world, along with mountains made of jewels, beautiful forest hermitages, and the sweet fragrances of heaven. All of these offerings are presented as an act of homage and service to the Buddha, the Buddha's teaching (Dharma), and the Buddha's community (Saṃgha). Literally, there is no way for the worshiper actually to gather these objects and place them before an image of the Buddha, and the text itself acknowledges that the gestures of worship can only be carried out by the "mind." But what does the text mean by "mind"? The mind (*citta*) is not only the central focus of the worshiper's own meditation; it also has the potential to be the worshiper's most precious offering. Incipiently, it is "the mind of enlightenment" (*bodhicitta*). As in the call to repentance in the book of Joel, this act of Buddhist devotion begins in the world of external action, then moves inside the worshiper in a gesture that is simultaneously one of humility and self-affirmation. The worshiper acknowledges his own inadequacy, in that he is incapable of making the offerings in a literal sense, but the acknowledgment of the worshiper's limitations and inadequacies puts the stress right where the ritual itself intends it to be put, on the internal cultivation of the mind that aspires to enlightenment.

The same movement from external action to internal transformation takes place in the ritual of confession itself. The worshiper first takes "refuge" in the Buddha, Dharma, and Saṃgha, using a verse form of the basic Buddhist devotional formula: "I go for refuge to the Buddha until [I achieve] the throne of enlightenment. I go for refuge in the Dharma and likewise to the congregation of bodhisattvas." The Buddha, Dharma, and Saṃgha are externalized in a double sense. Spatially, they are objects or entities that one has to "go" to in order to find refuge. Temporally, the act of refuge is meant to continue until the worshiper reaches the state of enlightenment. The commentary explains that the act of refuge has to continue until the worshiper actually becomes a Buddha. The moral force of the action comes from the way the text and the ritual together put these dualistic assumptions in question. The Buddha, Dharma, and Saṃgha are not outside the worshiper but within, and the act of confession and self-scrutiny develops precisely the qualities of mind and heart that, in their full perfection, transform the worshiper into a Buddha.

The text makes this point by turning back to the worshiper's past lives—especially lives in which the worshiper was born as an animal—and visualizing all the evil deeds that the worshiper committed directly or elicited from others. The text contemplates the terrors of death, then ends with the worshiper's invocation of the power and compassion of the great celestial bodhisattvas[22] of the Mahāyāna, including Avalokiteśvara, the bodhisattva of compassion. The net effect is to reduce the worshiper not only to a state of self-abasement but to a state of fear. Death can come at any moment, and the only thing that can stand in the way of a terrifying rebirth is the power of a compassionate savior. The movement away from this state of fear takes place at the beginning of the next chapter when the worshiper seizes the mind of enlightenment as his own. The turn depends initially on feelings of altruism toward others: the worshiper "rejoices" in the success of others and then visualizes himself as a physician who can heal others' ills. In focusing on others, the worshiper begins to visualize himself as if he played the same role that was attributed to the Buddha and bodhisattvas in his own act of confession. In other words, the worshiper begins to function as a compassionate savior. Here the "Buddha" is again transformed from an external object of devotion to an inner state, and the temporal sequence of the path begins to erode. The worshiper may still have a great distance to go on the path to enlightenment, but it is possible already for the worshiper to identify himself as Buddha and experience Buddhahood as if it were already making itself present.

The Introduction to the Practice of Enlightenment also gives a good introduction to some distinctive features of the Dalai Lama's program of moral and political reformation. The Dalai Lama insists, for example, that one should combine moral outrage about the Chinese treatment of Tibet with a commitment to compassion and nonviolence, as if the process of meditating on the injustices Tibetans have suffered in the last few decades were not only a challenge to resist great evil but to deepen one's own sense of compassion. The Dalai Lama says, "Learning to forgive is much more useful than merely picking up a stone and throwing it at the object of one's anger, the more so when the provocation is extreme. For it is under the greatest adversity that there exists the greatest potential for doing good, both for oneself and others."[23] These words echo the verses in *The Introduction to the Practice of Enlightenment* that describe enemies as an opportunity to practice patience, and advise a person to give thanks for them as if they were companions on the way to enlightenment.[24]

The Dalai Lama reflects this point of view not only in the account of his own attitude toward the Chinese but in his words about Pope John

Paul II: "Any man who can call out 'Brother' to his would-be assassin
. . . must be a highly evolved spiritual practitioner."[25] Here the drama
of repentance and reformation, of course, cuts in both directions. It
calls for a deepened sense of moral awareness on the part of the person
who is being asked to repent, but it also involves a transformation of
attitude on the part of the person who is called to forgive. The perme-
ability and malleability of Buddhist attitudes toward the personality
make this double process particularly appropriate. If the act of confession and repentance involves a visualization of one's sins, followed by
a visualization of one's own identification with the Buddha, then forgiveness involves a visualization of sin, followed by a visualization of
one's own identification with the sinner.

Another useful way to explore the process of spiritual development
that is being mapped in *The Introduction to the Practice of Enlightenment*
is to focus on the role of memory. In his biography of St. Augustine,
Peter Brown commented about the way Augustine's act of confession
led him to reinterpret his past in light of the present by winding
"round and round in [his] present memory the spiral of [his] errors."[26]
Augustine's intention was to build out of the raw material of memory
a new sense of himself. Buddhist acts of self-scrutiny and self-transfor-
mation also wind round and round through the spiral of memory.
When the confessional liturgy of *The Introduction to the Practice of Enlightenment* turns back to the worshiper's past lives and visualizes the
history of evil deeds, it recalls an even more searching investigation
of the past that appears in the story of the Buddha's enlightenment.
Buddhist tradition says that, on the night of his enlightenment, the
Buddha journeyed back through all of his previous births and recalled
them in detail before he finally moved forward into an enlightened
state.[27]

Enlightenment seems to grow from a searching of the past, as it does
from a focused attention on the present. The Buddhist word for
"memory" (*anusmṛti*) can be used to refer not only to a recollection of
the past but also to the practice of "mindfulness" that belongs to each
moment in the meditative process. In this conjunction of past and
present, one is reminded of McNamara's retrospective vision of Vietnam, his winding round and round through the remnants of the past
not just to set the historical record straight but also to center himself
in the present and visualize a future that is free from the errors of the
past. Repentance, it seems, involves an act of retrospection in service
of a new image of the present and future.

These comments about Buddhist views of repentance, as brief as they may be, should show how rich a tradition the Fourteenth Dalai Lama and Aung San Suu Kyi have at their disposal as they promote their programs of communal reform and reconciliation. When Aung San Suu Kyi says that "the quintessential revolution is that of the spirit, born of an intellectual conviction of the need for change," she is turning inward, as the Buddha himself once did, to find the mental clarity and the moral conviction to bring about moral change. For her, as for the Dalai Lama, this mental attitude involves "resisting the corrupting influences of desire, ill will, ignorance, and fear" not just in others but in herself. Here mind and heart go together, as do a person's inner orientation and external action. Whatever success these two Buddhist leaders have been able to achieve seems to be tied in no small part to their ability not merely to express these values but also to embody them in lives of political practice.

I began this chapter by calling attention to the differences that seem to separate the Buddhist tradition from the religious traditions of the West. How deep should we now take these differences to be? Certainly, the Buddhist tradition envisions a process of repentance and moral transformation in which the concept of God plays little role. The stories of Asoka and Aṅgulimāla, along with the rituals of monastic confession, depict a drama of guilt, remorse, confession, and transformation that lacks any reference to any transcendent, divine sanction. The Buddhist stories challenge the idea that repentance requires confrontation with a personal, creator God. But how serious is this difference?

It is not impossible to interpret Buddhist moral thinking in a way that minimizes the significance of the absence of God. Wilfred Cantwell Smith has argued that the Buddhist concept of Dharma plays the role in Buddhism that God plays in the theistic traditions of the West.[28] Dharma functions as a universal moral law that insures not only retribution for evil but the possibility of moral reformation and freedom. It would not be too farfetched to say that Aṅgulimāla and perhaps even Asoka felt the need for repentance only when they became aware that their actions had serious moral consequences, and they could escape the force of these consequences only if they made a radical change in their way of life. Certainly this was the implication of the Buddha's confrontation with Aṅgulimāla: "If you do not stop now, you will be stopped in hell." It is not God who will bring Aṅgulimāla to hell; it is simply the Dharma or the law of moral retribution that is embodied in the Buddha's teaching.

Another possible source for an external moral sanction, particularly in the Aṅgulimāla story, is the Buddha himself. Aṅgulimāla's aware-ness of the Dharma did not come to him as an abstract intellectual realization. It was mediated through the personality of the Buddha, and it was reinforced by the feelings of surprise, reverence, and awe that seem to accompany Aṅgulimāla's transformation from serial killer to Buddhist supplicant. Richard Gombrich has argued that Buddhist cultic life in Sri Lanka (where the modern version of the Aṅgulimāla story is found) is based on an "affective" apprehension of the Buddha as a powerful deity.[29] Buddhists may "know," in other words, that the Buddha is not a deity, but they "feel" as if he were, and from this feeling grow many of their most important religious actions and moral choices. Those who know the Buddhist doctrine of the Buddha will know that this position has strong affinities with Wilfred Cantwell Smith's position about the Dharma. In one of the most important doc-trinal statements of the Pali Canon, the Buddha is reported to have said, "What is there, Vakkali, in seeing this vile body? Whoso sees Dhamma sees me; whoso sees me sees Dhamma. Seeing Dhamma, Vakkali, he sees me; seeing me, he sees Dhamma."[30] Here the Buddha is identified with the Dharma and vice versa: to see or be affected by one is to see or be affected by the other.

There is much truth in the approaches Smith and Gombrich take to Buddhist tradition, but it is misleading to think that they have or would even want to turn the Buddhist tradition into some form of devotional theism. Think simply of the story of the Buddha himself. You could argue that the future Buddha encountered the Dharma as an external reality when he saw the four sights and decided to re-nounce his role as a prince, but the process of discipline that led to his awakening did not continue to treat the Dharma as a reality external to himself. To become a Buddha, he had to realize the Dharma in his own experience: he had to reach the state, in other words, in which he and the Dharma were one. This inward movement in the Buddha's development was mirrored by the inward focus in the monastic ritual of confession. Thanissaro Bhikkhu's explanation of the ceremony stressed that the act of confession functioned as a means of spiritual growth for the confessing monk. *The Introduction to the Practice of En-lightenment* gave this inward movement poetic and rhetorical form in the relationship of self-abasement and self-affirmation: to humble one-self in the act of confession was to anticipate one's identification with the Buddha. The Dharma and Buddha may have a certain "external" force at certain stages of discipline and in certain aspects of Buddhist practice, but the Buddhist tradition remains focused on the task of working out the Dharma in one's own experience. In this process the image of God might be more of a distraction than a help.

Then is the Buddhist condemned to play the role of the perpetual "other" in this discourse about repentance? Let me respond to this question by considering once again the complexity that lurks beneath the surface of Mr. McNamara's flat, American account of the act of repentance. The McNamara book closes with a quotation from Rudyard Kipling.

When I was a King and a Mason—a Master proven and skilled—
I cleared me ground for a Palace such as a King should build.
I decreed and dug down to my levels. Presently under the silt,
I came on the wreck of a Palace such as a King had built.

There was no worth in the fashion—there was no wit in the plan—
Hither and thither, aimless, the ruined footings ran—
Masonry brute, mishandled, but carven on every stone:
"After me cometh a Builder. Tell him, I too have known."

Swift to my use in my trenches, where my well-planned groundworks
    grew,
I tumbled his quoins and his ashlars, and cut and reset them anew.
Lime I milled of his marbles; burned it, slacked it, and spread;
Taking and leaving at pleasure the gifts of the humble dead.

Yet I despised not nor gloried; yet, as we wrenched them apart,
I read in the razed foundations the heart of that builder's heart.
As he had risen and pleaded, so did I understand
The form of the dream he had followed in the face of the thing he had
    planned.

When I was a King and a Mason—in the open noon of my pride,
They sent me word from the Darkness. They whispered and called me
    aside.
They said—"The end is forbidden." They said—"Thy use is fulfilled."
"Thy Palace shall stand as the other's—the spoil of a King who shall
    build."

I called my men from the trenches, my quarries, my wharves, and my
    sheers.
All I had wrought I abandoned to the faith of the faithless years.
Only I had cut on the timber—only I carved on the stone:
"After me cometh a Builder. Tell him, I too have known!"[31]

McNamara explains that he heard this poem nearly sixty years before he set out to write his book, and the words had grown so much in meaning that he found them almost haunting. His final comments about the poem speak eloquently of unrealized dreams, unfulfilled objectives, and the hope that others will be instructed and moved to action by the telling of his tale. It is not difficult to see why Kipling's image of the decay of British imperial ambitions should occupy a central place in the imagination of an official who watched American imperial ambitions fall to ruin. It is as if McNamara were signaling that he, too, had scoured the foundations of another culture only to threaten the foundations of his own. By writing his own book, he could have been putting his own inscription on the stones: "Tell them, I too have known."

Where does the poet's vision of ruin come from? The obvious source would be in the English literary tradition itself, where Shelley's "Ozymandias" gave ironical expression to the same sense of failed imperial ambition: "My name is Ozymandias, king of kings: Look on my works, ye Mighty, and despair!" I am inclined, however, to extend the search for influences and predecessors in another direction altogether. Kipling is the source of the claim that "East is East and West is West, and never the twain shall meet." No doubt there were many American officials during the Vietnam War who felt that Kipling's dictum was more true than they had thought and who wished that the East and West had never met. But Kipling's work challenges the force of his own words. His stories and verses come alive with images from the India of the British Raj. Is it possible that McNamara was haunted in his recollection of the Vietnam War by an echo of a story that came as much from the "East" as it did from the "West," the story of Indra and his palace? Could we have in McNamara's book an expression of Indra's "cognitive shock," with the same revision of his sense of self and the same distaste for the pride and ambition of the world? If so, it is not the first time such a cross-cultural connection has been made.

Historians have pointed out that the story of the Buddha's life was carried into Christian lore by John of Damascus under the name of St. Josaphat (a corruption of the word *bodhisattva*).[32] One of the best-known admirers of the story of St. Josaphat in the modern West was Tolstoy, who attempted to leave his own "palace" near the end of his life and become a wandering saint. Mohandas Gandhi was sufficiently impressed by this aspect of Tolstoy's life to name his first ashram in South Africa "Tolstoy Farm." Could it be that Gandhi's own program of political action, based as it was on a practice of compassion, humility, self-criticism, and fearlessness, was a gift from the Buddha back to India, made by way of Damascus, Moscow, and South Africa?

Historical influences are neither simple nor easy to chart. Hamilton Gibb has pointed out that cross-cultural borrowings require the presence of a predisposition or readiness in the receiving culture before it can borrow new ideas from another.[33] This is another way of saying

that the culture has to be asking similar questions and be close to for-
mulating similar answers before it can "borrow" something from the
outside. It would be foolish to think that Kipling or McNamara had to
turn to the traditions of India to reflect on the decay of human desires
and the reality of death. There were more than enough resources in
the cultural traditions of Europe and America to provoke McNamara's
bracing look at his own past. But there is a suggestion and a reminder
in McNamara's book that the boundaries between Western and Eastern attitudes toward issues of repentance need not be as sharp as they
once were. The time is coming and may, in many respects, already be
here when the Buddhist voice in America is not the voice of an "other"
but a voice that belongs very much to "our" community's tradition of
moral reflection.

Notes

1. These words are spoken by the narrator in "Buddhism: Footprint of
the Buddha—India," an episode in *The Long Search*, a video series produced
by the British Broadcasting Corporation, 1977.

2. Edward Said, "East Isn't East: The Impending End of the Age of Orien-
talism," *Times Literary Supplement*, 3 February 1995.

3. Robert S. McNamara with Brian VanDeMark, *In Retrospect: The Tragedy
and Lessons of Vietnam* (New York: Random House, 1995).

4. "The Abuse of McNamara," *New York Review of Books*, 25 May 1995,
16–17.

5. Aung San Suu Kyi, *Freedom from Fear and Other Writings*, ed. Michael Aris
(Harmondsworth, Middlesex: Penguin, 1991), 183.

6. Tenzin Gyatso, the Fourteenth Dalai Lama of Tibet, *Freedom in Exile:
The Autobiography of the Dalai Lama* (New York: HarperCollins, 1990), 270.

7. N. A. Nikam and Richard McKeon, ed. and trans., *The Edicts of Asoka*
(Chicago: University of Chicago Press, 1959), 27–30.

8. The account of Aṅgulimāla is based on G. P. Malalasekera, *Dictionary of
Pali Proper Names* (London: J. Murray, 1937–1938) and C. H. B. Reynolds, ed.,
An Anthology of Sinhalese Literature up to 1815 (London: George Allen & Unwin,
1970).

9. Reynolds, *Anthology of Sinhalese Literature*, 65.

10. For a useful account of the story of the Buddha's life, see Edward J.
Thomas, *The Life of the Buddha as Legend and History*, 3d ed. (1949; repr. London: Routledge & Kegan Paul, 1975).

11. Gerhard Kittel, ed., *Theological Dictionary of the New Testament* (Grand
Rapids, Mich.: Eerdmans, 1967).

12. Joel 2:12–13 in *The New English Bible with the Apocrypha* (Oxford: Oxford
University Press, 1970).

13. Kittel, *Theological Dictionary*, s.v. *metanoeo, metanoia*, 1000.

14. Translation quoted from John Ross Carter and Mahinda Palihawadana, trans., *The Dhammapada* (New York: Oxford University Press, 1987), 116.

15. I discuss these and similar verses in more detail in *To See the Buddha: A Philosopher's Quest for the Meaning of Emptiness* (San Francisco: HarperCollins, 1992; repr. Princeton: Princeton University Press, 1994).

16. "*Samvega:* Aesthetic Shock," in *Coomaraswamy 1: Selected Papers: Traditional Art and Symbolism*, ed. Robert Lipsey (Princeton: Princeton University Press, 1977), 179–83.

17. Heinrich Zimmer, *Myths and Symbols of Indian Art and Civilization*, ed. Joseph Campbell (Princeton: Princeton University Press, 1972).

18. Thanissaro Bhikkhu, *The Buddhist Monastic Code: The Patimokkha Training Rules* (Valley Center, Calif.: Metta Forest Monastery, 1994), 20.

19. Thanissaro Bhikkhu, *Buddhist Monastic Code*, 20.

20. Thanissaro Bhikkhu, *Buddhist Monastic Code*, 154.

21. Thanissaro Bhikkhu, *Buddhist Monastic Code*, 21–22.

22. A "bodhisattva" is a being who is on the way to Buddhahood but has not yet attained it. A "celestial bodhisattva" is one who has achieved such extraordinary power, through its practice of compassion and wisdom, that it functions almost as one of the Hindu gods.

23. Gyatso, *Freedom in Exile*, 261.

24. P. L. Vaidya, ed., *Bodhicaryāvatāra of Śāntideva* (Darbhanga: Mithila Institute, 1960), verses 6.107–8.

25. Gyatso, *Freedom in Exile*, 202.

26. The words are from *Confessions*, chapter 4, quoted by Peter Brown in *Augustine of Hippo: A Biography* (Berkeley: University of California Press, 1969), 164.

27. This story has been analyzed by Donald S. Lopez, Jr., "Memories of the Buddha," in *In the Mirror of Memory: Reflections on Mindfulness and Memory in Indian and Tibetan Buddhism*, ed. Janet Gyatso (Albany: State University of New York Press, 1992), 21–45.

28. Wilfred Cantwell Smith, "The Buddhist Instance: Faith as Atheist?" in *Faith and Belief* (Princeton: Princeton University Press, 1979), 20–32.

29. Richard F. Gombrich, *Precept and Practice: Traditional Buddhism in the Rural Highlands of Ceylon* (Oxford: Clarendon Press, 1971).

30. *Samyutta-nikāya* 3.120, translation quoted from Edward Conze, ed., *Buddhist Texts through the Ages* (New York: Harper & Row, 1964), 103.

31. *Rudyard Kipling's Verse: Inclusive Edition: 1885–1932* (London: Hodder and Stoughton, 1933), 379.

32. A summary of this material can be found in Wilfred Cantwell Smith, *Towards a World Theology: Faith and the Comparative History of Religion* (Philadelphia: Westminster Press, 1981).

33. From Hamilton Gibb's three "laws" of cultural influence, quoted by W. Montgomery Watt, *Muhammad: Prophet and Statesman* (Oxford: Oxford University Press, 1961), 42.

8

Repentance, Punishment, and Mercy[1]

Jeffrie G. Murphy

PROSPERO: At this hour
Lies at my mercy all mine enemies.

ARIEL: Your charm so strongly works 'em,
That if you now beheld them, your affections
Would become tender.

PROSPERO: And mine shall.
Hast thou, which art but air, a touch, a feeling
Of their afflictions, and shall not myself,
One of their kind, that relish all as sharply
Passion as they, be kindlier moved than thou art?
Though with their high wrongs I am struck to the quick,
Yet with my nobler reason, 'gainst my fury
Do I take part: the rarer action is
In virtue than in vengeance: they being penitent,
The sole drift of my purpose doth extend
Not a frown further.

These brief passages from the closing of Shakespeare's *The Tempest* contain many profound but controversial thoughts about the nature and justification of mercy. Prospero realizes that mercy may be exercised only by someone who has power over another ("at my mercy"), sees mercy as particularly difficult for someone who has been wrongfully injured ("struck to the quick"), sees mercy as involving greater virtue than vengeance, but seems to view even virtuous acts of mercy as *conditional*—that is, as requiring some precondition that must be satisfied by the wrongdoer before the granting of mercy is appropriate. Two such conditions are suggested: that the wrongdoer has gone through punishment or suffering sufficient to generate our compassion (the

143

point raised by Ariel) or that the wrongdoer has become *repentant* (the point raised by Prospero).[2]

The idea that repentance may open the door for mercy is a common theme in Christian thought—where it is perhaps in tension with the equally Christian idea that mercy is a free gift of grace and is thus unconditioned—and Shakespeare clearly writes within the context of this theological tradition.[3] Such ideas also find expression in contemporary secular culture, however, and in the United States find themselves revealed in criminal sentencing, most dramatically when life imprisonment or capital punishment is a possibility. Sentencing judges or juries may be swayed by criminal defense lawyers who use the defendant's supposed repentance as a ground for mercy or (perhaps more likely) by prosecutors who use the lack of such repentance as a ground for the refusal of mercy and the imposition of the harshest possible sentence. For example:

> As any trial attorney will attest, serious prejudice could result if medication inhibits the defendant's capacity to react and respond to the proceedings and to demonstrate remorse or compassion. The prejudice can be acute during the sentencing phase of the proceedings, when the sentencer must attempt to know the heart and mind of the offender and judge his character, his contrition or its absence, and his future dangerousness. In a capital sentencing proceeding, assessments of character and remorse may carry great weight and, perhaps, be determinative of whether the offender lives or dies.[4]

> The vicious acts you committed on December 7, 1993, were the acts of a coward. What could be more cowardly than entering a train filled with unsuspecting, homebound commuters and systematically shooting them at point-blank range. . . . What is even more remarkable is your total lack of remorse.[5]

> Have you observed any repentance by Mr. McCleskey? Has he exhibited to you any sorrow? Have you seen any tears in his eyes for this act that he has done?[6]

One might, of course, question the legitimacy of raising such questions in the context of the legal system of a contemporary liberal and secular state. To what degree, if at all, is a criminal's repentance relevant to the punishment or mercy that the criminal should receive? Perhaps the state should simply be concerned with compliance to its rules and should regard such issues as the defendant's sorrow and tears as private matters—matters between the defendant and his God, perhaps, but not between the defendant and his government.

In the book *Forgiveness and Mercy*, I tried to accept the constraints of secular liberalism and still leave room for the possible legal relevance of repentance. I argued that a person cannot be said to deserve mercy in the sense that he has a right to mercy and that others have a (perfect) duty to accord it to him. I also argued, however, that a person may exhibit certain characteristics that make him more *eligible* for mercy than he otherwise would have been. Chief among these attributes, I argued, is *repentance*.[7]

My purpose in the present chapter is to expand on the brief discussion of repentance contained in the book—an expansion that involves substantial rethinking and modification of the view presented there.[8] I will explore the concept of repentance, reasons for thinking that it is morally important, and ways in which it might be incorporated into our thinking about the philosophy of the criminal law—not merely as a possible justification for mercy but as a possible justification for punishment itself.

Repentance and Modernity

As the millennium (in at least one sense of that word) approaches, the newspapers are filled with talk of repentance. Pope John Paul has suggested that the Catholic Church repent for some of the injustices against non-Catholics to which it has been party during its history; the American Southern Baptist Convention has publicly repented its role in American slavery and racism; and French president Jacques Chirac has attempted to express, for France, repentance for its cooperative role in the Nazi extermination of French Jews. The government of Japan has struggled with developing a public response to its World War II atrocities against other Asian nations—some officials advocating full repentance and others more cautious expressions of sorrow or regret—and the government of Argentina is still struggling with the nature and degree of its public response to the atrocities committed against its own citizens in the "dirty war" during the regime of the generals. America, though taking a qualified public stand of repentance with respect to its wartime internment of Japanese Americans in concentration camps, has so far not taken such a stand with respect to slavery (a stand perhaps appropriate only for some states), genocide against Native Americans, or the terror-obliteration bombing of German and Japanese cities during World War II. All of these possible acts of repentance have been advocated, however, by some voices of influence in American politics and opinion.[9]

In sharp contrast to this talk about what might be called *collective* or *group* repentance (and all the logical and moral problems in which such talk is immersed), we rarely hear much talk these days about *individual* repentance. These two facts may be related, since a stress on collective responsibility could well have a tendency to weaken feelings of individual responsibility. Living (at least in America) in what some have called a "culture of victims," we have seen in recent years the development of various strategies to allow wrongdoers to avoid responsibility for their wrongdoing by claiming victim status for themselves, and a world without responsibility is a world in which repentance lacks logical space.[10]

Gone, it seems, are the days in which we could comfortably refer to prisons as *penitentiaries*—as places to which we would send responsible wrongdoers in order to encourage their repentance. We simply do not value repentance the way we once did; and the world has, in my view, suffered a loss thereby. Perhaps we see the concept as some vestigial relic of a religious worldview to which many people now, at most, pay only lip service. Or perhaps, even if we accept the value of repentance in certain contexts, we do not see an important place for the concept in a system of criminal law and punishment organized around secular values. It is even possible—given the realities of crime and punishment in America—that we cannot in honesty see prisons as anything more than fortresses in which we warehouse an alienated underclass that is perceived, often quite accurately, as highly dangerous to the stability of ordinary life.

Given this background, an essay on repentance and criminal punishment may seem to be little more than an exercise in historical nostalgia—an exercise having little relevance to the realities of the world in which we live. Such a skeptical assumption would be premature, however, because it is possible that the skepticism could at least partially be laid to rest by a detailed discussion of the concept of repentance in the light of contemporary thinking and contemporary realities. Such an exploration is the object of the present chapter.

The Concept of Repentance

Repentance may be conceptualized either as an interior mental act or as an act with an essential social dimension. As an interior act, it may be seen simply as the remorseful acceptance of responsibility for the evil that one sees in one's character, the repudiation of that evil, and the sincere resolve to do one's best to extirpate it. Montaigne, in his essay "Of Repentance," expressed the interior view when he wrote, "Repentance is nothing but a disavowal of our own will and an opposition to our fancies."

It is easy to see why repentance so conceptualized could be seen as an important moral or religious virtue—for example, as a step toward that "purity of heart" of which Kierkegaard spoke—but it is hard to see why the state, particularly the modern secular state, should concern itself with such matters. Indeed, Kierkegaard saw the state and the social relations over which it presides as a positive *enemy* of repentance in this purely interior sense because it will tempt a person to confuse "the improvement toward society" with what really matters for the sinner: "the resigning of himself to God."[11]

If repentance is to have important consequences for the social community—and for the legal system that partially binds that community together—it will be necessary to develop a concept of repentance that moves beyond the purely inner sphere and into the arena of social relations.

Consider this definition: Repentance is the remorseful acceptance of responsibility for one's wrongful and harmful actions, the repudiation of the aspects of one's character that generated the actions, the resolve to do one's best to extirpate those aspects of one's character, and the resolve to atone or make amends for the harm that one has done. Here the social dimension is obvious—both in the matters over which one is remorseful (wrongful harm to others and not merely a sinful character) and in the final steps of the repentance process (a recognition that one's evil had a *victim*—either a discrete individual or the entire community—and a desire to make that victim whole again).[12]

Even if we grant the social dimension of this sense of repentance, however, it still requires quite a leap to tie such repentance to the institution of *criminal punishment*. Should the very aim or purpose of punishment be to provoke repentance in the wrongdoer? Might this be, if not the primary aim, at least a permissible subordinate aim? If so, just how is punishment—the coercive infliction of *suffering*—supposed to accomplish this? (When people hurt me I tend to get angry and resentful, not remorseful.)[13] And even if the purpose of punishment is not to provoke repentance, may such repentance—when it is found— legitimately affect such matters as sentencing and pardon? These are the questions to which I shall now turn.

The Purposes of Punishment

Most contemporary philosophical discussions of the justification of legal punishment see it as a practice driven by two not totally consistent values: deterrence and retribution.[14] Deterrence looks to the future and justifies the punishment of the criminal as an effective way of providing him with an incentive not to commit crime again (special deterrence) or of providing others who are aware of his punishment with an incentive not to commit crime at all (general deterrence).[15]

Retribution, on the other hand, is not concerned with future consequences. Rather it looks to the past and seeks to impose on the criminal the level of suffering he *deserves*—that is, a level of suffering properly proportional to the wrongfulness of his criminal conduct.

These two values will often produce consistent guidance—in cases where the amount of punishment needed to deter is approximately the same as the amount deserved—but may sometimes point in opposed directions. For example: Strict criminal liability (punishment without regard to *mens rea* or other aspects of moral fault) might well be an effective way to deter certain activities (e.g., production of child pornography); but, by definition, a person without moral fault (e.g., one who photographed a naked minor whom he reasonably believed to be an adult) could not *deserve* any punishment at all.[16]

Both of these justifications of punishment are problematic. Deterrence is open to the Kantian moral objection that it is willing to use people merely as means to produce social benefit and to the empirical objection that the law's capacity to deter may be more of a hope than a fact grounded in solid evidence.

Retribution is open to the conceptual objection that the concept of desert is difficult to analyze with any precision—indeed is perhaps little more than a metaphor left over from old theological notions of cosmic or divine justice—and that a just society will not impose suffering on people in pursuit of a mere metaphor. Also, it is not at all clear why the secular state—not in the business of playing God—should be concerned with punishing on the basis of moral desert anyway.

Problematic or not, the ideas of deterrence and retribution are likely to remain as the dominant contemporary justifications of punishment. Thus, for our present purposes, it will be useful to inquire into the degree to which, if at all, repentance fits comfortably within these justifications.

It might seem that, with respect to special deterrence, repentance has an important role to play; for it seems obvious that repentant people are less likely to commit crimes again than are those criminals who are unrepentant. Indeed, one might even suggest that controlling crime by provoking repentance is just another way of describing the idea of special deterrence.

This pattern of thought, though tempting, is hasty and superficial. Repentance surely means not merely a resolution not to commit wrong again, but a resolution that includes a desire to make amends and that is based on certain virtues of character—for example, *remorse* over the wrong that one has done. If one's concern in punishing is merely to deter future criminal conduct, however, then one may consistently (and perhaps would realistically) ask much less from punishment than this.

Punishment as deterrence is essentially a system of *threats*, and threats appeal not to the softer and more virtuous aspects of our character, but simply to our capacities for *fear* grounded in *self-interest*. (It is for this reason that economists are drawn to deterrence theories of punishment.) Also, deterrence theorists might well advocate punishments where the demand for remorse would be utterly inappropriate. The person who commits a strict liability offense, for example, may have much to regret, but since he acted without moral fault, nothing to be remorseful about. In short, a deterrence justification of punishment might under certain circumstances welcome repentance as an extra incentive, but a rich concept of repentance—one meaning more than merely being disinclined to commit crime again—will not be a central idea in such an outlook.

What about retribution? Do repentant people deserve less suffering than those who remain hard and unrepentant? Here we must distinguish two different versions of retributivism. According to what I will call *grievance retributivism*, punishment is deserved for responsible wrongful acts—acts that occasion legitimate grievances against the wrongdoer and that place the wrongdoer in a kind of debt to his fellow citizens.[17] According to what I will call *character retributivism*, one's deserts are a function not merely of one's wrongful acts, but also of the ultimate state of one's character.[18]

Repentance will have less obvious bearing on grievance retributivism than on character retributivism. In general, the wrongfulness of conduct at one time will not be affected by repentance at a later time. I typically do not cease to have a grievance against you simply because you are now sorry that you wronged me; nor do your debts to me disappear merely because you now lament those acts that put you into debt to me.

There are, however, some exceptions to this. Sometimes the wrong-fulness of an act is a function of the harm that it brings to a victim, and sometimes this harm may be lessened through an act of repentance. This is because (as I have argued elsewhere)[19] the harm experienced by the victim is sometimes (e.g., in some rapes) perceived in part as an insult or a degradation—the unwelcome message that the wrongdoer regards himself as superior to the victim and may use the victim, like a mere object, for his own purposes. Such an insulting message hurts; and this message may be withdrawn—and thus the hurt lessened—when the wrongdoer repents. This is why such repentance often opens the door to forgiveness; since, had forgiveness been granted earlier by the victim (prior to repentance by the wrongdoer), the victim might well fear that he was accepting, in a servile way, the insulting message contained in his victimization.[20]

Often, of course, victims of wrongdoing will not see their hurt less-ened by acts of repentance. Perhaps they will see the injury done (e.g., harms to their children, or harms that leave them with serious physical handicaps, or harms that leave them poor) as involving harms having little to do with insult or degradation, and thus will be unmoved by any change in "message" conveyed by the wrongdoer. Or perhaps they will see the injury and degradation they have suffered as being so grave as to be "unforgivable."

As Simon Wiesenthal asks in his book *The Sunflower*, How many Jews will be or should be moved by the difference between a repentant Nazi exterminator and an unrepentant Nazi exterminator? And if they are moved, in what direction will they be moved?[21] Cynthia Ozick, in her essay in *The Sunflower*, suggests that the repentant Nazi reveals a moral nature that he must have repressed in order to engage in unspeakable practices. This, by her lights, makes him worse than someone who is simply a crude and unreflective thug and prompts Ozick to say of him: "Let him go to hell. Sooner the fly to God than he." Or consider Elie Wiesel's prayer at ceremonies marking the fiftieth anniversary of the liberation of Auschwitz: "God of forgiveness, do not forgive those who created this place. God of mercy, have no mercy on those who killed here Jewish children."[22]

In short, although repentance may play some role around the edges, it will—at least initially—not seem central in those versions of retributivism that emphasize a concept of desert based mainly on wrongdoing, grievance, and debt.[23]

What about those versions of retributivism that seek to target a con-cept of desert based not merely on wrongdoing, but also on ultimate character? Here repentance might well play a crucial role; for a repentant person seems to reveal a better character than an unrepentant person.

A concern with such nuances of character, however, is not likely to affect the basic design of the criminal code itself. Criminal punishment is, after all, an exercise of political or state power. It is easy to see why such power will be mainly concerned with wrongdoing (either to prevent it or to give it what it deserves in the sense of removing a debt or righting a wrong), but hard to see why the state—particularly the liberal secular state—should be concerned with ultimate character independent of wrongdoing.[24] It would seem that it could at most address this concern as a subordinate goal—perhaps as a way of constraining, through fine-tuned individuation, a system mainly concerned with other matters. Thus it is not surprising that, in a legal world dominated by the values of deterrence and politically relevant retribution (i.e., grievance retribution), a concern with issues of deep character will more likely be regarded as relevant, if at all, at the level of sentencing or pardon or restoration of rights for parolees (issues to be discussed in a later section of this chapter) than at the level of the basic design and purpose of the criminal code itself.

Punishment as Moral Improvement

It was not always this way, of course. Plato, although he made some place for general deterrence and incapacitation in his account of punishment in his great dialogue *Laws*, rejected retribution (which he could not distinguish from vengeance) as utterly barbaric.[25] He offered instead, as the dominant value that should govern criminal punishment, the value of *moral improvement*—punishment as a means of transforming the character of the criminal from a state of vice to a state of virtue. The goal of punishment is future oriented, but not mainly as a device for securing future compliance to law. Compliance is not the primary aim of punishment but will rather be secured as a by-product of the value that is the primary aim: instilling in the criminal, not a fear based on self-interest, but rather a true sense of justice—a desire to do the right thing for the right reason. The goal is to confer upon the criminal a good (the greatest good: a good character), and this is why the theory is sometimes referred to as a "paternalistic" theory of punishment.

This Platonic theory, until recently rejected by legal philosophers as quite implausible, has now been powerfully resurrected—particularly in the recent writings of R. A. Duff, Herbert Morris, and Jean Hampton.[26] Since repentance has a central role to play in such a theory—particularly in Duff's version—it will be useful to consider it in our discussion.

First of all, it is worth considering why, for a long time, the theory that punishment may function to generate repentance was understandably rejected as implausible. There are several reasons. The most obvious is that our primary methods of punishment are so brutal as to make repentance either impossible or unlikely. (In spite of Dr. Johnson's quip that the prospect of being hanged tends to focus the mind, the death penalty and incarceration in the pesthole of the modern prison seem primarily to brutalize all those who come in contact with the system.) Also, contemporary criminal law (at least in America) tends toward radical overcriminalization—punishing many offenses with absurd excess and regarding some actions as crimes that, since their moral wrongness is doubtful, are also doubtful objects of repentance. The Georgia penal code, for example, provides that consensual homosexual sodomy may be punished by up to twenty years in prison, but it is by no means obvious that the homosexual has done evil of a kind for which repentance may legitimately be demanded by a secular community. Also, the criminal process will sometimes result in the conviction of persons who are actually innocent. To demand repentance of such persons is simply to add insult to the injury that they suffer from being unjustly punished. Consider finally the crimes (e.g., criminal trespass, unlawful assembly) that may be committed by persons whose motives are those of nonviolent civil disobedience. Do we really want to seek repentance from the Martin Luther Kings and Gandhis of the world?[27]

The answer to these worries is, I think, to insist that the paternalistic theory of punishment is an *ideal* theory—not a description of the world in which we live but rather the portrait of a world to which we should aspire. A state or community properly using the criminal law to provoke repentance would have only just laws (laws organized around a respect for fundamental human rights) and would use only methods of punishment that would assist genuine moral rebirth and not simply reflex conformity or terrified submission. Thus, the fact that most of our present penal practices are not of this nature will be seen—by someone committed to the paternalistic theory—as a condemnation of those practices and not as a refutation of the paternalistic theory itself. The Chinese demand for criminal repentance under the regime of

Mao was morally disgusting, not because it sought repentance for a violation of community norms, but because the norms themselves were often very evil and the means used to secure repentance were degrading.[28]

Even as an ideal theory, however, the paternalistic theory is open to serious challenge. Punishments that are not brutal and inhumane must still, if they are truly to be called punishments, inflict some serious deprivation—some hard treatment—on offenders. (Otherwise, how would punishment be distinguished from reward or from psychiatric therapy as a means of reform?) How is this hard treatment to be justified as a step toward repentance and reform?

There is an obvious connection between repentance and suffering. Repentant people feel *guilty*, and a part of feeling guilty is a sense that one ought to suffer punishment. Thus, guilty and repentant people may well seek out, or at least accept willingly, the punishment that is appropriate for their wrongdoing.[29]

This connection, by itself, will not yield the paternalistic theory, however. For the connection thus far establishes only that repentance will naturally lead to an accepting of punishment (or other penance). The paternalistic theory, however, requires that the connection go in the other direction—that punishment itself will produce repentance. How could this be so?

There is a traditional answer here, but it is not one that is likely to appeal to the contemporary mind. A certain kind of Platonist, committed to soul/body dualism, might argue that tendencies to wrongdoing arise from the desires of the body when those desires are not under the proper control of the rational soul.[30] St. Paul was no doubt under the influence of this kind of Platonism when, in Romans 8:23, he described his own moral failings by saying "I see another law in my members, warring against the law of my mind, and bringing me into captivity to the law of sin which is in my members." Given such a view, it is not difficult to imagine that the infliction of suffering that mortifies the body might well cause one to grow to hate the body and focus more upon the soul and the life of virtue that the soul makes possible.[31]

Such an account is highly problematic. It is hard for the contemporary mind to embrace a sharp soul/body dualism and even harder to accept the claim that wrongdoing typically arises from desires of the body. (This may work for rape, but it seems highly implausible for treason.) Some vice is highly intellectual in nature and results far more from a corrupt mind or will than from slavery to the body.[32] Thus, if one wants a theory that follows in Plato's spirit without embracing the metaphysics of his letter, one might see punishment as reforming not merely by subjecting the body, but also by curtailing the power of whatever aspect of the personality is responsible for vice. As Herbert Fingarette has argued, the wrongdoer has assumed a power greater than is his right to assume, and thus it is important that he have his will humbled.[33] Punishment makes him suffer (in the sense of *endure*), and such suffering not only gives him what he deserves but also provides him with an important lesson in the legitimate scope of his power.

But how does punishment itself make the lesson *take*? Unless we can imagine a plausible mechanism to explain how the infliction of suffering itself generates repentance and reform, it looks as though we will at most be able to claim that punishment provides us with an *opportunity* to do *something else* to a person (provide therapy, education, religious instruction, etc.) that might be reformative. But then we would be justifying punishment, not in terms of its own reformative potential, but simply in terms of the opportunities that it provides—hardly the challenging promise originally held out by the paternalistic theory.

R. A. Duff is sensitive to this problem and makes a very promising start toward salvaging the paternalistic theory from the many objections that have been raised against it. He makes no pretense that punishment can guarantee repentance and reform (and neither can other interventions, such as psychotherapy, that also aim at reform). In this sense, he would agree that punishment can do no more than offer criminals an opportunity for moral rebirth. In his view, however, the opportunity is presented by the punishment itself and not by some other devices that might be employed while punishment is being endured.

How could this be? It is, claims Duff, because punishment must be understood in *communitarian* terms, as an *act of communication* between the community and a person who has flouted one of that community's shared norms.[34] The suffering endured is that of separation from a valued community—a community that the criminal values (perhaps without realizing it until he experiences its loss) and to which he would like to return—and communicates to the wrongdoer the judgment that his actions have made him, at least temporarily, unworthy of full participation in the life of the community. It requires that he experience the pain of separation so that he can come to see, in his heart, the appropriateness of that separation and thus seek, with the appropriate humility, reconciliation with the community that he has wronged. In other words, the hope is that a kind of compulsory penance will be replaced by a voluntary penance. Voluntary penance is a sincere act of reattachment or allegiance to community values—an act that will allow the wrongdoer to be welcomed again and reintegrated into community life. And what makes this paternalistic? Simply this: Punishment on such terms will benefit the wrongdoer because severance from a community—if it is a *just* and *decent* community—is a genuine harm to the individual who is isolated, and reintegration is a genuine good for him.[35]

According to Duff, the *right sort* of prison may help the wrongdoer to achieve the good of reintegration because it "removes the criminal from his corrupting peers, and provides the opportunity for and the stimulus to a reflective self-examination which will [ideally] induce repentance and self-reform."[36] Also worth considering are such alternatives to prison as community service and restitution.[37]

Duff's theory is rich and in many ways compelling. It cannot be the whole story on the justification of punishment, but it is—in my judgment—an important and largely neglected part of the story.[38] It may be highly unrealistic to attempt an application of the theory to the crime problem in a society such as that found in contemporary America. It is not at all clear to what degree there is a genuine community of values in our society; and, even where there may be a community of values, it is sometimes the case that those who flout those values feel so alienated (perhaps because of poverty or racial injustice or cultural exclusion) that they could not reasonably see reintegration into the community as a good to be secured by their punishment because they never felt truly integrated into the community in the first place.[39] However, if the paternalistic theory really is a compelling ideal theory, then even a serious gap between theory and practice will not be a legitimate ground for rejecting the theory. Rather, it will be an occasion for mourning the community that we have lost and for seeking to regain it—or for seeking to create it if we have never had it. Those committed to the paternalistic view will argue that we should work to create a community of mutual concern and respect wherein punishment, if needed at all, could—without self-deception or hypocrisy—be defended on paternalistic grounds.

But suppose that we are sufficiently charmed by the paternalistic theory that we want to get started now and not wait for the ideal world. How might we proceed? Perhaps the best arena in which initially to attempt to apply the theory is to be found not in the adult criminal law, but in the law dealing with juvenile offenders. Juvenile offenders are probably more open to radical character transformations than are adults. Also, as David Moore has suggested, the more informal and discretionary proceedings might allow—in encounters between offender (and family) and victim (and family)—the use of empathy to build a sense of community that more abstract and formal proceedings might mask.

It is also possible that one might be able to draw on subcommunities in ways that would ultimately benefit the larger community by developing in juvenile offenders a sense of self-worth through "belonging." For example, in 1994 a state court in Washington placed the punishment of two Tlingit teenagers guilty of robbery and assault in the hands of a tribal court—a court that banished the teenagers for eighteen months to separate uninhabited Alaskan islands in the hope that the necessity of surviving on their own, with only traditional tools and folkways to guide them, would build their characters and allow them reintegration into the community. Ideally, of course, one would want all citizens to feel a sense of belonging in the larger national community. One has to start somewhere, however, and since self-esteem cannot grow in an asocial vacuum, why not (before gangs come in and assume the role) take advantage of the opportunities offered by particular cultural subgroups? Such experiments are surely worth a try.[40]

Legal Mercy: Sentencing, Pardon, and Restoration of Rights

In the present world we will no doubt continue to employ a system of criminal punishment that is driven by a variety of different values. Even if we seek to introduce paternalistic concerns as one of our justifications, concerns with crime control (deterrence and incapacitation) and retribution will also loom large. In a system driven by these non-paternalistic values, even full repentance on the part of the criminal will frequently be viewed as not sufficient to remove the need for punishment. Punishing even the fully repentant might well serve general deterrence values, and it almost certainly will be demanded by crime victims who believe, on grievance retributive grounds, that the injuries that they have suffered require a response that is proportional to the wrongs that have produced those injuries.

If repentance is to play any role at all in our present system of criminal punishment, then it will probably be as one reason bearing on whatever *discretion* officials are allowed within a punitive range that satisfies the legitimate demands of crime control and grievance retribution. If, for example, we have grounds for believing that society's legitimate general deterrence and retributive objectives with respect to a specific offense could be satisfied by any punishment within a particular range (e.g., three to eight years), then sincere repentance could provide an authority with discretion (normally a sentencing judge or an executive with the power of pardon) with a good reason for choosing a punishment at the lower rather than the higher end of the range. I shall refer to decisions to impose a reduced sentence as acts of mercy when they are based on some relevant aspect of the offender rather than on factors of a purely external nature such as jail overcrowding.

But in what sense is repentance a relevant aspect? The obvious answer is to be found within the context of what I earlier called character retributivism. The repentant person has a better character than the unrepentant person, and thus the repentant person—on this theory— simply deserves less punishment than the unrepentant person. This basis for mercy—meaning here simply a reduction of sentence—is easy to understand, and may even be conceptualized as an aspect of justice.

Less immediately apparent, however, is a way in which repentance can be a basis for mercy (again as sentence reduction) even within the context of what I earlier called grievance retributivism. Victims of wrongdoing often want the person who wronged them to suffer. If these victims are moral and rational, however, they will not desire that the wrongdoer suffer to any degree greater than he deserves.

But what is deserved suffering? I have neither the space nor the talent to present a complete theory of this matter here, but one thing should be obvious: there will, on any theory of deserved suffering, be a prescription that a certain overall *amount* of suffering be experienced by the wrongdoer as what he deserves.

We normally expect the proper amount of suffering to be administered by the state through legal punishment. However, if there is reason to believe that the individual has already experienced a significant amount of relevant suffering through nonlegal channels, it is not unreasonable to suggest that the suffering he experience at the hands of the state be reduced to that degree—perhaps eliminated entirely in those cases where we are inclined to say "he has suffered enough." If mercy, in the sense of reduction of legal punishment, is extended on these grounds, this will not compromise the legitimate claims of grievance retributivism but will instead be required by them.

Of course, not all suffering is relevant—for example, the suffering that a wrongdoer might experience from losing a position (e.g., loss of professional reputation) that his criminal conduct showed that he had no right to enjoy in the first place.[41]

I am inclined to think that the suffering that one imposes upon oneself through repentance is very different from this, however. The sincerely repentant person tortures himself—hates at least that aspect of himself that allowed him to engage in the wrong he now laments—and the pain that this produces is arguably relevant in a way that a painful loss of an undeserved honorific status is not. Unless the victim's injury is one that is regarded as simply unforgivable, then the self-generated suffering experienced by the repentant wrongdoer might well be accepted by an aggrieved victim as a part of what he is owed in the way of suffering from the person who wronged him. If he does not accept this, then it would seem that the burden of argument now shifts to him to explain why, if the amount of relevant suffering is proper, it matters in any deep moral sense what percentage of it comes from the state.[42]

We can now see how repentance could be a basis for sentence reduction even on grievance retributive grounds. The actual use of this basis, however, is tricky. We normally consider granting mercy or pardon when someone begs or petitions for it. A truly repentant person, however, would normally see his suffering punishment as *proper* and might, as noted earlier, even seek it out. Why then is he begging for mercy and trying to avoid more punishment? Is the fact that he wants us to reduce his punishment perhaps evidence that he is not repentant; and are we then faced with the problem that the only persons who are truly eligible for mercy on grounds of repentance will almost never get it because their repentance will cause them not to ask for it?

There are reasons for being cautious here, and many practical problems of distinguishing real from counterfeit repentance exist.[43] In my judgment, however, there are no insoluble problems of principle, and I think this for two reasons. First, we might have sufficient grounds to grant mercy in cases where the person (perhaps because of neurotic desires for too much self-punishment) refuses to ask for it. Second, if we take the trouble to inquire, we might find that some repentant persons ask for mercy, not so that they can avoid some deserved suffering, but in order that they can leave prison and do something useful and good with what remains of their lives. We should not simply assume that all such expressions are disguises for self-interest, although some of them certainly are.[44]

In summary, a truly repentant wrongdoer is recommitted to community values, requires no additional special deterrence, and clearly—on the theory of character retributivism—deserves less punishment than a wrongdoer who is unrepentant. When one could promote the goods represented by these considerations without

compromising the law's legitimate interest in crime control and grievance retribution (to which repentance, I have argued, may also be relevant), it would seem irrational—even cruel—not to do so and bestow
mercy.

There are degrees of mercy, of course; and the grounds that justify
letting a person out of prison may not require that the community
treat the freed individual exactly as he would have been treated prior
to any criminal conduct. Heavyweight champion Mike Tyson served
his sentence for rape and was properly released from prison. Football
and movie star O. J. Simpson, charged with murdering his wife and
her friend, was acquitted at trial and was properly released from
prison. Substantial segments of the American public refuse to welcome
these two men back into American society, however, because they are
viewed as wrongdoers who refuse to acknowledge and repent of their
wrongdoing. Although both men maintain their innocence, many people simply do not believe them and thus, while agreeing that they must
be freed from jail, still refuse to accord them their previous levels of
respect. One proof of this is that they are no longer employed for commercial endorsements.

Also consider the case of Tonya Harding. She did express remorse
for what she claimed to be her limited role in the criminal assault on
fellow Olympic skater Nancy Kerrigan, but the American public—
while no doubt generally content with the plea bargain that allowed
her to avoid jail time—still continues to treat her with contempt.[45] Is
this because of a belief that she minimized her actual role in the crime,
or a belief that she is not truly repentant, or an unwillingness to forgive
her even if she is truly repentant? There is no way of knowing for sure;
and I mention this and the previous cases simply to make the point
that "we will let you out of jail" does not always lead to "we will fully
welcome you back into the community." No doubt the former generally should lead to the latter; but sometimes there are perhaps under-
standable reasons why it does not.

The reentry problems faced by Tyson, Simpson, and Harding are
mainly concerned with the private responses that other citizens choose
to make to them—responses (such as refusals to offer opportunities for
commercial endorsements) that are clearly within the rights of those
citizens.

But what if it is the *state* that refuses to allow—even for the repentant
and freed criminal—full reentry into the rights and privileges of society? Even this, I think, is a matter of considerable complexity.

Consider the issue of the restoration of certain rights to paroled felons—a matter that, in the absence of specific legislative enactments, is often left in the hands of officials of state agencies that are neither judicial nor executive.

For example, a couple of years ago, the admissions committee of the College of Law at my university admitted a paroled murderer into the first-year class. The outcry from alumni and legislators was enormous—including a still-simmering threat to withdraw funding from the college and shut it down. Both the parole board and the admissions committee believed that the individual, who had served a very long prison term, was sincerely repentant and fully rehabilitated, and desired to make the rest of his life of some use to society. Critics regarded this argument as irrelevant either because they doubted the sincerity of the repentance or, more commonly, because they believed that even fully repentant murderers owed a lifetime debt to their victims and to the community that could not be overcome by any change of character.

Who is right here? It is, I think, very hard to say. Although I supported and continue to support the admission of this person to the College of Law, the decision was a close call for me because I think that reasonable people can be on either side of an issue of this nature. Even those who advocate reintegration of repentant criminals into the community might have reasonable grounds for limiting this reintegration. Although it would surely be unconscionable to deny such individuals access to state medical care or even general state programs of university education, it does not strike me as comparably unconscionable to adopt, if not an absolute rule, at least a strong presumption against allowing such individuals access to such a scarce and costly community resource as a tax-funded legal education.[46]

What this discussion shows, I think, is that much more thinking needs to be done on the relationship between mercy and repentance. Repentance may earn a reduction in sentence—perhaps even a full release from prison—but may understandably be viewed as not sufficient to earn complete reintegration into the community. It may get you out of the fire and into the frying pan, but—as I think J. L. Austin remarked somewhere—it may be a frying pan that is still in a fire.

A Closing Second Thought on Collective Repentance

When one thinks of repentance in connection with criminal punishment, one tends to think that all demands for repentance must be addressed to the criminal. But surely the community—through its patterns of abuse, neglect, and discrimination—sometimes creates a social environment that undermines the development of virtuous character and makes the temptations to crime very great, greater than many of us might have been able to resist if similarly situated.[47]

The important idea here is not that criminals, if they are from social groups that are poor or despised or abused or discriminated against, are not to any degree responsible for their criminality. They are. As a part of their dignity as human beings, they must be seen as responsible agents and not merely as helpless victims. But their responsibility is, in my view, sometimes *shared* with those of us in the larger community. In these cases, we too may be legitimately called upon for repentance and atonement—attitudes of mind that should prevent us from thinking of criminals as totally other, and should thus moderate our tendencies to respond to them with nothing but malice.

At present, however, unrepentant viciousness toward criminals has become an increasingly pervasive feature of American society. So out of control is this passion that Chief Judge Richard A. Posner, hardly a bleeding heart sentimentalist, powerfully condemned it in a recent opinion:

There are different ways to look upon the inmates of prisons and jails in the United States in 1995. One way is to look upon them as members of a different species, indeed as a type of vermin, devoid of human dignity and entitled to no respect. . . .

I do not myself consider the 1.5 million inmates of American prisons and jails in that light. This is a non-negligible fraction of the American population. And it is only the current inmate population. The fraction of the total population that has spent time in a prison or jail is larger. . . . A substantial number of these prison and jail inmates . . . have not been convicted of a crime. They are merely charged with crime, and awaiting trial. Some of them may actually be innocent. Of the guilty, many are guilty of sumptuary offenses, or of other victimless crimes uncannily similar to lawful activity (gambling offenses are an example), or of esoteric financial and regulatory offenses (such as violation of the migratory game laws) some of which do not even require a guilty intent. It is wrong to break even foolish laws, or wise laws that should carry only civil penalties. It is wrongful to break the law when the lawbreaker is flawed, weak, retarded, unstable, ignorant, brutalized, or profoundly disadvantaged, rather than violent, vicious, or evil to the core. But we should have a realistic conception of the composition of the prison and jail population before deciding that they are scum entitled to nothing better than what a vengeful populace and a resource-starved penal system chooses to give them. We must not exaggerate the distance between "us," the lawful ones, the respectable ones, and the prison and jail population; for such exaggeration will make it too easy for us to deny that population the rudiments of humane consideration.[48]

Even though we cannot always grant mercy, we should always be open to it—even disposed toward it—because, at some level, we all require it and should hope that our repentance might be seen as a ground for it. Annie, in the Oscar Hijuelos story, maintained that "in her opinion the troubles in life were started by people who never looked into their own souls."[49] All of us would be well advised to take her words to heart and, as we demand repentance of the criminal, demand it also of ourselves. If we find that we are unwilling or unable to demand it of ourselves, perhaps we should conclude that we have forfeited our right to demand it from the criminal.[50]

Notes

1. A slightly different version of this chapter originally appeared in *The Quality of Mercy*, edited by Andrew Brien (Rodopi Press, 1997). It is reprinted here with permission.

2. One of the puzzles about this play is the fact that Prospero seems simply *wrong* in some of his assessments here. Of the "three men of sin" who have wronged Prospero, only Alonso repents. Antonio and Sebastian do not. A theory to be pursued later in this chapter is the Platonic claim that punishment itself may provoke repentance. Perhaps Prospero subscribes to some version of this theory, thinking that the suffering he has inflicted on his three enemies as punishment should have been sufficient to generate their repentance and thereby render them eligible for mercy.

3. Shakespeare's sensitivity to the idea that mercy may be a free act of grace is revealed in Portia's often quoted claim in *The Merchant of Venice* (Act IV) that "the quality of mercy is not [con]strain'd; It droppeth as the gentle rain from heaven upon the place beneath: it is twice blessed."

4. Concurring opinion by Justice Anthony Kennedy in *Riggins v. Nevada* (504 U.S. 127, 143, 112 S.Ct. 1810, 1819).

5. Nassau County Court, 22 March 1995. These remarks were offered by Judge Donald E. Belfi as he defended the sentence of two hundred years that he had imposed on Colin Ferguson. Ferguson, identified by numerous eye witnesses, was convicted on six counts of murder and nineteen counts of attempted murder in an attack on commuters on a Long Island Railroad train.

A truly bizarre man (so bizarre that many questioned Judge Belfi's decision that he was sane enough to serve as his own attorney), Ferguson offered a totally unbelievable theory of mistaken identity in a hopeless attempt to establish his innocence. He claimed that his refusal to show remorse was appropriate because, being innocent, he had nothing over which to be remorseful.

6. These rhetorical questions were raised by Atlanta assistant district attorney Richard Parker as he argued before the jury that Warren G. McCleskey, convicted of murdering a police officer, should be shown no mercy but should be sentenced to death. After two hours of deliberation, the jury sentenced McCleskey to death. The quoted passage is from the transcript of the 1978 trial. The death sentence was appealed (unsuccessfully), not because of a claim that the prosecution erred in focusing on McCleskey's lack of repentance, but on totally different grounds: the claim that McCleskey, a black, might be receiving the death sentence in part because his victim was white. This argument was rejected by the United States Supreme Court in *McCleskey v. Kemp*, 481 U.S. 279, 107 S.Ct. 1756, 95 L.Ed.2d 262 (1987), rehearing denied 482 U.S. 920, 107 S.Ct. 3199, 96 L.Ed.2d 686 (1987).

7. *Forgiveness and Mercy* by Jeffrie G. Murphy (chapters 1, 3, and 5) and Jean Hampton (chapters 2 and 4), Cambridge University Press, 1988. I developed this account of repentance in connection with forgiveness and argued that it applies to mercy only to the degree that mercy is not a virtue separate from forgiveness. For an argument that there is a sense in which a person can deserve mercy, see Andrew Brien's "Mercy and Desert" (*Philosophical Papers* 20, no. 3 [1991]: 193–201). For an argument (grounded in Christian theology) that repentance should *not* be viewed as a precondition for forgiveness, see *Embodying Forgiveness, A Theological Analysis* by L. Gregory Jones (Grand Rapids: Eerdmans, 1995). I am sorry that I did not become aware of this book until I was in the process of meeting the deadline for the present volume.

8. When I wrote my chapters for *Forgiveness and Mercy*, I was on the whole still convinced that the retributive theory of punishment is the correct theory of punishment and that such a theory can sit comfortably within the confines of liberal theory. I had already started to develop some doubts about this, however, and these doubts have recently become quite serious. See my "Retributivism, Moral Education and the Liberal State" (*Criminal Justice Ethics* 4, no. 1 [Winter/Spring 1985] and reprinted in my book *Retribution Reconsidered* [Boston: Kluwer, 1992]) and my "Legal Moralism and Liberalism" (*Arizona Law Review* 37, no. 1 [Spring 1995]).

9. For an illuminating discussion of some of the issues involved in collective repentance and forgiveness, see *An Ethic for Enemies, Forgiveness in Politics* by Donald W. Shriver, Jr. (New York: Oxford University Press, 1995).

10. See Charles J. Sykes, *A Nation of Victims: The Decay of the American Character* (New York: St. Martin's Press, 1992). This book is often shrill and filled with political and rhetorical overkill, but it introduces a useful perspective.

11. Søren Kierkegaard, *Purity of Heart Is to Will One Thing, Spiritual Prepara-*

tion for the Office of Confession, trans. Douglas V. Steere (New York: Harper and Row, 1948), chapter 2: "Remorse, Repentance, Confession."

12. Note that repentance thus defined, in spite of its social dimension, still retains inner elements—such as remorse. In this way it differs from the purely social (indeed ritualistic) act of *apology*. Repentant people generally feel inclined to apologize, but people who apologize are often not repentant. For a rich discussion of apology, see Nicholas Tavuchis's *Mea Culpa: A Sociology of Apology and Reconciliation* (Stanford, Calif.: Stanford University Press, 1991).

13. As usual, Nietzsche is instructive here: "True remorse is rarest among criminals and convicts. . . . By and large, punishment hardens and freezes; it concentrates; it sharpens the sense of alienation; it strengthens resistance." Friedrich Nietzsche, *The Genealogy of Morals*, section XIV, trans. Francis Golffing (New York: Doubleday, 1956).

14. This is, of necessity, a very sketchy and superficial survey of the theory of punishment. For a more detailed treatment see chapter 3 of Jeffrie G. Murphy and Jules L. Coleman, *The Philosophy of Law: An Introduction to Jurisprudence*, rev. ed. (Boulder: Westview Press, 1990). I have tried to give a more detailed characterization of retributivism in some of my other writings. See, for example, "Legal Moralism and Liberalism," *supra* note 8.

15. Although the attempt to control crime through punishment depends mainly on a belief in the deterrent efficacy of punishment, punishment may also be used to control crime in a more direct way: incapacitation. Incapacitation is the attempt to make it *impossible* for a person to commit crime (through maximum security incarceration or even death).

16. Strict criminal liability is (in my view) always unfair, but it may indeed have general deterrence value. A requirement of *mens rea* (e.g., intent or knowledge) is one more thing that the state has to prove and thus one more thing defendants might be able to exploit in attempting to establish reasonable doubt in the minds of a jury. When strict liability (e.g., absence of *mens rea*, one kind of absence of fault) governs activity in a particular area, then entering the area becomes more risky for potential criminals than it otherwise would have been (since they have one less avoidance strategy to exploit with respect to punishment) and thus entry becomes a less eligible option.

17. See, for example, Herbert Morris's "Persons and Punishment," *The Monist* 52, no. 4 (October 1968). This essay has been reprinted in *Punishment and Rehabilitation*, 3d ed., ed. Jeffrie G. Murphy (Belmont: Wadsworth, 1995).

18. See, for example, Michael Moore's "The Moral Worth of Retribution," in *Responsibility, Character and the Emotions*, ed. Ferdinand Schoeman (Cambridge: Cambridge University Press, 1987). This essay has been reprinted in *Punishment and Rehabilitation*, 3d ed., ed. Jeffrie G. Murphy (Belmont: Wadsworth, 1995). For an essay that explores the possible inconsistencies between this kind of retributivism and a liberal theory of the state, see Jeffrie G. Murphy's "Legal Moralism and Liberalism," *supra* note 8.

19. *Forgiveness and Mercy, supra* note 7.

20. Although I am here discussing harm to an individual victim of crime, it is important to note that the harm of crime may befall the community as a whole. Treason is a dramatic example where the harm is essentially harm to the entire community, but many crimes will have this community dimension—a fact that in part explains the nature of the state as the complaining party in criminal prosecutions. The idea of wrongdoers as traitors to the ideal of community is pursued in a rich (if often obscure) way by Josiah Royce in his 1918 *The Problem of Christianity* (Chicago: University of Chicago Press, 1968). See especially chapter 6 ("Atonement").

21. Simon Wiesenthal, *The Sunflower* (New York: Schocken Books, 1976). In this book, Wiesenthal tells the story of his experience when a dying Nazi begged forgiveness for the atrocities that the Nazi had committed against Jews. After the story, a variety of writers comment on it.

22. Suppose Wiesenthal or some other Nazi hunter had a list of escaped Nazis who ran death camps—each responsible for the deaths of the same number of Jews. Suppose some are repentant and some are unrepentant and that time and resources allow the capture of only some of them. Does one go for the repentant ones first or last? I owe this puzzle to Cynthia Ward.

23. I say "at least initially" here to make room for an issue I wish to explore later in the chapter when I consider possible repentance-based grounds for mercy. Those with grievances against wrongdoers often want the wrongdoers to suffer punishment. But is it not the case that a truly repentant wrongdoer inflicts suffering *upon himself*—through feelings of self-loathing, perhaps? If this is so, perhaps this suffering could be used to justify a reduction in the amount of suffering inflicted by the state as punishment since what is deserved is arguably an overall amount of suffering. I am not sure that it is legitimate for aggrieved persons to demand that those who wronged them suffer. If this is legitimate, however, it would require a separate argument to render legitimate their demand that all the suffering be imposed by the state and that none that is self-imposed should be allowed to count. I am grateful to Andrew Brien for calling this issue to my attention, and I hope that my later—and very tentative—treatment of it in the section of the chapter on mercy and sentencing will advance the discussion in a useful way.

24. See "Legal Moralism and Liberalism," *supra* note 8.

25. The two best discussions of Plato's philosophy of punishment are Mary Margaret Mackenzie's *Plato on Punishment* (Berkeley: University of California Press, 1981), and Trevor J. Saunders's *Plato's Penal Code* (New York: Oxford University Press, 1991).

26. Herbert Morris, "A Paternalistic Theory of Punishment," *American Philosophical Quarterly* 18, no. 4 (October 1981); Jean Hampton, "The Moral Education Theory of Punishment," *Philosophy and Public Affairs* 13, no. 3 (1984); R. A. Duff, *Trials and Punishments* (Cambridge: Cambridge University Press, 1986). (The Morris essay and a chapter from the Duff book are reprinted in *Punishment and Rehabilitation*, 3d ed., ed. Jeffrie G. Murphy [Belmont: Wads-

worth, 1995].) Although emphasizing punishment as a means of educating and reforming character, Duff, Morris, and Hampton—unlike Plato—make room for retributive values as well.

27. Professor Uma Narayan makes the point about the unavoidability, in a system of punishment aimed at repentance, of sometimes improperly seeking repentance from the innocent in her unpublished paper "Contrition and Criminal Punishment."

28. Of course, as Plato noted in *Laws*, it is of some embarrassment that an ideal society should have to punish at all. An ideal Platonic society is, after all, structured to produce virtuous citizens. Why then are there still criminals? And, if virtuous socialization has not yet taken, why suppose that it will take in the process of punishment? Plato says that punishment in such an ideal society is needed mainly to deal with slaves and foreigners—persons who, as outsiders, have not undergone the processes of socialization that will attach them to shared community values.

Contemporary multicultural societies exhibit diversity of value, of course, and the list of shared community values may be shorter than we might initially have hoped; thus the use of a paternalistic criminal law, and its demand for repentance, may to that degree be restricted. We should not too quickly overestimate such diversity, however, for there may be a core of basic moral agreement lying beneath the surface of apparent disagreement. The urban teenager, whose only possible legal employment may be working for minimum wage at McDonald's, may initially think that he is justified in selling drugs. Would he still hold this view if directly confronted with a young and innocent life destroyed by the drugs he sold? Diversity of value (and associated self-deception) is easier to maintain about some issues than others.

29. In a later section, I will explore the relation between this idea and mercy in sentencing and pardon.

30. Plato only sometimes (e.g., in parts of *Phaedo*) talks in this simplistic dualistic way. At other times (e.g., in *Republic*) he offers a more complex picture of the nature of motivation and the origin of wrongdoing.

31. As my colleague Michael White has pointed out to me, similar ideas may be found in the Christian ascetic tradition (e.g., in Pascal). In general the ascetic tradition is speaking of acts of mortification that are voluntarily assumed. Pains that are not voluntarily assumed (e.g., illness, acts of punishment) may also lead to spiritual improvement if they are accepted in the proper spirit, but it is hard to see how the pains themselves can generate the proper attitude of acceptance.

32. Aristotle, at *Nicomachean Ethics* 1129a, locates the cause of much wrongdoing in *pleonexia*—the desire to have more than one's fair share. This desire can hardly be understood as having its origin in the body.

33. Herbert Fingarette, "Punishment and Suffering," American Philosophical Association Presidential Address, 1977.

34. For the pursuit of a similar idea from the perspective of social science,

see the discussion of "reintegrative shaming" in John Braithwaite's *Crime, Shame and Reintegration* (Cambridge: Cambridge University Press, 1989).

35. The importance of the constraints of justice and decency cannot be overstressed. Too often communitarians fail to make sufficiently clear that it is only communities organized around the right values, and not all communities, that are worthy of allegiance.

36. The idea of prison envisioned by Duff—a place providing an opportunity for and stimulus to repentance—is not without problems. Maimonides distinguished coerced from deliberative repentance. The former arises when the conditions for indulging in sinful behavior are no longer present. Coercive repentance is "imperfect" because it does not secure a sincere change of heart on the part of the wrongdoer. As such it is contrasted with the "perfect" repentance that arises from the exercise of free choice in an environment where it is still possible to succumb to the relevant temptation. It is thus hard to see how incarceration could provide more than an opportunity for imperfect repentance. (See Pinchas Peli, *Soloveitchik on Repentance* [New York: Paulist Press, 1984]. This is a treatise on Rabbi Soloveitchik's teachings on Maimonides.)

37. In correspondence (1995) Duff says,

> I'm inclined now to place less weight on imprisonment as a mode of communicative punishment (though it can have *some* place in such an account), and more weight on con-custodial punishments: both on standard kinds of sentence like community service and probation, and on more experimental kinds of programme such as victim-offender mediation programmes, and programmes which aim to confront offenders with the effects and implications of their offenses. These are often portrayed by their advocates as *alternatives* to punishment (often as "therapeutic" rather than "punitive"), but I think they are better understood, and should operate, as communicative punishments.

38. Here is one reason why it cannot be the whole story: The paternalistic theory, by placing so much emphasis on the way in which criminality severs ties with the community, perhaps tends to underemphasize that crime also poses special threats to and imposes special injuries upon individual victims. It is not clear that a proper concern with the victim can be adequately addressed by an account of punishment that focuses mainly on the wrongdoer and on what would be good for him. How, on a scale of severity of punishment, will criminal offenses be ranked on Duff's account—by the harms they cause to the victim or by what it would take to secure penance from the offender? The latter can hardly be expected to satisfy all crime victims. For a discussion that gives emphasis (too much I am now inclined to think) to the concerns of the victim, see "Getting Even: The Role of the Victim" in Jeffrie G. Murphy, *Retribution Reconsidered* (Boston: Kluwer, 1992).

39. For a discussion of the ways in which social inequality can undermine the application of theories of punishment, see Jeffrie G. Murphy, "Marxism and Retribution," *Philosophy and Public Affairs* 2, no. 3 (Spring 1973), and re-

printed in Jeffrie G. Murphy, *Retribution, Justice and Therapy* (Dordrecht: Reidel, 1979).

40. According to the *New York Times* (11 September 1995), the Tlingit experiment was unfortunately not allowed to run its full course. According to a tribal judge, the teenagers were making definite improvements when the conditions of their banishment were being enforced. After a few months, however, the enforcement became lax and they began more frequent interactions with their families and friends—even coming into town on occasion. According to tribal judge Elbert James, "They're [no longer] out on their own. They're not by themselves. They're not thinking about things. They're not digging around getting food, not working hard to cut wood to make their own fire. At first, when we had them out by themselves, you could see a definite improvement in those boys. But then their families came in and got their hands on them, and they quit being dependent on themselves."

For an extremely insightful attempt to apply communitarian theory to issues in juvenile justice (with examples from New Zealand and Australia), see David B. Moore's "Shame, Forgiveness, and Juvenile Justice" in *Criminal Justice Ethics*, Winter/Spring 1993. For the newsletter of a group attempting to give Moore's ideas an application in America, see *Real Justice Forum*, P. O. Box 500, Pipersville, Penn., 18947. For a skeptical critique of victim-offender mediation, see Jennifer Brown's "The Use of Mediation to Resolve Criminal Cases: A Procedural Critique," 43 *Emory Law Journal* 1247.

41. One thinks here of President Gerald Ford's decision to pardon former president Richard Nixon on the grounds that Nixon, forced to leave office because of his criminal conduct, had already suffered enough by losing the presidency.

42. If one accepts Herbert Fingarette's view (*supra* note 33) that punishment is justified in order to "humble the will" of the wrongdoer by making him submissive to the legitimacy of the very power he thwarted, then one might have the basis of an argument that state punishment cannot be replaced by self-punishment, since self-punishment could be viewed as an exercise of the very faculty that needs to be humbled: autonomy. The person who would impose his own punishment perhaps still has too much of a "these matters are up to me" attitude.

43. It is important that any system that rewards repentance (and thus, like our present system of plea bargaining, gives defendants strong incentives to fake it) develop safeguards against counterfeit repentance. As Montaigne observed, "These men make us believe that they feel great regret and remorse within, but of amendment and correction or interruption they show us no sign. . . . I know of no quality so easy to counterfeit as piety."

Legitimate caution here, however, should not lead one to adopt the radical skeptic view that we can *never* have reasonable grounds for thinking that repentance is genuine. It is indeed hard to know another's mental states; but, as our reasonably comfortable use of *mens rea* in the criminal law illustrates, we do not generally regard it as impossible.

44. It is often said that genuine mercy grows out of *compassion* rather than

a sense of justice and, because of this, may lead us into injustice—revealing itself thereby as a vice rather than the virtue it is usually claimed to be. Following Saint Anselm, I raised this worry in *Forgiveness and Mercy, supra* note 7.

I am now inclined to think that this move against mercy is far too hasty and probably rests upon an ambiguity in the concept of compassion.

If compassion means nothing more than "feeling sorry for," then it may be nothing but a piece of personal sentimentality that has no place in thinking about punishment and mercy.

The root meaning of compassion, however, is *to feel with*—that is, empathy. Being a compassionate person in this sense involves taking the trouble to view the wrongdoer (indeed all others) through trying to understand his life from inside, his life as it actually is, rather than in terms of the general category "criminal" and the application of a few hasty assumptions and socially accepted cliches about persons in this class. This will involve efforts at individuation both of the criminal ("Is he really just an evil piece of scum?") and of oneself as victim ("Have I really experienced an injury that is truly unforgivable?"). As David Moore has observed (*supra* note 40), vicious sentiments directed toward criminals—so easy to express in the world of public politics—often drop away when the criminal and victim can be brought together in such a way that they can relate to each other as individual people. In many (but, of course, not all) cases, these encounters allow the victim to move toward forgiveness and mercy as the criminal moves toward repentance. We would do well to adopt the wise perspective that Felicia (in the William Trevor story) adopted toward the man who tried to murder her: "Lost within a man who murdered, there was a soul like any other soul, purity itself it surely once had been" (William Trevor, *Felicia's Journey* [London: Viking, 1994], 212). For further insight on these matters, see Martha Nussbaum's "Equity and Mercy" in *Philosophy and Public Affairs* 22, no. 2 (1993) (reprinted in *Punishment and Rehabilitation*, 3d ed., ed. Jeffrie G. Murphy [Belmont: Wadsworth, 1995]).

45. In a pitiful attempt to begin a career as a singer, Harding was recently pelted with rotten fruit while she was performing on stage.

46. The entering law school class is limited to under 150 students, and only medical school education is more limited and more costly. In the modern world, some college education is increasingly important in assisting people to develop into fully autonomous citizens and to lead rich and meaningful lives, and to deny paroled felons access to such programs would undermine the possibility of the very kind of self-improvement in them that we want to see continue. It is harder to defend legal and medical education in such terms, however, since it is fairly easy to make great strides in self-improvement, develop full autonomy, and lead a rich and meaningful life without becoming a lawyer or doctor. I would not favor an absolute ban on admission of paroled felons, however, since I would (for example) want to leave open the possibility of admitting such a person who expressed a desire to develop expertise in issues of prisoners' rights and could argue that his own experience behind bars would be a great asset in such a practice.

47. "If society lets any considerable number of its members grow up mere children, incapable of being acted on by rational consideration of distant motives, society has itself to blame for the consequences" (John Stuart Mill, *On Liberty* [London: Penguin Books, 1995], 212).

48. *Johnson v. Phelan*, No. 93-3753, United States Court of Appeals, Seventh Circuit, 1995 WL 621777 (7th Cir.[Ill.]).

49. Oscar Hijuelos, *Mr. Ives' Christmas* (New York: HarperCollins, 1995), 48.

50. An earlier version of the present chapter was presented at a conference on repentance sponsored by the Communitarian Network, and the participants at the conference provided many helpful comments. A highly abbreviated version of the chapter, with the title "Crime and Punishment: Where Does Repentance Fit?" was published in their journal, *The Responsive Community* (5, no. 4 [Fall 1995], 15–24). I also received valuable discussion when I presented the essay to the Arizona State University Workshop in Moral, Political, and Legal Theory. Andrew Brien, Antony Duff, David Moore, and Eleonore Stump were kind enough to read a later draft and provide me with insightful comments. I am extremely grateful to all of these persons and to my two splendid research assistants, Mary Sigler and Bahar Schippel.

9

Repentance in Criminal Procedure: The Ritual Affirmation of Community

Robert Wuthnow

In *The Elementary Forms of the Religious Life*, Emile Durkheim argued that societies define and periodically renew their basic values by drawing distinctions between the sacred and the profane and by performing rituals that dramatize these distinctions.[1] Sociologists and anthropologists have extended this insight to discussions of criminal behavior and other forms of deviance, arguing that the labeling of such behavior and its punishment through the confinement, torture, execution, or expulsion of criminals can be understood as ways in which community values are reaffirmed. Kai T. Erikson developed this argument as an explanation for the witch trials that occurred in seventeenth-century Massachusetts.[2] Mary Douglas contended that social boundaries were often symbolized by physical bodies and Michel Foucault offered graphic examples of how the torture of criminals in eighteenth-century Europe dramatized the authority of the totalitarian state.[3] Albert Bergesen demonstrated that political witch hunts in the twentieth century have been used by national leaders to shore up collective values during times of uncertainty,[4] and James Inverarity showed that lynchings in Southern states coincided with moments of popular support for stronger communal commitments.[5] Retributive theories of criminal justice often adopt a similar logic, arguing that punishment of criminal behavior expresses the community's disapproval of such activities and restores moral balance to the community.[6]

It is curious that this literature has paid virtually no attention to repentance, emphasizing instead that communities purify and restore themselves by physically or symbolically expelling criminals from their midst. One would think that communities might also restore themselves by calling on criminals to repent and by ritually reincorporating deviant members into full rights and responsibilities of the community. Indeed, a rehabilitated criminal, just as a repentant sinner, might well serve more clearly than an excluded one as evidence of the community's power. Yet in practice, far more attention is devoted to the prevention and punishment of crime than to ways in which criminals might be encouraged to repent and resume normal lives. Fifteen states, for instance, currently make no provision for ex-felons even to regain basic rights of citizenship, instead disenfranchising them for life, and most states restrict ex-offenders from working in occupations as varied as banking, teaching, bartending, and barbering.[7]

Over a longer period, however, the fact is that repentance and rehabilitation have, indeed, been important ways in which societies exercise control over their members. The nature of repentance reflects what the society values most highly in its members and the process of absorbing criminals back into the society provides an occasion for many of the operating principles of that society to be dramatized. By considering the changing expectations surrounding the rehabilitation of criminals, we can gain an understanding of both the way in which deviance itself is treated and the broader dilemmas that must now be confronted in efforts to strengthen community obligations. These considerations are intended not as recommendations for the revision of judicial procedure itself, but as a way of initiating further discussion of this important topic.

My argument is that repentance remains potentially significant as one of the means by which the United States can address its ever-deepening problems of crime. For that potential to be realized, however, it is necessary to regain an appreciation of the role of *ritual* in affirming community. If Durkheim and his followers are correct, community loyalties are affirmed not simply by the expulsion of deviant elements, but also by the ritual activities surrounding such expurgations. By the same token, repentance is unlikely to have benefit for the society as a whole if penitent offenders are expected only to quietly resume their roles as citizens and as breadwinners; here, too, ritual must be part of the reassimilation process.

How much of a role ritual has played in the past—and the reasons why its role is attenuated—can be understood by tracing some of the historical changes in modern criminal procedure. A preliminary clue, however, is evident in an episode that recently absorbed the attention of a suburban community in central New Jersey.

   This episode involved the tragic slaying of a seven-year-old girl on 29 July 1994 by a convicted sex offender (who confessed to the killing).[8] Outraged by the fact that a sex offender had been able to move into their community and live what appeared to be an ordinary life, citizens drew up a petition—subsequently enacted as "Megan's Law" by the state legislature—that would require public notification (of local police, school officials, churches, and neighbors) when any such offender attempted to take up residence. Critics of the law said it would stigmatize rehabilitated sex offenders, making it harder for them to assimilate into community life; those favorable to the law pointed out that sex offenders have an exceptionally high rate of recidivism, and thus notification made sense. In any event, the new law was immediately challenged in the courts and was eventually upheld by the New Jersey Supreme Court. In its final version, Megan's Law did take implicit account of repentance by requiring wider and more visible forms of notification for repeat offenders than for first-time offenders, and the discussion surrounding it raised broader questions about the treatment of other kinds of criminals who may have repented and tried to resume ordinary lives in their communities.[9]

   The important part of the story, however, is that the community in which the crime occurred sought to cleanse itself in a manner reminiscent of Durkheim's thesis on ritual: community organizations, pizza parlors, and schools raised money to purchase and demolish the house in which the murder took place, and then transformed the space into a community park. Local residents said they could not feel that things were back to normal until the site had been cleared.[10] This part of the story provided a perfect illustration of Durkheim's point about ritual: cleansing itself of the effects of this horrid crime required the community not only to punish the criminal but to engage collectively in some effort to move beyond the crime, such as destroying the house and creating a public park.

   If such collective activity is necessary for a community to rid itself of having been violated by crime, would it not make sense that ritual activity would also need to be present for a convicted criminal to repent and to be reintegrated into the community? That is, a repentant person who has served a full sentence for having robbed a bank or engaged in mail fraud (or whatever the crime may have been) and who now wishes to resume a normal life probably needs some kind of help from the community in order to do so, perhaps even help that brings the crime once again to the public attention of others. And if the criminal needs such help from the community, the community probably needs to provide this help for its own sake, at least if Durkheim is right about people needing rituals in order to affirm their common values. Yet it is clear that an argument of this kind runs contrary to common practice. Either no means of repenting is made possible or it is assumed that the best way to assimilate repentant criminals is to maintain abject silence about their previous life. Thus, we need to examine some of the popular conceptions that govern our habits about repentance and rehabilitation. The barriers preventing repentance from being part of community rituals can best be understood by placing our time in historical context.

Criminality and Repentance

The modern connection between repentance and society's treatment of criminals is rooted historically in the Jewish understanding of *teshuvah* (or atonement) and in early Christian teachings about the redemption of individuals from sin.[11] Drawing inspiration from Jesus' admonition to "go and sin no more," the apostolic writers described possibilities of rebirth in which a new, cleansed being could replace the sinful nature in which all humans were immersed. By the third century, penitential exercises such as fasting, wearing sackcloth, almsgiving, and lying in ashes had spread throughout the Roman world as a ritualistic means of demonstrating repentance.[12] These exercises provided a powerful means for controlling the behavior of believers; during subsequent centuries, religious and secular leaders alike encouraged their observance, making them obligatory (for example, during Lent) and by imposing fees for absolution. By the late Middle Ages, pilgrimages, merits, and indulgences had become part of the penitential system.[13] The Protestant Reformation was, among other things, an effort to eradicate from the penitential system the worst of its abuses. Protestants and Catholics alike used religious admonitions as well as secular authority in efforts to curb social disorder.[14]

Until the nineteenth century, repentance was closely linked with collective rituals of accusation, trial, and punishment, thereby permitting the offender to make public restitution to assembled community representatives and for the community to declare its acceptance of an appropriate plea of repentance. In medieval and early modern Europe, offenders were often asked to recant as a way of making restitution for heretical beliefs and to mitigate divine punishment, even though death was still inflicted by the community. This kind of repentance, often occurring under duress, gave evidence to the community that its sacred beliefs were intact. The following example, one of nearly fifty thousand recorded in Spain between 1540 and 1700, illustrates how closely accusations, penance, and community ritual were associated:

> All the reconciled went in procession, to the number of 750 persons. . . . With the bitter cold and the dishonour and disgrace they suffered from the great number of spectators . . . they went along howling loudly and weeping and tearing out their hair. . . . Then they went into the church [and] a notary stood up and began to call each one by name, saying, "Is x here?" The penitent raised his candle and said, "Yes." There in public they read all the things in which he had judaized. The same was done for the women. When this was over they were publicly allotted penance and ordered to go in procession for six Fridays, disciplining their body with scourges of hempcord, barebacked, unshod and bareheaded.[15]

When their period of penance was complete, the accused were accepted back into the community, but denied certain public roles, and ordered that if they relapsed, they would be burned at the stake.

After the Enlightenment, freedom to express heretical beliefs was more often tolerated, but criminal trials remained venues in which repentance could be expressed. Hegel believed, for instance, that offenders underwent a kind of penance by condemning their own wrongdoing during judicial proceedings.[16] In the United States, preachers and town leaders often worked closely with judges and wardens: criminals were put on display in village squares and executions drew sizable crowds. The logic of punishment stressed deterrence; yet these public events also provided occasions for protestations of remorse and repentance.[17] In principle, at least, American criminal justice followed Locke in seeking to make crime "an ill bargain to the Offender, give him cause to repent, and terrifie others from doing the like."[18]

During the nineteenth century, the rehabilitation of criminals to function again as responsible members of society came to be favored in place of penal theories emphasizing retribution and punishment. Religious leaders were often in the forefront of efforts to promote rehabilitative practices. Such practices were deemed to be an extension of the idea that people who had done wrong could, under the right circumstances, repent of their wrongdoing, turn away from it, and lead a better life in the future. Rehabilitation was defended as a more humane approach to crime and, indeed, as a way of cutting costs of imprisonment and restoring offending citizens to the community. It was, however, the individual, rather than the community, who received greatest attention. Rehabilitation required sentencing to be tailored to the individual, rather than being prescribed by law for entire categories of crimes. Variable sentences took into account the differences in circumstances and attitudes that would influence whether—and over what period of time—a particular criminal could be rehabilitated.[19]

The prospect of rehabilitation became a prominent argument for abolishing capital punishment during the 1840s and 1850s. Prisoners should not be put to death, according to this argument, because of the likelihood that they would repent and make a new life for themselves. Opponents of capital punishment also argued that true repentance seldom came about as a result of fear or torture, but was a process of enlightenment best furthered by paying attention to harmonies and goodness in human nature.[20] The possibility of prisoners receiving pardons was also extended as a way in which repentance and rehabilitation might be recognized.[21]

Thus, it is evident that in the past repentance has generally been considered an important aspect of the process of dealing with criminals, and that repentance has never been considered a purely private (or subjective) act on the part of the individual criminal alone but has consisted of *social activity* involving the local community, churches, courts, and other institutions. It is also evident in these examples that understandings of repentance have changed dramatically over the centuries and that the treatment of repentant criminals has always reflected understandings, not only of the crime itself, but of the broader values on which a good society is presumed to function. With the perspective provided by historical distance, torturing criminals is likely to seem an odd way of helping them to repent, just as are religious customs that require people to flagellate themselves in public parades. Readers schooled in the culture of late twentieth-century America are likely to ask, how could their repentance possibly be sincere? Yet, the fact that these historic practices seem strange should suggest that our own practices are also shaped by the culture in which we live.

Repentance and Rights

At the end of the twentieth century, the rehabilitation of criminals is still a professed goal of many community leaders; however, it has become increasingly problematic to ascertain how this goal is best accomplished or even whether or not it should be a high priority in criminal procedure.[22] With fears of crime ranking high among public concerns, opinion appears to have shifted away from rehabilitation and repentance toward punishment. For example, a national poll asking Americans about the juvenile justice system found that interest in punishment outweighed interest in rehabilitation by a margin of 52 to 31 percent.[23] By an even larger margin (61 percent to 13 percent), another poll found that the public views prisons as places to keep criminals away from society, rather than as places of rehabilitation.[24]

In addition to popular sentiment, views among criminologists and attorneys have also become less favorable toward rehabilitation. One concern is that rehabilitation can actually work against the rights of both criminals and their victims by placing too much discretionary power in the hands of professional administrators. According to this criticism, sentences may vary widely, for instance, depending on administrators' views of how much progress the criminal is making toward full rehabilitation. In our interest to make laws equitable, we have thus sought to standardize sentences, rather than taking into account the individual circumstances of the criminal. This concern pertains only to sentencing and to the decisions of parole boards, of course, but it has overshadowed concerns about what happens *after* a full sentence has been served to the point that subsequent repentance and rehabilitation are neglected.

Another problem is that the relationship between attitudes and behavior is now considered more difficult to determine. As recently as the 1950s, personality theories generally regarded attitudes and values as deep predispositions to behave in certain ways; subsequent research has raised questions about these theories, suggesting that attitudes are frequently in conflict with one another and that behavior may not reflect deeper inclinations at all. The question I mentioned earlier about sincerity illustrates how sharply we have come to differentiate attitudes and behavior: rather than assuming that action accurately reflects what is inside a person, we imagine that people are simply playing a role or that they are presenting a public side of themselves that may not be who they really are.

In criminal proceedings, it is thus possible to see increasing skepticism about attitudes as reliable evidence of true repentance. On one hand, courts assert that protestations of remorse should not be the basis for lighter sentences, while on the other hand, critics of the penal system point out that administrators may abuse prisoners' rights by requiring deferential attitudes as conditions for parole. These problems, among others, have led increasingly to the view, as one judge observed, that "the notion of repentance is out of fashion."[25]

Insofar as repentance is explicitly associated with a religious conversion, the courts have also been reluctant to take into consideration such evidence on grounds that doing so may show partiality to certain religious perspectives. In Charles Colson's disbarment case, for instance, the judge refused to take Colson's religious conversion into account, but did note his sincerity and moral character.[26]

The disjuncture between attitudes and behavior is also of special concern in dealing with sex offenders. One of the reasons why Megan's Law was upheld in the courts is that sexual offenses are assumed to arise from such deep and often repressed personal dispositions that an offender who claims to have repented can still not be trusted to behave as an ordinary person. Freudian psychology has taught us repressed desires can be both powerful and unpredictable.

In other kinds of crimes, it may be more likely that a repentant offender can more easily control his or her behavior and thus be trusted to act as a responsible member of the community. Yet Freudian insights color the treatment of these offenders as well. For example, a white-collar criminal who claims to have repented may be suspected of having such an unstable personality that he or she cannot be placed in a position of responsibility. Or a plea such as "I've gone straight" may be met implicitly with the response, "Yes, but are you *really* sorry for what you did?"

Yet another orientation that has diminished the importance of repentance in the handling of criminal cases in recent years is the view that such behavior arises less from explicit wrongdoing on the part of the individual offender and more from structural defects in society at large. To suggest that a criminal might repent and reenter society as a law-abiding citizen seems naive to those who believe that crime is rooted more fundamentally in entire neighborhoods or in economic patterns that perpetuate an underclass of impoverished citizens.[27] Recognizing the effects of these larger social conditions, some authorities argue that it is pointless to talk about repentance because most criminals do not understand that they have done something wrong in the first place. Again, the penchant for generalizations makes it harder for the exceptional, but truly repentant ex-criminal to be rehabilitated.

Rehabilitation has also become problematic because of the effect of imprisonment itself on subsequent criminal behavior. Whereas it was once hoped that confinement would serve as a time of self-examination and repentance or (later) that social workers and other professionals could effect repentance in criminals through a process of resocialization, it has become more commonly accepted that imprisonment functions mainly to stigmatize, imprint a deviant identity, and impart skills for further acts of crime.[28] As one critic writes, veterans of the punishment system leave it "more deeply entrenched in a criminal culture, more hostile to society and its values, and less fit to meet the problems of a life in free society."[29] Repentance is thus assumed to be less likely after imprisonment than before, and in any case is further removed as an issue with which the courts themselves are likely to be concerned.

The probability that ex-convicts will be repeat offenders has also increased in the public mind as a result of new inquiries about the effects of early childhood training, dysfunctional family backgrounds, and even genetics on the propensity to engage in violence. Sexual offenses have been particularly subject to such scrutiny. Legislatures have passed new laws requiring public disclosure of the identities of convicted sex offenders and governors have become more wary of pardoning criminals.

Finally, proponents of deterrence point out that repentance should not be considered in sentencing because the purpose of criminal prosecution is not so much to mete out punishment on the basis of the offender's own character but as an example to other potential offenders. This argument does not rule out repentance as a desirable outcome at some point after due punishment has been received.

These, then, are some of the contemporary assumptions about criminal behavior that make it hard to focus public attention on repentance. My point is not that these assumptions are wrong; indeed, there is much evidence to support all of them. Nevertheless, the fact that most criminals do not repent but commit crimes again, or the need to question professions of repentance to make sure that behavior and attitudes are consistent, should not rule out the possibility that sincere repentance can take place.

The Rehabilitation of Repentance

It is perhaps only a slight exaggeration to say that criminal procedure has become preoccupied with questions of sentencing, fairness, and rights to the point that little room remains for any serious consideration of repentance as part of such procedure itself. Throughout the twentieth century, the courts have adamantly insisted that repentance, even to the point of failing to carry through a crime to conclusion, does not constitute grounds for overlooking the fact that a crime has been committed.[30] But this position says nothing about criminals who have served their sentences, turned over a new leaf, and endeavor to regain full membership in the community. Whether or not criminal procedure itself can anticipate and encourage such acts is the question.

One basis on which repentance may be brought back into criminal proceedings (perhaps ironically) is through the postmodernist, deconstructionist view of the decentered or multiple self. In this view, personal identity is malleable, shaped by its linguistic constructions and by circumstances, and presenting itself differently from situation to situation. Arguments as varied as Charles Horton Cooley's looking-glass self, Freudian conceptions of multiple personalities, neomarxist ideas of false consciousness, Goffman's emphasis on the presentation of self, and popular therapeutic notions of retraining the inner child all provide new ground for thinking that the self that commits a crime at one time may undergo some process of transformation and become a different self at a later time.[31] The irony is that these are the same perspectives that have raised skepticism about the relationship between attitudes and behavior and thus cast doubt on protestations of sincere repentance. Yet, if taken to their logical conclusion, these perspectives would suggest that a person can turn over a new leaf, indeed, that behaving *as if* one has turned over a new leaf is tantamount to having done so. The deconstructionist emphasis on language, for example, implies that a person who professes loudly and often enough that he or she has repented actually becomes a repentant person. Or the idea that we become the roles we play means that someone who functions as a responsible member of the community for a few years should be regarded as *being* that kind of person, rather than focusing on the fact that this person may have committed a crime at some point in the past.

Yet the concept of successive selves has raised more questions about repentance than it has supplied answers.[32] Recognizing that defendants may indeed manipulate the presentation of their selves, courts have generally been reluctant to agree that a person who commits a crime may become a different person at a later point except where there is evidence of acute mental disorder.[33] Even proponents of malleable-self arguments, therefore, have tended to emphasize continuities in the self, such as physical identity and psychological traits.[34] In their view, repentance may still be possible, but it requires harder work than simply learning a new role and, ultimately, it requires coming to terms with the fact that one has committed a crime and that the consequences of having done so will continue throughout a person's life.

A more workable understanding of repentance thus stems from philosophical conceptions of the self that emphasize responsibility deriving either from some transcendent aspect of personhood, such as the idea of a soul, or from the self's inescapable relationship with the human community of which it is a part.[35] In this conception, repentance does not constitute a denial of the past, but acceptance of responsibility for one's deeds.[36] Direct restitution to one's victims or indirect proof of one's repentance through exemplary behavior become important features of repentance.

Most of the ways in which repentance has been brought into criminal procedure in recent years have been voluntary, although some have been suggested or required by the courts. Some repentant criminals, for example, have placed notices in the newspapers stating that they were sorry for their behavior and asking victims and others to forgive them. Another option has been to require rehabilitated criminals to "notify" the community of their past by having special bumper stickers or license plates on their automobiles. These notifications of course are often criticized as being less about repentance and more about using public pressure as a means of deterrence. In other cases, repentant criminals have been able to demonstrate their change of heart by writing books or engaging in socially beneficial behavior. For example, in recent years several ex-prostitutes have gained publicity for becoming involved in community programs to combat prostitution.

Of all the various alternatives, community service has become an increasingly popular way of thinking about repentance because it offers criminals a means of taking responsibility for their actions and of making restitution to the community in deeds rather than in words alone.[37] In many instances, community service is explicitly linked with other means of determining the extent to which repentance occurs. For example, a 1988 case in California required an attorney who had been convicted of embezzlement to do two hundred hours of community service, to undergo psychotherapy, and to pass a professional responsibility examination. Explaining his decision, the judge wrote,

> Forgiveness and rehabilitation are not mutually exclusive from the necessity to safeguard and protect society, recognizing the fact that there are recidivists, and that until Respondent proves himself by his acts rather than by his words alone, he remains suspect and should exist to the extent necessary subject to the scrutiny, examination and supervision of those to whom he may pose a threat.[38]

Critics of community service argue that it often constitutes little more than a slap on the wrist, rather than carrying sufficient stigma to express the community's full disapproval of the crime that has been committed. Another potential weakness of community service is that the deeds themselves overshadow the idea of repentance to such an extent that criminal behavior is in effect excused by the possibility that offenders may still make a positive contribution to society. On such grounds, for instance, Nobel Prize winners who commit crimes may be given token sentences because they are deemed to be of good moral character by virtue of their deeds, whereas ordinary mortals committing similar crimes are punished more severely.[39] It is for this reason that the courts have often required doctors, lawyers, politicians, and others who might easily be able to serve the community through their work to perform menial tasks as punishment for wrongdoing. In such instances, the symbolic meaning of menial service is assumed to be more important than the sheer contribution to the community itself.

Yet another concern about community service as a court-mandated means of paying for criminal activity is that the broader significance of community service is thereby demeaned. This concern is similar to that expressed by critics who argue that community service requirements—say, in high schools—undermine the very idea of service. What is lost, clearly, is the *voluntary* dimension of service and, implicitly, the sincerity of such service. Thus, if someone is compelled to help others, we wonder if such compulsion may introduce utilitarian or legalistic concerns to the point that altruism is undermined.[40]

Community service appears to be used most successfully when there is a specific source of wrongdoing that can be monitored and corrected, such as an addiction to gambling or drug use.[41] In such cases, evidence of repentance need not consist merely of personal avowals, but can be determined through a prescribed procedure of counseling, medication, and/or testing. Such procedure thus becomes a kind of ritual, generally carried out by professionals who are entrusted by the community to vouch for the criminal's rehabilitation. Community service itself may be little more than make-work designed to give the criminal something constructive to do while the process of rehabilitation takes place. Insofar as community service is limited to certain white-collar crimes in which repentance can be certified by professional experts, its applicability to whole varieties of crime and to wide sections of the community is inevitably diminished.

The idea that crime is part of a larger system of social relationships suggests that repentance may also need to be conceived as an act of contrition, not only on the part of individual offenders, but by the entire community. For law-abiding, middle-class Americans to accept responsibility for social conditions that may encourage crime is not a popular idea. Nor is any thought of "paying for one's sins" by paying higher taxes in order to promote redistributive economic policies. Yet it is clear that the victims of crime pay dearly for the sins of the wider society in these respects. It is also part of the American tradition to believe that we are, in a sense, responsible for the collective well-being of our society. In many religious communities, believers still gather regularly to confess their sins and to ask divine forgiveness and absolution. Paying more serious attention to what is being confessed—and to what true repentance may require—is perhaps one way in which all citizens can become involved in the struggle to rescue their communities from crime.

A somewhat broader conclusion also derives from these considerations. Repentance has traditionally held meaning because it was understood within particular cultural (often religious) traditions and reinforced by the practices of those traditions. It cannot easily be put into purely legal contexts without losing much of its traditional meaning. Those who argue that religious arguments should simply be accorded greater respect by the judicial system radically oversimplify the problem. But those who argue on the basis of religious membership and attendance figures that America is fundamentally a religious society also miss the extent to which secularization has taken place. If the community, stripped of its traditional religious connotations, is now reemerging as a sacred concept, some method of reintegrating deviant members and transforming them into full citizenship will need to be rediscovered. But it will probably not be called repentance; or if it is, we will have to think of repentance in ways that take account of our present legal and institutional complexities.

For repentance to be an effective means of reintegrating criminals into the community, it must be embedded in rituals that dramatize a change of heart and that provide community members with evidence that such a change is in fact sincere. The case of a Chicago assessor convicted of taking bribes is instructive. In addition to paying a $50,000 fine, the assessor was required to do five hundred hours of community service, which he performed at a shelter for the homeless. In their petition for reinstatement as a licensed assessor, his attorneys noted that he had demonstrated his sincere repentance by continuing to work at the shelter after the community service requirement had been fulfilled. They also called four witnesses to testify on his behalf: a clergyman who was director of the homeless shelter, a psychiatrist who had treated him for four years, an attorney who headed a character and fitness committee, and the petitioner's present employer.[42] In cases such as this, the court itself provides occasion for the ritual affirmation of repentance.

Yet the courts should not be expected to serve this function alone or in every case. Concern about rights and sentencing, not to mention overcrowded dockets, prevents the courts from paying full attention to the ways in which communities may affirm their values and reinforce the identities of their members. As the foregoing illustrates, homeless shelters, churches, synagogues, and professional associations are important means by which communities maintain themselves. Such associations provide firsthand contact as well as special expertise, thus equipping them to certify the extent of repentance. In contrast, newspaper and television accounts are generally ill-suited to provide such evidence: by their nature, they raise skepticism about the actions and intentions of strangers. In addition to formal community associations, informal gatherings can also provide venues for the ritual affirmation of repentance. The many Alcoholics Anonymous and other twelve-step groups that exist in most communities, for example, routinely encourage participants to remember and turn away from their addictions.[43] Such gatherings function well because they bring relatively homogeneous segments of the community together; whether or not they can bridge increasingly diverse segments of society is a more difficult question.

In the end, it is worth emphasizing that Durkheim was correct in arguing that beliefs amount to little unless they are supported ritually. The judicial system reflects a similar concern when it takes a skeptical view of mere verbal protestations of remorse and when it attempts to ensure that repentance is reinforced by community rituals. Through collective events, the community is made whole and its individual members are strengthened. Such events may include testimony by clergy and therapists or involve community service for the homeless, all of which constitute genuine work. But the point of ritual is that instrumental tasks also convey expressive messages. Weddings and funerals communicate a change that has taken place in the social order; so do executions. Ritual occasions for repentance can be a vital way in which communities affirm themselves.

Notes

1. Emile Durkheim, *The Elementary Forms of the Religious Life* (New York: Free Press, 1965; originally published in 1915).

2. Kai T. Erikson, *Wayward Puritans: A Study in the Sociology of Deviance* (New York: Wiley, 1966).

3. Mary Douglas, *Purity and Danger: An Analysis of Concepts of Pollution and Taboo* (London: Penguin, 1966); Mary Douglas, *Natural Symbols* (New York: Vintage, 1970); Michel Foucault, *Discipline and Punish: The Birth of the Prison* (New York: Vintage, 1979).

4. Albert Bergesen, "Political Witch-Hunts: The Sacred and the Subversive in Cross-National Perspective," *American Sociological Review* 42 (April 1977): 220–33; Albert Bergesen, *The Sacred and the Subversive: Political Witch-Hunts as National Rituals* (Storrs, Conn.: Society for the Scientific Study of Religion Monograph Series, 1984).

5. James M. Inverarity, "Populism and Lynching in Louisiana, 1889–1896: A Test of Erikson's Theory of the Relationship between Boundary Crises and Repressive Justice," *American Sociological Review* 41 (April 1976): 262–80; James M. Inverarity, Pat Lauderdale, and Barry C. Feld, *Law and Society: Sociological Perspectives on Criminal Law* (Boston: Little, Brown, 1983).

6. Andrew von Hirsch, *Past or Future Crimes: Deservedness and Dangerousness in the Sentencing of Criminals* (New Brunswick, N.J.: Rutgers University Press, 1985); Jeffrie G. Murphy, *Retribution Reconsidered: More Essays in the Philosophy of Law* (Boston: Kluwer Academic, 1992); Marvin Henberg, *Retribution: Evil for Evil in Ethics, Law, and Literature* (Philadelphia: Temple University Press, 1990).

7. David T. Stanley, *Prisoners among Us* (Washington, D.C.: Brookings Institution, 1976).

8. "States Lock in Laws Addressing Fear of Crime," *Los Angeles Times*, 3 January 1995, A16.

9. "Sex Offender Law Temporarily Blocked by Judge," *Reuters World Service*, 4 January 1995, on-line.

10. "Turbulence Marks Headlines of 1994 in N.J.," *Bergen Record*, 25 December 1994, N4.

11. Chaim Nussbaum, *The Essence of Teshuvah: A Path to Repentance* (Northvale, N.J.: J. Aronson, 1993); on the various biblical meanings of repentance, see David Daube, "Judas," *California Law Review* 82 (January 1994): 95–108.

12. Justo L. Gonzalez, *The Story of Christianity*, vol. 1, *The Early Church to the Dawn of the Reformation* (New York: Harper & Row, 1984).

13. Sandra J. McEntire, *The Doctrine of Compunction in Medieval England: Holy Tears* (Lewiston, N.Y.: Edwin Mellen Press, 1990).

14. Michel Mollat, *The Poor in the Middle Ages: An Essay in Social History*, trans. Arthur Goldhammer (New Haven: Yale University Press, 1986).

15. Henry Kamen, *Inquisition and Society in Spain in the Sixteenth and Seventeenth Centuries* (Bloomington: Indiana University Press, 1985), 191.

16. R. A. Duff, *Trials and Punishments* (New York: Cambridge University Press, 1986).

17. Timothy L. Hall, "Roger Williams and the Foundations of Religious Liberty," *Boston University Law Review* 71 (May 1991): 455–65.

18. John Locke, *Two Treatises of Government* (New York: New American Library, 1965), 315.

19. *Williams v. New York*, 337 U.S. 241, 247 (1949).

20. Anthony Davis, "The Movement to Abolish Capital Punishment in America, 1787–1861," *American Historical Review* 63 (1957): 23–33.

21. Kathleen Dean Moore, *Pardons: Justice, Mercy, and the Public Interest* (New York: Oxford University Press, 1989).

22. Torsten Eriksson, *The Reformers: An Historical Survey of Pioneer Experiments in the Treatment of Criminals* (New York: Elsevier, 1976).

23. Public Opinion Online (28 September 1994).

24. Public Opinion Online (21 October 1994).

25. Marvin Frankel, quoted in *United States v. Grayson* (U.S. Supreme Court, No. 76–1572, 22 February 1978).

26. Colson, 412 A.2d 1160 (D.C. Cir. 1979).

27. Jack Katz, "Criminals' Passions and the Progressive's Dilemma," in *America at Century's End*, ed. Alan Wolfe (Berkeley and Los Angeles: University of California Press, 1991), 396–420.

28. F. A. Allen, *The Decline of the Rehabilitative Ideal: Penal Policy and Social Purpose* (New York: Cambridge University Press, 1981).

29. J. Andenaes, *Punishment and Deterrence* (New York: Oxford University Press, 1974), 179.

30. Joseph Goldstein, Alan M. Dershowitz, and Richard D. Schwartz, *Criminal Law: Theory and Process* (New York: Free Press, 1974).

31. Michael S. Moore, *Law and Psychiatry: Rethinking the Relationship* (New York: Cambridge University Press, 1984).

32. Jon Elster, *The Multiple Self* (New York: Cambridge University Press, 1986).

33. Rebecca Dresser, "Personal Identity and Punishment," *Boston University Law Review* 70 (May 1990): 395–445.

34. Derek Parfit, *Reasons and Persons* (Oxford: Clarendon Press, 1984).

35. Sydney Shoemaker and Richard Swinburne, *Personal Identity* (Oxford: Basil Blackwell, 1984).

36. Loren E. Lomasky, *Persons, Right, and the Moral Community* (New York: Oxford University Press, 1987).

37. Stephanie Gardner Holder, "Criminal Procedure," *University of Arkansas at Little Rock Law Journal* 16 (Winter 1994): 99–108.

38. Basinger, No. S004072, Supreme Court of California (18 July 1988).

39. John Buchanan, "Advance Directives and the Personal Identity Problem," *Philosophy and Public Affairs* 17 (1988): 277–94.

40. For a more extended discussion, see my book *Learning to Care: Elementary Kindness in an Age of Indifference* (New York: Oxford University Press, 1995).

41. *Florida Bar v. Thompson*, No. 66,399, Supreme Court of Florida (30 October 1986).

42. Alexander, No. 67737, Supreme Court of Illinois (24 May 1989).

43. Robert Wuthnow, *Sharing the Journey: Support Groups and America's New Quest for Community* (New York: Free Press, 1994).

Index

About the Editors

Amitai Etzioni is the first University Professor of the George Washington University. From 1987 to 1989, he served as the Thomas Henry Carroll Ford Foundation Professor at Harvard Business School. He served as senior advisor at the White House from 1979 to 1980. He was guest scholar at the Brookings Institution in 1978–79. For twenty years (1958–78), he served as professor of sociology at Columbia University, part of the time as chairman of the department.

In 1991, he founded the Communitarian Network, and he is the editor of nineteen books, including *The Spirit of Community: Rights, Responsibilities, and the Communitarian Agenda* (1993) and the upcoming *The New Golden Rule* (1997).

Outside of academia, Dr. Etzioni is familiar to readers of the leading news media and viewers of network television.

David E. Carney is currently a student at the William and Mary School of Law, where he is on the staff of *The William and Mary Bill of Rights Journal*. He was a research associate with the Center for Communitarian Policy Studies and an assistant editor of *The Responsive Community*.

About the Contributors

Mahmoud Ayoub is a professor of Islamic studies in the Department of Religion at Temple University. He is the author of a number of books, including *Redemptive Suffering in Islam* and *The Qur'ān and Its Interpreters*. In addition, his articles have appeared in *The Muslim World*, *Journal of the American Oriental Society*, *Bulletin of the Institute of Middle Eastern Studies* (Tokyo, Japan), and *Islamochristina* (Rome, Italy), among others.

Guy L. Beck taught Eastern religions and Hinduism at Louisiana State University from 1990 to 1995. In addition to many articles published in academic journals and encyclopedias, and a book chapter on reincarnation in Hinduism, his ground-breaking book on sacred sound, *Sonic Theology: Hinduism and Sacred Sound* was published in 1993. He is currently teaching world religions at Loyola University in New Orleans.

Harold O. J. Brown holds the Franklin Forman Chair of Ethics in Theology at Trinity Evangelical School in Deerfield, Illinois, where he is also professor of biblical and systematic theology. He is the director of the Center on Religion and Society at the Rockford Institute.

Harvey Cox is Victor S. Thomas Professor of Divinity at Harvard University. He is the author of several books, including *The Secular City* (1965), *Religion in the Secular City* (1984), *The Silencing of Leonardo Boff: Liberation Theory and the Future of World Christianity* (1988), *Many Mansions: A Christian's Encounters with Other Faiths* (1988), and *Fire from Heaven: The Rise of Pentecostal Spirituality and the Reshaping of Religion in the Twenty-First Century*.

Malcolm David Eckel is associate professor of religion at Boston University and the author, most recently, of *To See the Buddha: A Philosopher's Quest for the Meaning of Emptiness.*

John Lyden is associate professor of religion at Dana College in Blair, Nebraska. Dr. Lyden has published articles on a wide range of topics in religious studies, including Jewish-Christian dialogue, religious pluralism, the teaching of religion, and philosophical theology. He is the editor of *Enduring Issues in Religion*, published in 1995.

Jeffrie G. Murphy is Regents' Professor of Law and Philosophy at Arizona State University. He is the author (with Jules Coleman) of the book *The Philosophy of Law: An Introduction to Jurisprudence* (1990), the author (with Jean Hampton) of the book *Forgiveness and Mercy* (1988), and the editor of the anthology *Punishment and Rehabilitation*, 3d ed. (1995). Two collections of his essays have been published: *Retribution, Justice and Therapy* (1979) and *Retribution Reconsidered* (1992).

Jacob Neusner is Distinguished Research Professor of Religious Studies at the University of South Florida, Tampa; a member of the Institute for Advanced Study, Princeton, New Jersey; and a Life Member of Clare Hall, Cambridge University.

Robert Wuthnow is the Gerhard R. Andlinger Professor of Social Sciences and director of the Center for the Study of American Religion at Princeton University. His recent books include *Acts of Compassion: Caring for Others and Helping Ourselves* (1991), *Rediscovering the Sacred* (1992), *Christianity in the Twenty-First Century* (1993), *Sharing the Journey: Support Groups and America's New Quest for Community* (1994), *Producing the Sacred: An Essay on Public Religion* (1994), *God and Mammon in America* (1994), and *Learning to Care: Elementary Kindness in an Age of Indifference* (1995).